Understanding
A Separate Peace

The Greenwood Press "Literature in Context" Series
Student Casebooks to Issues, Sources, and Historical Documents

UNDERSTANDING
A Separate Peace

A STUDENT CASEBOOK TO ISSUES, SOURCES, AND HISTORICAL DOCUMENTS

Hallman Bell Bryant

The Greenwood Press
"Literature in Context" Series
Claudia Durst Johnson, Series Editor

GREENWOOD PRESS
Westport, Connecticut • London

Library of Congress Cataloging-in-Publication Data

Bryant, Hallman Bell, 1936–
    Understanding A separate peace : a student casebook to issues, sources, and
historical documents / Hallman Bell Bryant.
        p.   cm. — (The Greenwood Press "Literature in context" series, ISSN 1074–
598X)
    Includes bibliographical references (p.   ) and index.
    ISBN 0–313–31165–X (alk. paper)
    1. Knowles, John, 1926–   Separate peace.   2. Preparatory schools—United
States—History—20th century—Sources.   3. World War, 1939–1945—Literature
and the war—Sources.   4. World War, 1939–1945—Literature and the war.
    5. Preparatory school students in literature.   I. Title.   II. Series.
PS3561.N68 S439   2002
813'.54—dc21   2001018024

British Library Cataloguing in Publication Data is available.

Library of Congress Catalog Card Number: 2001018024
ISBN: 0–313–31165–X
ISSN: 1074–598X

First published in 2002

Greenwood Press, 88 Post Road West, Westport, CT 06881
An imprint of Greenwood Publishing Group, Inc.
www.greenwood.com

Printed in the United States of America

∞™

The paper used in this book complies with the
Permanent Paper Standard issued by the National
Information Standards Organization (Z39.48–1984).

10 9 8 7 6 5 4 3 2 1

Copyright Acknowledgments

Contents

Introduction

Since its publication in 1959, John Knowles's *A Separate Peace* has acquired the reputation of a minor classic of American literature, and is now read in many English courses by both high school and college students. Young people enjoy this novel and read it with relish. Its prose style is highly engaging, it has characters with whom they can identify, and it has a message they can comprehend without difficulty. *A Separate Peace* deals with feelings most teenagers are familiar with on the simplest level—fear of failure, disillusionment, and the sense of guilt—but most important, it is a story of friendship set against the violence of a world at war in the early 1940s. The crisis that faced the nation in those years is juxtaposed against the personal crisis undergone by the two central characters.

A Separate Peace, which has never gone out of print and has sold nearly 10 million copies to date, was not an immediate success. Knowles started work on the novel in 1954 and the writing came easily and quickly—as Knowles said, it "flowed from my mind and into words"—and was completed by 1956 (*Esquire* 1985). However, it would be several years before the manuscript was accepted by a publisher. All the editors who saw the book apparently wondered if a story about a group of prep school boys during the war years would interest anyone. After the manuscript was rejected

by eleven publishers, Knowles submitted it to the London publisher of Secker and Warburg, which published it early in 1959.
Like so many other American artists before and since, it took a
foreign eye to see the merits of a native author's work. The literary
press in England gave *A Separate Peace* an enthusiastic response,
and it received positive reviews from all the leading journals and
papers, the most important one coming from the London *Times*
(May 1, 1959), which called it "a novel of exceptional power and
distinction." A number of reviewers were attracted to what they
perceived as an antiwar theme in the novel and saw pacifism as a
subtext.

   Although Knowles has continued to write novels, nothing has
equaled the success of his first one, which has achieved a place in
the hearts and minds of its millions of readers of all ages and both
sexes, though it is mostly young people who love and treasure *A
Separate Peace*.

   The purpose of the novel, Knowles revealed in an interview, was
to unscramble, plumb, and explain what had happened during a
very "peculiar summer" at Phillips Exeter Academy in New Hampshire when he was a sixteen-year-old summer school student in
1943. What began as an account of competition between two
schoolboys became an allegory about war. In *A Separate Peace*,
Knowles revealed emotions and fears that he and his generation
felt as they faced the prospect of going to war as soon as they
reached their eighteenth birthday. Thus, the book captured an experience that would be universal for millions of American boys at
that period of history.

   On the other hand, there is much that is unique or special about
the situation described in *A Separate Peace*. The setting is an exclusive eastern preparatory school and concerns characters from
privileged backgrounds. Yet there is the theme of growing up in
troubled times that transcends these facts. One of the central ideas
that the story conveys is that we all lose something in growing up.
As the English romantic poet William Blake shows us in his *Songs
of Innocence and Experience*, we start out in a state of ignorance
of evil, which is taken away as the world forces us to see reality as
we grow up. In the adult world, the harmony and selflessness of
innocent childhood are replaced by the selfishness and hostility of
adulthood. Knowles's novel and Blake's poems show the same
nostalgia for the lost world of pastoral peace, which is set against

the growing awareness of a violent world that awaits these boys beyond the groves of academe.

A Separate Peace can be read as a war novel, and in fact takes its title from a war novel. Ernest Hemingway's *A Farewell to Arms* has a scene where the hero, Lieutenant Frederic Henry, says that he has made "a separate peace" and deserts the Italian army. It is not actual warfare that Knowles depicts, however, but the impact of the war on the lives of the school boys who feel the changes and upheavals that the war has caused in American society.

Some of the changes that the war has brought about are described by Gene Forrester, the narrator of the novel, who notes that we all have a particular period of time or history that we believe belongs exclusively to us and our generation:

> For me, this moment—four years is a moment in history—was the war. The war was and is reality for me. I still instinctively live and think in its atmosphere . . . America is not, never has been, and never will be what the songs and poems call it, a land of plenty. Nylon, meat, gasoline, and steel are rare. There are too many jobs and not enough workers. Money is easy to earn but rather hard to spend, because there isn't very much to buy. Trains are always late and always crowded with "servicemen." The war will always be fought very far from America and it will never end. (32)

The war that Gene is speaking of is World War II, fought over fifty years ago, though still within the memory of many living Americans. The generation that fought this war, which was one of the defining events of the twentieth century, is now passing away at the rate of 30,000 a month. Of the 6.3 million remaining, most of these veterans will be gone by the year 2008. This is the generation that Tom Brokaw calls the greatest generation any society has ever produced in his best-selling book by the same name. As Tom Hanks says in the radio/television promotion for a monument to be built in Washington honoring the men and women who contributed to the Allied victory in World War II, they are our fathers, our grandfathers, our mothers and grandmothers who grew up in the Depression, left their classrooms, offices, and farms, and went off to the factories and battlefields to fight a war for freedom in which over 400,000 gave their lives. It is hard to comprehend the sacrifices that all Americans made during the war years because it was so different from the Korean War and the war in Vietnam, which were unpopular, limited, undeclared wars. So that students will be able to understand *A Separate Peace* more completely, I have provided information that connects this novel to the world in which events in the book took place, showing how the novel was shaped by the milieu of an exclusive prep school atmosphere that nevertheless was not a sanctuary from a violent world that was engaged in total war.

Chapter 1 provides practical criticism of the book through an analysis of the basic elements of a work of fiction: setting, plot, characterization, and theme as conveyed through images and symbols. As Cleanth Brooks and Robert Penn Warren said in *Understanding Fiction*, "A piece of fiction is a tissue of significances, some great and some small, but all of them aspects, finally, of the total significance of the piece" (xviii). By studying the text closely, students can learn to enjoy their reading of *A Separate Peace* and explore in greater depth the issues that Knowles raises.

The relationship of the author to his novel is examined in Chapter 2 in order to show how Knowles came to write the book, which is strongly autobiographical. Drawing on his own prep school experiences, Knowles also developed many of the novel's characters from real people, whom he has identified in magazine articles and newspaper interviews included in this book. The definition of "preppyness" is also considered, using excerpts from school papers and institutional histories to reveal how private schools manifest a special sense of eliteness and project a culture of status.

In Chapter 3 the focus is expanded to show how America's prep schools were forced to make many adjustments to wartime conditions. In the early days of the war, the sense of crisis was acute, and many different programs were launched to try to meet the national emergency. Included in this chapter are several government documents issued to the schools concerning "victory" programs and selections from institutional histories of various schools that describe the impact of the war on their campuses.

Chapter 4 examines official directives concerning military service and the draft, as well as private letters showing what young men were facing as they reported to the military training camps for duty. Many young soldiers broke down under the impersonal regimentation and sometimes brutal conditions of barracks life, which is revealed in U.S. Army medical documents published shortly after the war. These were not released by the War Department during wartime because of the strict censorship of any information that was deemed harmful to morale.

In Chapter 5, readers hear from individuals who recount their experiences in the military during the war. Over 6 million Americans answered the call to arms, and each one has story. Some of these veterans put their experiences down in letters to relatives at home, some kept journals, and some have provided oral histories. Some of the sources cited come from the period and provide a contemporary perspective; others are taken from more recent accounts and have a retrospective cast on the events that shaped lives.

Chapter 6 considers several contemporary issues that are latent in the novel but not an overt part of the plot, such as post-traumatic stress disorder, athletics versus academics, crime on campus, and single-gender education. All of these are important topics today. Examining them sheds additional light on *A Separate Peace* and enrich our grasp of Knowles's remarkable novel.

NOTE

Page numbers in parentheses indicate quotations from the 1975 edition of *A Separate Peace* produced by Dell Publishers.

SUGGESTED READINGS AND WORKS CITED

Blake, William. *Songs of Innocence and Experience*. New Rochelle: Peter Pauper Press, 1935.

Brooks, Cleanth, and Robert Penn Warren, eds. *Understanding Fiction*. New York: Appleton-Century-Crofts, 1959.

Knowles, John. "My Separate Peace." *Esquire* (March 1985).

"A Novel of Exceptional Power." (Review of *A Separate Peace*.) *London Times Literary Supplement*, May 1, 1959.

1

A Literary Analysis of *A Separate Peace*: A Novel of Conflicts

Academic fiction has a long tradition as the subject of literature. Novelists especially have begun to use campuses of schools and colleges increasingly as a setting and subject for their work. As character types, professors and students fascinate readers. Indeed, if one looks back across the span of English literature, we see that some of the most memorable and famous literary figures have been linked to academe. Hamlet, for example, was a student and Doctor Faustus a professor. Some of Chaucer's funniest *tales*—"The Miller's Tale" and "The Reeve's Tale"—are devoted to the antics of Cambridge and Oxford students. Ben Jonson's *The Alchemist* depicts a bogus scientist, who if he were on a contemporary campus would be a member of the research faculty of a modern university. A more notorious student of science was Victor Frankenstein, who created the horrible android that bears his name. Poets have also expressed their feelings about their school years. Wordsworth, Tennyson, Bryon, Shelley, and Arnold all felt a sense of alienation. Even before the Middle Ages and Renaissance, there was a tradition of dealing with intellectuals, pedants, and students in literary vein, and it was largely satirical. The classical comedies of the Greek poets Mennipus and Lucilius and the Roman playwright Terence often focused on comic character types such as rowdy students and pedantic professors. If we restrict ourselves for the moment to American treatments of the academic scene, we will discover that though the times have changed, some things remain fairly constant in dealing with campus life.

There are hundreds of books about campus life. Many are written by academics; some are written by undergraduates or recent graduates and differ in tone and point of view from those written by professors. In campus novels about students, the pursuit of an education appears to be mechanical, bureaucratic, absurd, or irrelevant; true growing up and learning take place in the dorm, the tavern, or town—anyplace except the classroom. These academic novels ironically take a negative perspective and eschew the "best years of our lives" sort of nostalgia one would expect. John Osborne's *The Paper Chase* (1971), Ken Kolb's *Getting Straight* (1967), and John Nichols's *The Sterile Cuckoo* (1965) are all written from the student's point of view, and each shows the author's disgust with the superficial grandeur of academic life even at top-rung institutions.

Two of the most widely read novels that deal with academic situations at prep school are J. D. Salinger's *The Catcher in the Rye* (1951) and John Knowles's *A Separate Peace* (1959). Both books are written from a first-person point of view, and each narrator gives a qualified account of life in a boarding school. Salinger's narrator, Holden Caulfield, is much more cynical in his appraisal of Pencey Prep School than Gene Forrester, the narrator of *A Separate Peace*, is of the Devon School. In fact, to Holden, everything about prep school life is "phony" (his word), even down to the school's advertising in magazines featuring horseback riding. Gene is less censorious of his school, although he also has had a negative experience while attending Devon. As Harold Bloom points out in his introduction to *Modern Critical Interpretations of John Knowles's* A Separate Peace, Knowles's novel is a masterpiece of the limited genre of prep school fiction and yet is also a period piece that encapsulates the particular time and place it describes.

The historical and particular settings of *A Separate Peace* contribute much to the appeal of this novel. Almost all of the events described in the book take place in a fictional academy, the Devon School, located somewhere in New England. The characters are almost entirely boys, with a few adults appearing as teachers and parents; there are no girls or romantic interests. Basically the novel is about the relationship between the two main characters, Gene Forrester, the narrator, and his roommate and best friend Phineas, or "Finny" as he is usually called. The focus is on these teenagers and the world of the school, a microcosm of the larger world during the early days of World War II.

The story begins with a matter-of-fact statement. Gene says, "I went back to Devon School not long ago, and found it looking oddly newer than when I was a student there fifteen years ago" (1). Gene returns neither to be reunited with old classmates nor to seek out favorite teachers. His is not a normal homecoming by any means, because he has come back to see two places that have fearful memories for him; a staircase and a tree.

Gene's anxiety on his return is conveyed by his initial impressions of his school. The place looks too new to him, and there is a disconcerting aura of sedateness that now pervades the campus. It strikes him that Devon has become "shinier and more upright" (1) than he recalled it being. Everything is in such a good state of preservation that Gene says the school reminds him of a museum. His emotions at this point are exactly like those of any other person who has ever gone back to a place where he or she no longer belongs; he feels like a relic from the past.

At this point in the narrative, Knowles is preparing readers for the retrospective cast of the novel. As we discover in these opening paragraphs, Gene has returned to Devon School to seek out his past and confront it. Several times he refers to the fear that he experienced while a student, and we assume that it must have been a result of the normal fear that a boy on the verge of draft age would have felt during the war years. However, it soon becomes apparent that Gene's anxiety stemmed not from the historical situation but from a series of events that took place at two sites on the campus: a set of stairs in an academic building and a huge tree that stood on the bank of a river.

In accord with the somber purpose that has brought Gene back to his old school, the weather on this late November day of gray clouds and gusty winds is raw and cold. The day is described as "self pitying" (2) and mournful, which conveys the mood that Gene is in as he approaches the first place he seeks—the oldest building on campus, the first Academy Building, a building in eighteenth-century-style architecture with an inscription over the entrance in Latin: *Hic venits pueri et viri sitis* ("Here enter boys to become men"). The application of this motto to Gene's case is one of the central themes of the novel.

At this point, Gene reveals exactly what he has come to see

here—"a long white marble flight of stairs" (3)—but all we are told about the stairs is that the stone seemed especially hard, "a crucial fact" (3) Gene had previously overlooked. Readers do not have enough information at this point in the story to understand Gene's remark fully or see the irony of it, but will later learn that a tragic event took place here that deeply influenced his life. Fifteen years ago, Gene had been brought to this building in the middle of the night to be accused by a group of his schoolmates of causing an accident that crippled Finny, his roommate and best friend. On these stairs, another accident would happen that same night that would cause the death of Finny.

Although readers are told little about the narrator's purpose for confronting this scene, it later becomes apparent that Gene's purpose in returning is to make a judgment on himself and reconcile himself with the past.

Leaving the school grounds, Gene makes his way to the river as the weather worsens. His progress is impeded by the mud and mist as he crosses sodden fields in search of his second objective, the tree. Gene feels a chill, as if the ghosts that had haunted his youth are still about, and he is confused because the trees along the edge of the river all look the same. He cannot locate the one he seeks. In his mind's eye he remembered this tree as "a huge lone spike dominating the riverbank" (5), a tree so tall it was to him like Jack's mythic beanstalk, full of threat and danger to anyone who dared to climb it. The tree that had once appeared so large and intimidating now seems shrunken and like all the other trees. The only way he can identify the particular tree is by small nail marks, left like scars in the trunk.

Symbolically, the changes in the physical appearance that Gene notes on the school grounds and in the tree indicate the psychological changes that have taken place in him over time. He realizes that change is a necessary part of nature and human life, and he is encouraged by the perception that nothing remains the same, "Not a tree, not love, not even a death by violence" (6), so he takes hope that he has changed as well and now can come to terms with the past.

In the chapters that follow, we are taken back to the days that Gene had found so fearful by a flashback to the summer of 1942, the first year of U.S. participation in World War II.

As a novel about coming of age in a time of national crisis, Knowles is concerned with the loss of innocence that occurs with growing up and facing the reality of military service in wartime. The early plot events are made up of Gene's memories of the events of the summer of 1942 and the academic year of 1942–43. He recalls the jumping game that the boys played at the tree, the tree that he has returned to find, but now it is seen from the perspective of the sixteen-year-old Gene. He perceives it as a "tremendous, irate, steely, black steeple" (6) that Finny has challenged him to climb. He is irritated and angry that his roommate should propose such a risky stunt, which he resents because he sees it as a personal challenge to him rather than just a proposal to have some fun. Gene is jealous of Finny's confidence and courage, which make him think that leaping out of a tall tree into the river below will be a "cinch" (7). Many of Gene's negative traits are revealed in this opening scene: his fear of not measuring up, his sarcasm, which allows him to make verbal retaliations against Finny, and his envy of his friend's persuasive powers and hypnotic charm. Urged on by Finny, Gene makes a jump, feeling as though he is risking his very life. However, when he emerges from the water, he feels proud of his bravery and full of self-satisfaction.

This first jumping scene is important because it introduces the two main characters of the novel and reveals how the two boys are alike and yet very different. Although he is not very big, Finny is the best athlete in the school. In fact, he and Gene are about the same size, but Gene is not very athletic and is more concerned with academics. The two boys are almost identical physically. They are both five feet, eight-and-one-half inches tall, although Gene claims to be five feet, nine inches until Finny forces him to admit the truth. This detail is significant, because it indicates Gene's basic insecurity.

In addition, Finny's weight is given as 155 pounds, a fact that is said to be "crucial," perhaps because Finny is a larger person than Gene, who weighs 150 pounds. This extra weight might suggest Finny's greater heart than Gene's. Another detail that helps to characterize Finny is his pronunciation of the word "yes" by saying "aey-rh." This New England affirmative amuses Gene, which is the means that Finny uses to influence Gene—by making him lighten up and laugh, breaking down his resistance.

Another episode from the summer of 1942 deserves mention: the scene in Chapter 2 at the tea party given by the headmaster, Mr. Patch-Withers. This chapter reveals animosity developing between Gene and Finny. On this occasion Finny has had the temerity to wear a pink shirt to this stuffy, formal affair. In addition to violating the dress code, which permitted only white or blue ox-ford cloth button-down collars, he has put the school tie through his pants as a belt. Finny is untroubled by the taunts that his attire causes, least of all that he might appear effeminate by wearing a pink shirt. In fact, he is amused that he would be thought a ho-mosexual by his classmates because he is so self-confident about his own sexuality. Gene, however, who might harbor submerged homoerotic feelings for Finny, is unsettled by the pink shirt and projects his own sexual anxiety onto Finny.

Actually Finny is not wearing the shirt to attract attention. He confides to Gene that he is wearing it in lieu of flying a flag. He explains to the headmaster's wife, who is aghast at his ensemble, that his purpose is patriotic. Gene watches with amazement as Finny glibly extricates himself from a potentially embarrassing sit-uation. His reason, as he tells Mrs. Patch-Withers for using his tie as a belt and for the unusually colored shirt is to "tie in" with a successful Allied bombing raid on Central Europe and thus show how the school supports the war. Everyone is so amused by Finny's illogical reason that he escapes censure, much to Gene's chagrin that Finny gets off the hook by his charm.

This episode, like the earlier scene at the river, reveals how much the war has changed the norms of the school. The boys are being prepared to go into military service by jumping from obsta-cles like the tree and taking accelerated academic work so that they can get their diplomas by the time they turn eighteen. Also con-ventions are in abeyance. As Gene observes, adults know that in two years, these sixteen-year-old boys will be sent to war, and so they are more tolerant of teenagers.

The attitude of adults toward the war is further revealed in a conversation about an air raid. In 1942 the Allied cause was bol-stered by two raids that had little significance except as morale raisers: the Doolittle raid on Tokyo and the U.S. Air Force strike against oil fields in Romania. Finny is most likely referring to the latter, which was cause for some elation because there previously had been no Allied victories to celebrate. Most of the U.S. Fleet had been sunk at Pearl Harbor, and in the Philippines, thousands of U.S. soldiers were made prisoners of war by the Japanese.

The adults' reaction to the war news is revealing of how little the home front understood the war. One of the faculty wives voices the view that the bombers should not hit women, children, or older people and should avoid hospitals, schools, and churches. She is deeply concerned that works of art of permanent value to civilization should be spared. Her husband corrects her naive assumptions by pointing out that it is impossible to bomb without doing collateral damage to civilians and nonmilitary targets, adding condescendingly that there is no permanent art in Central Europe.

More important than revealing the war news, this scene in the novel shows that Gene's feelings for Finny are ambivalent. He admires his roommate and feels affection for him, but there is also a building countercurrent of resentment and jealousy. He especially envies Finny's knack for breaking the rules and getting away with it, but he thinks that such envy is harmless. Although he is not aware of it even himself, readers are aware that Gene covets those characteristics in Finny that he lacks: his spontaneous and imaginative response to life and his courage to follow his own impulses.

To celebrate the fact that Finny has made the headmaster laugh at his attire and antics, he proposes the creation of the "Super Suicide Society," whose members must be initiated by jumping out of the tree. The choice of name for his club has an all-too-literal implication, because on one occasion while attempting a double jump, Gene has a near-fatal slip on the limb when he panics. He is saved by Finny, who reaches out to steady him and allow a safe leap.

In addition to the nocturnal activities of the Suicide Society, Finny invents a new sport called "blitzball," a term taken from the newsreels of the period, which dubbed Germany's new methods of war *blitzkreig*, that is, "lightning war." This is an ironic name to link with a boys' game because it suggested the total war that the Axis powers—Germany, Italy and Japan—were waging against the world. Of course, Finny excels at his game because there are no rules, and players make things up as they go. It is little more than a free-for-all that requires the player with the ball to run with it until tackled or giving off the ball to another player. There are no winners or losers because, as Finny states, "You always win . . . everyone always wins at sports" (26). Finny's attitude toward competition is again noted at the swimming pool when he casually breaks the school's 100-meter swimming record and refuses to let Gene call attention to his feat. Gene is puzzled and suspicious, thinking that Finny is trying to trick him by some sort of reverse psychology. He can't believe that Finny would do something without an ulterior motive.

Gene's growing frustration at Finny's influence over him is brought out in the episode when they play hooky from school and slip off to the seashore on bikes, an easy ride since Devon (actually Exeter) is less than fifteen miles from the New Hampshire coast. Gene starts to believe that Finny has him under a spell. Nevertheless, he gives in to his friend and they make the trip, though it means Gene will miss an important math test. On this occasion, Finny confesses to Gene that he regards him as his "best pal" (40), which unnerves Gene, who does not know how to respond to these gestures of friendship and says nothing.

The defining event of the novel occurs shortly afterward, when Finny again insists that Gene should forget his studies and participate in a Suicide Society initiation. This insistence is especially irritating to Gene, because he has decided to compete for a scholarship—the *Ne Plus Ultra* prize for the top student at Devon. Gene's motive is not to be a scholar for the sake of scholarship; he is not an intellectual. Instead, he wants to rival Finny, the best athlete in the school, by standing out as the brightest student.

Gene suspects that Finny's motives for enticing him away from his studies are to ruin his ambitious plans to excel in his studies. When Gene protests to Finny that he needs to study, it becomes clear that Finny had no ulterior motive of spoiling his roommate's grades. When he reveals that he assumed that Gene was so bright he never needed to study, Gene is suddenly aware that there was never any hidden agenda and no rivalry between them except in his own mind. He had attributed his own negative feelings onto Finny. This insight demolishes Gene's self-concept; he feels very small and mean-spirited as he realizes that there never could have been any rivalry between them: "I was not of the same quality as he. I couldn't stand this" (51).

Against Finny's protests, Gene leaves his studies and joins the group going to the tree. Once they reach the tree, the crucial scene unfolds as Gene and Finny climb up the trunk to make a double jump. Inching their way out on the limb that hangs over the river, Finny is farther out and in the more dangerous position. As he balances on the unsteady limb, Gene bends his knees and shakes the limb, causing Finny to lose his balance and fall on the riverbank below instead of in the water. Gene's action is unexplainable—an act of impulsive vindictiveness and moral ambiguity that he cannot comprehend and will come to understand only much later.

Gene's act of treachery is unpremeditated; there is no indication that he intended to do any harm to Finny. His action is an attempt to make Finny look bad rather than to hurt him. It was caused by "a reflex," Knowles once explained in a lecture in 1991 at Clemson University. He jars his friend off the limb to bring him down to a level where they are equals. His ego could not handle the fact that Finny was a better person than he was, so he felt he had to cut him down to his own size. So Gene strikes out at Finny, who never suspects that he is considered a foe.

The fall causes serious injury to Finny's leg. It is "shattered," the doctor says; Finny is so badly crippled that sports will never be possible again for him. Gene is racked by guilt and also fears that Finny will expose what he did. But when he visits the infirmary, he discovers that Finny does not know that he was responsible for knocking him out of the tree. He decides to make a full confession but is prevented from doing so by the arrival of the ambulance to take Finny back home to Boston.

Although Finny has been the one who falls physically, Gene has fallen as well. His fall breaks no bones; rather, his injuries have a moral and psychological dimension. It seems apparent that these plot events that take place during the last summer of freedom and peace that these boys will know has parallels with the situation in the Garden of Eden, where there is also a tree that is forbidden (as this tree was off-limits to all except seniors). Gene's crime against Finny has aspects of original sin—the fall of man as described in the Book of Genesis as the sin Adam and Eve committed when they disobeyed God and ate the fruit of the forbidden Tree of Wisdom. His guilt alienates him from others and himself. In trying to take Finny down, he has ironically taken something vital away from his own nature: he has lost his innocence.

Gene's transgression against Finny is the central and defining event of the novel. Everything that follow is, as Knowles has said, "one long object confession, a *mea culpa*, a tale of crime—if a crime has been committed—and of no punishment. It is a story of growth through tragedy" (Knowles, 109). Gene has moved into a stage of shame that will require much time to atone for. The last part of the book shows Gene's steps toward that end as he tries to find a way to make up for what he has done to his friend.

The next part of the novel deals with the return to school after the disturbing events of the summer. As Gene returns to Devon, he stops off in Boston to see Finny, who is convalescing at home. His purpose is to tell Finny the truth about what happened. This time he is prevented from doing so by Finny, who threatens him with violence if he confesses; he cannot face the fact that Gene would have deliberately done such a thing to him. The confession attempt is frustrated by Finny's refusal to hear it.

With his guilt unpurged and still festering, Gene returns to school for the regular term. The relaxed rules of the summer session have given way to regular routines in the fall. Gene, without Finny to direct him, reverts to conformist tendencies. It is a bad time for Gene as he tries to redeem himself by self-abasement. His former ambitions to be a prominent student are forgotten, and he tries to bury himself in meaningless extracurricular activities. Although he has athletic potential, he goes out for assistant crew manager as if seeking humiliation. This results in a confrontation with an arrogant classmate whose ugly personality is hinted at by his name, Cliff Quackenbush, the crew manager. On his first day as crew manager, Gene gets into a fistfight with Quackenbush, who calls him "a maimed son-of-a-bitch" (71), which Gene sees as a reference to Finny. In the course of the fight Gene slips off the boathouse dock and falls into the dirty waters of the tidal Naguamsett River. Gene considers it fitting that his "baptism" takes place on the first day of the winter session (78).

With the approach of winter, the war makes its first real appearance in the novel. The change in the weather marks a changing outlook on the war. The season's first snowfall is described with military images—the big snowflakes gathering "like noiseless invaders conquering because they took possession so gently" (84). Gene sees the snow as a premonition of the changes that the war will make in the lives of his generation as they adapt to changing conditions caused by new, harsher climate of world history. In mid-October the boys are called on to help harvest the local apple crop. Although it seems part of the war effort, the task is too much like a holiday for it to be taken as anything patriotic. There is the hint, however, that these are "the last shining days" (89) for these young men, a last reprise before they will be expected to perform harsher tasks. And indeed the next work call is less pleasant. The school sends a group of students to shovel snow off the railroad tracks in the nearby railyards, where men and materials are being shipped off to war. In contrast to the skylarking in the apple orchard, the boys are put under the supervision of a grim old railroad man who dislikes the elitist prep school boys for their privilege and youth. After being yelled at and overworked, they finally clear the line late in the afternoon. Just then, a troop train full of soldiers pulls through the station. There is not much difference in age between the students and the soldiers, and the young men yell back and forth at each other with cheerful greetings. Nevertheless, the sight of these troops has a sobering effect on the Devon boys, who are suddenly aware that the time is not far off when they will be on such trains headed toward an uncertain fate.

This experience brings the reality of the war home with greater impact than anything that they have yet seen, and for the next few days the talk turns to the war and the various military options they have. Brinker, an important boy in the senior class who has become Gene's friend in Finny's absence, has an impulsive idea to enlist, which plants the thought in Gene's mind that this is the solution to his problem as well. Not only would entering the service put Gene's life in the hands of a simpler fate; it would also allow him to channel his latent aggression to the destruction of war.

At this point, Gene is on the verge of an irrational decision. Returning to his dorm, Gene finds Finny in the room at his desk, back just in time to save Gene from enlisting in the military and letting the war take care of everything. Finny ensures that Gene will stay in school and come to terms with his guilt. Gene gives up all plans of leaving school because he sees Finny's pain at finding out what had been his intention. Unwilling to hurt Finny again and perhaps realizing that he can find his true integrity in helping the person he has nearly destroyed, Gene determines to stay at Devon and work out his destiny.

The war becomes a distant and unreal thing due to Finny, and once again the boy's focus is on sports rather than combat. Even in the middle of winter, the recommitment to athletics reminds them of the summer peace that had prevailed. Finny's oddball theory that the war is a hoax even takes over Gene's thinking, and he willingly suspends his disbelief, as much to humor Finny as to beguile himself. The rejection of the war as a fact is, of course, a comic fantasy. Finny himself does not believe in his theory, but he is providing an illusion by which both boys can live in an unfallen world of peace.

In this episode the wave of war that had been about to engulf Gene prematurely as a result of his seeing the troop train and Brinker's patriotism is turned aside. He will be under the hypnotic power of Finny's imagination during the bleak winter of 1943.

Gene is told by Finny that he is going to have to be "the big star" now that he is on the sidelines. Finny's plan is to live vicariously through Gene's athletic exploits. In order for this transfer of power to take place, though, Gene not only has to perform like Finny; he must start to think like Finny. The first lesson that he has to learn is that war is not real but that sports are. Wars are for old men, for adults, while games are for boys, and Finny's instructions are aimed at keeping them boys long enough to accomplish his goal of returning the spirit of peace to the campus.

Had it not been for Leper's defection, Finny might have brought off his grand illusion, but the dreamy, overly idealistic Lepellier is the first of the class of 1943 to give up the life of the scholar for that of the soldier. Entranced by a recruiting film of ski troops who glide silently as angels across pure fields of snow, "white warriors of winter" (116), Leper falls in love with the vision, which is the turning point of his life. Only Finny questions the validity of Leper's epiphany, suggesting, with what seems a pun on his name, that the troops in the movie are really Finns who are skiing out to shoot down the bolsheviks, who are in fact allies. Here as elsewhere, Finny tends to disparage overblown patriotism and reveal a cynical reserve about the meaning of war, where loyalties are reversed overnight; the communists, former enemies, are now allies. Leper, however, is convinced by the propaganda. Without dramatic gestures or any fanfare, he makes the occasion seem antiheroic. Wearing his white stocking cap, Leper takes leave of his schoolmates, going into the army to find what he hopes will be a "recognizable and friendly face to the war" (117). Leper represents to Gene what all of the class was seeking: a way to cope with the violence of war that they could comprehend.

A few months later, a messenger arrives bearing bad news: a telegram from Leper saying he has gone AWOL—absent without leave—from the army and desperately seeks Gene's help. In this next episode, Gene undertakes a nighttime pilgrimage to Leper's home in Vermont, where he comes closer to the consequences of war than he has ever been. As Gene will discover, Leper has had a mental breakdown as a result of the traumatic experiences during basic training camp. The trip to Vermont, where even the homes seem afflicted by the freezing weather, is (as the mature voice of the narrator says) a portent of his own wartime experience, which entailed not fighting or marching but monotonous nighttime journeys across the country from one military post to another.

When he arrives in Leper's hometown, Gene must walk out in the keen winds and brilliant sunlight to the rural house where his friend lives. It is described as a "brittle-looking" (132) home, which aptly characterizes Leper as well. As Gene approaches, he sees in one window a small red, white, and blue flag with one star on it, indicating a son in military service; in another window on ground level, he sees Leper peering out. This one-star flag, which Leper's patriotic mother hung so proudly, is mocked by the grim face of her fugitive soldier son.

In his conversation with Leper, it becomes clear immediately that Leper has been reduced to a near psychotic condition by the pressures of military life. Gene attempts false humor and uses a hearty tone, but his efforts fall flat. The seriousness of Leper's condition is made apparent by his confession that he has gone AWOL in order to avoid being discharged as psychologically unfit for military service. Leper's revelation of his condition to Gene leads to a clash of wills. Leper, sensitive to Gene's disdain of him, turns on him with an accusation; he tells Gene that he has always felt that he was "a savage underneath" (137) and reveals that he knows that it was Gene who knocked Finny out of the tree. As if to confirm Leper's accusation, Gene springs forward and knocks Leper out of his chair, spilling him onto the floor, where he curls up in a fetal position, alternately laughing and weeping hysterically.

Gene's encounter with Leper is climactic for both of them; he is appalled at the sight of a person whose whole personality has collapsed. Whatever hope he had of helping Leper turns into an effort to maintain his own mental stability. During their walk across the snow-covered landscape following lunch, Leper reveals what has caused his breakdown. Gene hopes that the frigid, natural scene will have a stabilizing effect on Leper, and he has a momentary illusion that Leper could not be unbalanced in the midst of the wintery outdoors that he loved. Yet the crusty snow that crackles underfoot has ominous implications and seems to symbolize the fragility of the state of mind of both boys. In this tautly drawn scene, Knowles reveals several interesting points that bear on Leper's condition; most important, the nature of Leper's insanity seems to stem from fantasies of sexual transformation. In one instance, he is joking about Brinker's face on Snow White's body (this is the second time that Brinker has been the subject of a joke about his sexuality), and then he breaks down, sobbingly confessing to Gene that his psychological problem stems from his imagining a man's head on a woman's body or inanimate objects like a chair's arm turning into a human arm. The experience with army life has been a nightmare for Leper, during which everything is turned inside out. He reaches a breaking point because he loses contact with the reality of the identity of the people around him. He goes crazy after he imagines that an uncommissioned officer changes into a woman. The account of Leper's confused sexual orientation is more than Gene can stand, maybe because at some level it reveals his own confusion about his own sexual identity and his latent fears of homoerotic feelings. His own stability, like the frozen crust of snow he stands on, is in danger of cracking, and so he runs away, disavowing any connection between what has happened to Leper and himself. Leper's psychological disintegration is disturbing to Gene precisely because it bears so directly on his own struggle. Both Gene and Leper have attempted to avoid the reality of unpleasant facts; Leper has escaped by going insane, but Gene has not yet faced up to his situation. Thus, he strikes out at Leper first and then flees because he cannot accept the truth that he also has an irrational side to his being that he cannot control anymore than Leper can prevent his mind from projected disjointed sexual illusions. Gene's protest that Leper's case has "nothing to do with me" (138) is highly ironic because Gene is very much afraid that he too might not be able to stand the pressure of the war within, which he is fighting alone, or the stress of the war without, which he eventually will have to fight.

The episode in Vermont heightens the novel thematically and prepares for the events in the last three chapters in which the tragic climax of novel will turn on the reappearance of Leper. From the nighttime train trip to the description of rural Vermont, every physical detail is observed with perfect accuracy and endowed with metaphorical implications. For instance, the train ride through the night, which foreshadows Gene's own experiences in a seemingly mindless military bureaucracy, is written so as to convey the sense of time telescoped by the acceleration of events. Also Gene's leaving Leper alone in the frozen snowfields is his second act of betrayal of a friend in the novel. As he flees from Leper, the sounds of the cold cracking the limbs of trees remind him of "distant rifle fire" (142) and metaphorically suggest the parallel between Gene's abandoning his schoolmate and a frightened soldier's deserting the battlefield in a panic.

Gene's first sight of Finny upon his return is in stark contrast to his last glimpse of Leper. He finds his friend in the middle of a snowball fight. This childish activity and boyish joy in life are a world away from the adult conflict that has led to Leper's mental crippling.

After the confrontation with Leper's insanity and the reexposure to the ugly truth of his own guilt, Gene is deeply disturbed. His need to return to Finny and Devon is a reaction to the disorder and irrationality he experienced during his mission to help Leper. Paradoxically, Gene has helped Leper very little but he has gained self-insight and a glimpse into the "heart of darkness." Life to Gene has become a "tangled" business, and the more he experiences existence beyond the groves of academe, the more he would like to evade it.

Other scenes as well touch on the theme of war and reveal how the illusions Gene and Finny hold over the winter were only temporary stays from reality. As spring and graduation approach, the campus is host to many military officers who speak to the students about the merits of military service. To Gene, the various military programs established on college campuses appear more and more attractive because they seem very safe, peaceful and, he thinks, "almost like just going normally on to college" (150). The Devon class of 1943 is faced with the decision of which branch of the military to choose rather than a university, as would have been the case in peacetime. The crisis for seniors not which college will accept them or where they will attend school; rather, it is where they will go to be prepared for war. As Gene says, "There was no rush to get into the fighting; no one seemed to feel the need to get into the infantry. . . . The thing to be was careful and self-preserving. It was going to be a long war" (151).

At this point, Finny's pretense that the war is a hoax has to be admitted, since he has no choice but to believe that Gene's account of Leper's breakdown is true. In addition, he has seen the frightened Leper hiding in the bushes near the school chapel, and he confesses to Gene that he always knew the war was real, to which Gene replies that he, too, knew the war was real, but that he preferred Finny's version.

The trial scene that follows is the final episode of this chapter and precipitates the tragic catastrophe of the novel. Of all of the plot events in the novel, this one has seemed most problematical to commentators, who raise objections to the night court situation as a means to move the story to a conclusion. Although Knowles has foreshadowed the kangaroo court by the earlier episode at the smoking area where Gene faced uncomfortable questions about his past in the accident, here Brinker is shown as an unpleasant, oppressive sort of busybody and the motives that lead Brinker to convene his court are not adequately explained. We never learn why Brinker would so eagerly prosecute his friend Gene in such a sadistic manner. Perhaps more troubling to most readers than Brinker's reasons for investigating the accident is the tone of the court scene; it does not seem to be either a prank or wholly serious either. This scene is not fully comprehensible because there has been no previous indication that Brinker is concerned enough about the unsolved mystery of Finny's fall to go to the lengths that he does to solve it.

The questioning turns on where Gene was in the tree at the time of the accident. Gene claims he cannot recall exactly where he was, but Finny, in a flash of recollection, cuts through to the truth, recalling that they climbed up the tree together to undertake a double jump. The members of the tribunal are not satisfied and demand a witness who can testify to the facts. Then Finny remembers that Leper has returned to Devon and can clear up the matter because he was also at the tree.

Leper's testimony reveals what actually transpired. He tells that he saw both Gene and Finny standing on the limb in a blaze of light from the setting sun, whose rays were "shooting past them like—like golden machine-gun fire" (166). It is now clear to Phineas what happened, and he flees Assembly Hall as if trying to evade the truth with a desperate physical gesture that would shake off the facts as he once shook off tacklers. The sound of his body tumbling down the marble staircase tells us that he has taken a second terrible fall.

Chapter 12 contains the reconciliation of Gene and Finny and their coming to terms with the full facts about the fall, which each had resisted until Brinker's court of inquiry. The trial ultimately reverses the implications of the first fall because it makes possible Gene's acceptance of his guilt and his full confession to Finny.

After spending all night in the stadium rather than in his dorm, Gene returns to school and finds a note from Dr. Stanhope instructing him to bring Finny's personal items to the infirmary. This meeting between Gene and Finny is their final one, and for Gene it is his chance to atone for his sin against Finny.

Gene starts to talk, explaining that he had tried to confess his crime before and had been unable to bring it out in the open. This remark satisfies Finny that Gene is now telling the truth, and his face registers "a settled, enlightened look" (181). At this point Finny explains to Gene that he has been deceiving him about his belief that there was no war. All along, he has been trying to enlist in some branch of the armed forces, but without success. Gene's remark to Finny in response to his admission that he has been trying to get into the war while denying its existence is a summarizing statement that puts Finny's character into the fullest focus. Gene points out to Finny that he'd be worthless in the war, even if his leg had not been injured. "They'd get you some place at the front and there'd be a lull in the fighting, and the next thing anyone knew you'd be over with the Germans or the Japs, asking if they'd like to field a baseball team against our side. . . . You'd get things so scrambled up nobody would know who to fight any more" (182).

In Gene's estimate, Finny's innocence so totally represents the spirit of peace that his very presence would make war appear unacceptable. His goodwill and fundamental idealism would overcome the fear and hostility that fuel war. Finny is moved by Gene's honesty and is now willing to accept that his friend acted from a blind impulse rather than out of vindictive feelings. Thus both Gene and Finny accept what happened because they can understand it as a consequence of human weakness.

Although the injury to Finny's leg is a "clean break," when the leg is reset, some bone marrow gets into the bloodstream, causing Finny's death from heart arrest. As unexpected as Finny's death is to the reader, it has been anticipated by Knowles and is indeed almost inevitable. The symbolism of Finny's heart stopping is inescapable. He did not have the heart to keep up any longer the illusion of the world that had sustained him.

In the last chapter, Knowles moves the plot forward several months to June 1943 as the class graduates. His purpose for extending the story beyond the dramatic death of the main character is to introduce the war theme again and sound the generation gap motif. To do so, he brings in a new character, Brinker's father, a World War I veteran whose excessive patriotism is offensive to both his son and Gene. Combat duty will provide war memories to reminisce about in future years as they recall their heroic youth in the marines, paratroops, or as frogmen. To Brinker and Gene, the prospect of risking their lives in order to have some future bragging rights is totally unrealistic. Much to Mr. Hadley's dismay, Gene tells him he is going into the Navy to avoid fighting in foxholes with the infantry; Brinker's plan is to join the Coast Guard because he hopes it will be safest service. The scene, one of the only extended depiction of parents, with the exception of Leper's mother, is intended to draw a distinction between the older and younger generations. Paradoxically, the boys conclude that the World War I generation is childish and they are the mature ones. Their disillusionment is akin to Finny's view, which maintained the war was a joke that fat and foolish old men played on younger men. However, Gene forms an independent idea. To him, "it seemed clear that wars were made not by generations and their special stupidities, but that wars were made instead by something ignorant in the human heart" (193).

The arrival of the army air force parachute riggers detachment at Devon signals the end of all illusions of peace as the civilian campus becomes a military installation "for the duration" of the war, as the phrase of the day went. The soldiers do not look very bellicose to Gene in their rumpled khaki uniforms and struggling columns. They are singing a popular polka tune, "Roll Out the Barrel," and marching behind jeeps and trucks loaded with sewing machines rather than machine guns. The irony of the military occupation of troops who pack parachutes to ensure safe falls is certainly intended in the light of the one of the novel's major motifs: falling from trees and down stairs as well as the fallen nature of man. The military occupation of Devon soon makes the campus unrecognizable, as olive green trash barrels sprout and stenciled signs denoting military offices and areas appear everywhere, giving the school a changed atmosphere marked by the map of a "conscious maintenance of high morale" (193).

The last pages of the novel serve to extend Gene's awareness as narrator beyond the moment in time he is located and assure us that he has reached a point of understanding the experience he narrates. This part of the novel thus forms a conclusion that rounds out the meaning of the main plot much like Fitzgerald's ending of *The Great Gatsby*, which also conveys the author's evaluation of the meaning of the book.

Gene's recovery from the alienation that afflicted him depends on a process of spiritual transformation. Those qualities in Finny that were most vital and life giving are assumed by Gene, while his negative traits are exorcised by Finny's death. Gene's psyche is integrated and harmonized by the forgiveness and love that Finny extended to his friend. Thus, as he packs after graduation to enlist in the Navy, Gene comes to understand that Finny was never an enemy; rather, he was his own enemy and had been fighting a war within himself between two sides of his own nature. He leaves for war with the assurance that his friend's peace-loving and joyful outlook on life has become a permanent part of his own nature. The process of self-understanding and self-forgiveness has thus begun, and the novel ends with Gene's having made his separate peace.

Thus ends one of the most beloved American works of the mid-twentieth century. Gene has gotten in step with that side of his nature that was represented by Finny and an open outlook on life. The savagery and destructiveness that Gene had once harbored in his heart have been expunged and expiated. The inner conflict, which was a sort of war within his own being, has ended, and the good angels of his nature have taken possession of Gene's spirit. Although the inner strife that Gene experiences throughout the story is a major aspect of the theme of *A Separate Peace*, the novel also provides a paradigm for our sinful and problematic fallen nature as human beings, a defect in ourselves that causes violence and war. Only Finny, who is presented as having exemplary virtues and total absence of feelings of malice and jealousy, seems free from the sins that flesh is heir to. In fact, his goodness is almost too angelic, and that may weaken Finny as a character. He is too much a symbol who exists as a representative of qualities that we would all like to possess. Nevertheless, Finny is the most attractive of the book's characters and fulfills the role of the tragic protagonist whose death restores the capacity for life in others. While some may say that this role is too heavy for sixteen-year-old boys to play, no reader, especially young readers, would fault Knowles for having given American literature another one of those radical innocents like Huckleberry Finn, Daisy Miller, Jay Gatsby, and Holden Caulfield, whose virtues raise them above a morally ambivalent world and enshrine them in our hearts.

TOPICS FOR DISCUSSION AND RESEARCH

1. *A Separate Peace* contains biblical allusions to events in Genesis, especially the forbidden fruit and the Fall. How do these references help convey the themes of the novel?

2. Brinker, Leper, and Finny are nicknames of three of the important characters. Are their names in any way descriptive of character or symbolic? Give specific reasons.

3. What is the implication of Leper's telling Gene, "You were always a savage underneath!"

4. Develop in detail a comparison between two of the following sets of characters, taking into account likenesses as well as differences in each case: (a) Chet Douglas and Quackenbush; (b) Mr. Hadley and Mrs. Lepellier; (c) Rev. Carhart and Coach Phil Lathan; (d) Mr. Prud'homme or Mr. Ludsbury and Dr. Stanpole.

5. Gene finally understands that Finny is someone of high moral character. Are there things about Finny that would cause an objective observer to disagree with this view?

6. How would our conception of the novel be different if it had been narrated from an author's omniscient point of view and we knew what characters other than Gene were thinking? What if Gene were telling the story as it happened rather than fifteen years later?

7. If you have seen the 1972 movie version of the novel, you will note that the film script departs from the novel in several ways in key scenes. Compare (a) the accident at the tree, (b) the blitzball game, (c) the encounter with Leper at his home in New Hampshire, (d) the kangaroo court in the auditorium, and (e) the ending of the novel as they are treated in the book and in the film.

8. What is the difference between the Devon and Nuguamsett rivers? Do they have any symbolic value?

9. How is Mr. Hadley's attitude toward war and military service different from Brinker's and Gene's?

10. Do you see any irony in the fact that an army unit of parachute riggers is billeted at Devon School toward the end of the war?

11. Why do you think this novel is set at a private boys school? Do you think the wartime atmosphere would have differed at a public school?

TOPICS FOR FURTHER EXPLORATION

1. In *A Separate Peace*, Knowles depicts conflicts between the world of peace (the school, adolescence, or childhood) and the world of war

(the adults), which makes its influence felt by the boys by the war reports, shortages, and the threat of being drafted into military service at age eighteen. Show how the boys resist being overwhelmed by the grim reality they face by maintaining the illusion of peace in a world at war.

2. Develop in detail a comparison between the point of view in *A Separate Peace* and the first-person narrator in F. Scott Fitzgerald's *The Great Gatsby*, Nick Carroway, who judges and evaluates the events he describes as Gene does.

3. Compare *A Separate Peace* with William Golding's *The Lord of the Flies*, which also attempts to trace the defects of society back to defects in human nature.

4. Discuss the parallel with *A Farewell to Arms*, where the protagonist of Ernest Hemingway's novel makes a separate peace.

5. *A Separate Peace* uses techniques of the double or "doppelganger" story, in which a central character confronts a figure who is his physical or psychic counterpart. The two can complement or oppose each other; always, one character is instructed or altered by the encounter with the double, for better or worse. Apply this concept of doubles to Gene and Finny so as to explain the complex relationship between the two boys.

6. Knowles shows a great talent for describing local atmosphere in *A Separate Peace*, one of his main appeals as a writer. He frequently uses setting to forward ideas or themes that he wishes to develop in the story he is telling. Select at least three scenes from the novel, and show how the treatment of terrain, climate, and other background details serves a thematic purpose.

SUGGESTED READINGS AND WORKS CITED

There is only one book-length study of *A Separate Peace* but many insightful essays may be consulted, a few of which are included below.

Alley, Douglas. "Teaching Emerson Through *A Separate Peace*." *English Journal* 70 (January 1981): 19–23.

Bloom, Harold. *Modern Critical Interpretations of John Knowles's* A Separate Peace. Philadelphia: Chelsea House, 2000.

Bryant, Hallman B. *A Separate Peace: The War Within*. Twayne's Masterworks Series, No. 50. Boston: Twayne, 1990.

Ellis, James. "*A Separate Peace*: The Fall from Grace." *English Journal* 53 (1964): 313–18.

Halio, Jay. "John Knowles's Short Novels." *Studies in Short Fiction* 1
     (1964): 107–12.
Knowles, John. "My Separate Peace." *Esquire* (March 1985).
Nora, M. "A Comparison of Actual and Symbolic Landscape in *A Separate
     Peace*." *Discourse* 11 (1968): 356–62.
Webster, Ronald. "Narrative Method in *A Separate Peace*." *Studies in
     Short Fiction* 3 (1965): 63–72.

2

The Old School Tie: The Preparatory School as Setting of the Novel

Many readers of *A Separate Peace* are not aware that a number of episodes in the novel are based on real-life experiences and actual relationships with people the author knew while he was attending Phillips Exeter Academy in the early 1940s. Knowles has been candid about explaining the interconnections of fact and fiction in *A Separate Peace*. As is the case with many first novels, much in the book is semiautobiographical. In a 1972 interview with the school newspaper, *The Exonian*, Knowles admits how he adapted specific people and events to the plot and also projected some of his own personality into the nature of the narrator, Gene Forrester. He noted that he did not aspire to be a top student as Gene did and did not cause any bodily injury to his classmates.

In "The Young Writer's Real Friends" (1962), Knowles describes how he came to write *A Separate Peace*. He had written an earlier novel set in Europe with an exotic and symbolic setting in the mode of European existentialists like Camus and Gide, but gave up on the manuscript after being told by Thornton Wilder, who had become his literary mentor, to find a story and characters that he was interested in first and then let the symbolism take care of itself. Following this advice, Knowles set out to write another book, about which he says, "If anything I wrote tempted me to insert artificial complexities, I ignored it. If anything appeared which looked suspiciously like a symbol, I left it on its own. I thought that I wrote truly and deeply enough about certain specific people in certain places and at a particular time having certain specific experiences, then the result would be relevant for many other kinds of people" (14). Thus, Knowles started with characters and a setting that he knew well, a New England boy's school that he calls Devon but is in reality Phillips Exeter. A number of people have pointed to the many parallels between the fictional place and the real school, most carefully by Sister Mary Nora in "A Comparison of the Actual and Symbolic Landscape in *A Separate Peace*."

Because the nature of a boarding school like the one in the novel has changed so radically in the forty years since the book was published, it is instructive to look back at that world from a historical perspective to see what these elite schools were like in terms of their origins, curricula, attitudes, regimens, faculty, and place in the social and educational scheme of things in the United States. Schools like Andover and Exeter, which were founded in the late eighteenth century, were strongly influenced by the models of British public schools like Eton, Harrow, and Rugby as were other elite prep schools. American preparatory schools show other signs of British overtones in the way that classes were made up of "forms" rather than grades, the teachers were called "masters," and the students wore school uniforms, including ties. Also, some hazing or harassing of the younger boys by the older boys was traditional. In addition, the seniors were given a hand in the everyday running of the school and exercised authority over the lower grades.

The sense of the power and prestige that prep school conferred on their students strikes some as un-American and elitist, reflected in the following statement by a Groton graduate: "Here the American upper class sends its sons to instill the classic values: discipline, honor, a belief in the existing values and the rightness of them. Coincidentally it's at Groton one starts to meet the right people, and where connections which will serve well later on are forged" (David Haberstram, quoted in Cookson and Persell, 5).

There is a perception that prep schools are little more than educational country clubs because they are expensive and exclusive and have rural settings. Therefore, one would assume that life on the campuses would be idyllic—but that would be a misconception. Although Knowles describes life at Devon in the summer of 1942 as almost Edenic, life in most prep schools is full of stress. Like all other communal societies, whether military or religious, the members are expected to follow a strict regimen that is regulated by the clock. Students in boarding schools follow tight schedules. On school days they typically rise early, go to class during the morning hours, attend chapel daily, have athletics in the afternoon, spend two or three hours in the evening at required study period, and retire at lights out prior to midnight. The weekends are more relaxed, but the students' time is still structured. The institutions seek to strengthen character and expand the mind by keeping young people so occupied that they don't have time to get into trouble.

Prep schools make demands on more than students' time. There is also intense intellectual pressure. The business of education is taken seriously, and lazy or indifferent students do not last long. The academic climate is enhanced by stimulating and dedicated teachers, who try to instill in their students a desire for learning for its own sake rather than for grades alone. Since class sizes are small, usually around fifteen per class, instruction involves student participation, which means they must be prepared to express their ideas. Phillips Exeter was one of the first academies to move away from learning by memorization and recitation with the adoption of the "Harkness Plan," seminars where a small group of students sit around a table and are led in a discussion of a topic by a teacher. The Socratic method, in which teachers ask questions, is used for the purpose of forming and expressing ideas rather than "dispensing and receiving information."

The intense learning environment is often too much for some students, such as those who are slow learners or those who expect to make top grades, which are hard to come by because there is still harsh grading in prep schools. The complications of adolescence and rigid rules and academic pressure are too much for some students who develop psychological problems. These kinds of breakdowns are manifested as rebellion, withdrawals, or dropping out, as Leper does in *A Separate Peace*.

Although it is expected that students in elite prep schools are high achievers and are driven by ambition to excell, there is also a counterexpectation that studying too hard and long is not good form. Being someone who seeks high grades can result in one's becoming stigmatized, as Finny accuses Gene of "sweating" his grades too much at a critical point in the novel, putting him in a bind of having to conform to peer pressure or be excluded.

In addition to the academic training, prep schools also put a great emphasis on extracurricular activities, especially sports. Here again the model is the British public schools' philosophy of a sound mind in a healthy body and the promotion of the keen sense of competition that equips one for success in the world. Many of the sports played at prep schools are also derived from English prototypes, like rugby, soccer, and rowing. The pressure to excel in athletics is just as intense as it is in the classroom, and on the playing fields the emphasis is on winning.

As in other aspects of life, people with similar interests and attitudes tend to form themselves into groups, and prep school students tend to sort themselves out into cliques, such as those who go in for sports ("the jocks"), those who strive for grades ("the brains"), and those who are the student leaders ("the pols"—boys who participate in school politics).

Although there is little mention of the faculty in *A Separate Peace*, those who teach at boarding schools are special people in several senses. Many are themselves graduates of private schools and colleges and are educated beyond the level of public school teachers, the majority holding M.A. degrees and Ph.D.s, and most are male, whereas in public secondary schools, women usually make up the majority of the teaching staff. The prep school teacher is also expected to function as a friend to homesick students, live in a dormitory as a monitor, coach athletics, and carry out police duties to discover who is breaking the rules and to catch them at it. It is an all-absorbing occupation that requires them to be on duty seven days a week, so only those with dedication and a willingness to sacrifice something of their own private lives are likely to last as prep school faculty. The rewards are that teaching in a prep school is intellectually stimulating and one does not have to worry about keeping order in the classroom. The high ideals and purposes that instruction in boarding schools is grounded on are well illustrated by the words in deed of gift that Dr. Phillips wrote to the trustees of the academy he established at Exeter in 1782:

> It shall ever be considered as a principal duty of the instructors to regulate the tempers, to enlarge the minds, and form the morals of the youth committed to their care. But above all, it is expected that the attention of instructors to the disposition of the minds and morale of the youth under their charge will exceed every other care; well considering that though goodness without knowledge is weak and feeble, yet knowledge without goodness is dangerous, and that

both unified form the noblest character, and lay the surest foundation of usefulness to man kind.

In the 1980s there was a surge of interest in prep schools that coincided with the return of the Republicans to the White House under Ronald Reagan which ushered in the "Yuppie" decade. The Young Urban Professionals were products of the prep culture and Ivy League educations. The sense of power and prestige that they projected was satirized and mocked by Nelson Aldrich in *The Atlantic Monthly* (1979) and Lisa Birnbach in *The Official Preppy Handbook* (1980), which damn with faint praise the fashions and fads of preppiness. The trend to look preppy has had its day, however, replaced by the dressed-down grungy look.

The question is, Do prep schools still have a role to play in an increasingly democratic and diverse society? In such a world will there be any reason for the production of an elite class of people? Does the conservative approach to life and the holding on to tradition doom these boarding schools to the fate of the dinosaurs? As Darwin demonstrated, change is the order of nature and organisms that do not adapt to a changing environment will die, so the evolution that the prep schools are ungoing at the moment may signal their survival.

MINING THE PAST

The following article, which Knowles wrote in 1956 while on assignment for *Holiday* magazine, informed and shaped his descriptions of the grounds of Devon School in *A Separate Peace*. The trip he took back to Phillips Exeter made him start to think about some of his experiences at the school over a decade before. There are several connections between what he observes on his return to his alma mater and the novel. For example, Knowles reveals there is actually no school tie at Exeter, which makes it different from Devon, and he, like Gene in the novel, is annoyed by the sight of some new buildings on campus, which seem a blemish on the otherwise unchanging aspect of the school. Note how in the last paragraphs Knowles draws a parallel between the variety of weather that goes with the sharp changes in the seasons and the way these surroundings enrich the experiences of the students.

FROM JOHN KNOWLES, "A NATURALLY SUPERIOR SCHOOL"
(*Holiday*, December 1956)

The first fact to establish about Phillips Exeter Academy is that it does not have an old-school tie. This is quite a break with tradition for a school so old, so heavy with history and English associations. One would certainly expect the tie, the symbol of the separate, special group, the evidence of belonging. But there isn't one.

Certainly the school has an English look about it—courts surrounded by red-brick Georgian buildings, rambling old houses amid ancient trees, a low-lying English Gothic country church, playing fields reaching out toward the river and the woods. The faculty members tend to wear tweeds rivaling in shapelessness any Sussex gentlemen's. Even the surrounding little town of Exeter, New Hampshire, resembles an English village.

This impression of a transplanted Eton or Harrow could occur to any visitor arriving at the academy during a class period, when the boys are out of sight. After a while a bell high in a cupola will begin to ring. No one who has ever lived there can forget that bell.

It does not joyously peal or portentously toll. It simply announces that Exeter boys will now get out of bed, or go to morning chapel, or leave one classroom and go to another. Throughout their school years the Exeter bell calmly and ceaselessly rings the changes in their lives.

For a visitor contemplating how stately and English everything is, the bell shatters that illusion abruptly. Doors in the classroom building fly open and out stream the students, wearing ties to be sure, but any ties— no two alike. Instead of the uniform accent of an English school, the spoken word here is as varied as the United States and more. The English aim is to make the students more like each other, to stamp them permanently as Old Etonians or Old Harrovians. The Exeter aim is the opposite: to bring out what is individually promising in each of the students.

Then I knew that Exeter hadn't changed. The look of it hadn't changed, I had noticed that at once. In the eleven years since I had graduated there were just a few new structures—a long, low a maintenance building; an artificial hockey rink; a new art gallery. Nothing to disturb the reminiscing alumnus except a picture-windowed, ranch-type ell someone had tacked onto the simple, venerable First Academy Building. Aside from this outrage, it was all as it had been.

Exeter's policy has always been conservative. Its reputation was first made as a classical school, and while the curriculum has necessarily become more liberal to conform with that of the colleges its graduates enter, "No one," in the words of an old pillar of the school, "majors in sand pile." To graduate, a student must pass four years of English, three of mathematics, three of one foreign language, a year of American history and six additional major subjects. In 1946 the radical concession of not requiring Latin and Greek in any combination.

As a result of this scholastic pace, Exeter students often go straight into sophomore courses, and sometimes junior courses, when they enter college. But no harrowing adjustment to the freedom of college life is necessary. "There are no rules at Exeter," an old motto runs, "until they are broken." While juniors and lower middlers (freshmen and sophomores) must be in their dormitories at 8:00 P.M., upper middlers (juniors) may stay out until 9:00, and seniors until 10:00. While all must attend chapel at 8:00 each morning, no one is obliged to appear at any meal, although of course most do. After the wild brass-knuckle period, the faculty reined back on the student body, but since then has been gradually loosening up to see how much discipline the students will impose upon themselves. Study hall is compulsory only when work is not up to the mark.

A few years ago a newspaper, irked about something I had written, tried to indicate how out of touch I was by reporting that at an early age I had been "whisked off to exclusive Phillips Exeter Academy." The picture of spoiled little would-be aristocrats fenced off from American life came clearly through. But what actually happened at Exeter was that I found myself in a matter-of-fact school where democratic diversity was taken for granted. I was placed in one of the "houses," old New England manses which supplement the thirteen dormitories. A master and his family lived on the first floor, and six other boys and I lived on the two floors above. I think our different ways of talking indicated what a wide sampling of America we were. There was a Bostonian who, every morning as we make or beds, used to sing *St. James Infirmary* in regulation Harvard Yard diction. From downstairs the molasses accent of a boy from Florida would ooze up, usually complaining about the unreasonable peace of things. He was balanced by a twang from down the hall, one of those tart Vermont voices, dry and energetic. Between that room and mine there was a boy from Arizona who used a gruff, grunting way of speaking which sounds a little like Indian talk. Across from him a native of Poughkeepsie added the accent of metropolitan New York; I contributed a bit of West Virginia mountain drawl, and downstairs a Pennsylvania boy spoke unexceptionable American English.

There is no doubt that we were diverse, which is one aspect of democracy. But did we have poor as well as rich? I have just tried to remember, and now I realize that I never knew, although I naturally knew a great deal about all of them. Exeter is more democratic than that of many public high schools. No one is permitted to have a car, so that avenue of conspicuous consumption is cut. There is little variation in clothes; flannel slacks or khaki pants and a sports jacket are standard. Wealthy parents are not encouraged to send their sons large amounts of money; it would simply create the problem of where to spend it.

There are few places where money means less. The tuition is $1600 a year, but Exeter tries to mitigate it through scholarships. Almost 25 per cent of the students receive some scholarship help, from one fifth of the cost to the entire amount. Jobs are also available for boys who want to help pay their way.

Money is not the measure of value at Exeter. It is not the wealthy, but the active, boy who stands out, someone who can juggle several fields at once. There is a whole constellation of extracurricular activities, in addition to athletics—the student newspaper, musical groups, debating societies, literary, dramatic and political clubs, and many other organizations.

The strongest popularity comes to a boy who seems to be settled with himself, who is effective but not aggressive about it, friendly without backslapping, a good student but no pedant, a capable athlete without biceps flexing. There is a tremendous emphasis on being "knowing." I think one of the chief values of Exeter is the opportunities it offers for knowing about studies, about places, about people from every corner of the country and about different ways of life.

Yet Exeter isn't the warmest place in the world, especially at first. My first night there, the other six boys in the house and I were called down to the master's apartment. It happened to be my birthday. I was seven hundred miles from home, on my own for the first time, and as yet with no friend in the school. This wasn't especially harrowing, but could have improved with even a little friendliness and warmth. There didn't seem to be any around. The master sat at the end of his Colonial living room and, in a quiet, cold voice, read us the rules. He sat at right angles to us, as if we weren't there. I began to feel that I had been committed to Exeter.

The students aren't prize examples of brotherly love either. Their very diversity enforces a comparatively broad tolerance, but the fact remains that they are adolescents. Uncomplimentary nicknames spring up like witch grass. For every boy who raises some real or imagined claim for himself, there is a slash to cut it down. Only if he is ready with a swift counter-slash will he wind up no worse off than he began. The conflict of egos can be heard all over these peaceful acres.

But every afternoon all this energy is turned to sport. The school buildings empty; the students and many of the masters trek to the gym for basketball, swimming, wrestling; or to the hockey rink, squash courts, track cage; or to the Plimpton Playing Fields, for baseball, soccer, track, tennis; or beyond them to the Fields Beyond, for touch football or lacrosse. Some go to the tidewater river below the school for crew; in the winter the ski team seeks out snow-covered slopes.

This is for me the best moment in an Exeter day. The textbooks are closed, and toward the river dozens of teams practice and play; some lower middle forgets every nuance of *She Stoops to Conquer* when he throws his first successful block. Time, which has crept along during class after class in the morning, suddenly hurtles through the afternoon. Sports are credited with developing the body, the character, confidence, sportmanship and so on. Everyone gains some of these things from afternoons on the playing fields of Exeter.

Exeter is New England in essence. Many of the buildings bear the old Puritan names—Wheelwright, Peabody, Phillips, Abbot, Gilman, Jeremiah Smith. The town is one of those historic New England settlements which had an early leading role in the region and then lapsed into unchangingness. Never becoming big and famous, it preserved a certain flavor of colonial days. Churches loom everywhere as in the times when they were the center of social life; there has been no need to tear down the old house to make room for apartment buildings; ancient cemeteries have not been moved to provide space for parking lots.

Exeter's rival and brother school, the Phillips Academy at Andover, Massachusetts, has a more elaborate look, more civilized and urban—it might be in Pennsylvania or Virginia. But Exeter, with this more secluded and even provincial quality about it, is distinctly in New Hampshire. I always felt that we were far up in the north country, and that our woods extended on into the not-yet-completely-tamed wilderness.

The changes of season are more emphatic than almost anywhere in the country. Fall arrives with sharp-edged decision, and a luminous sky spreads over Exeter, so that in the crisp clarity of the air the autumn colors stand out sharply. Voices carry far, and everything—trees, rooms, clothes, hair—smells of the edged vigor of the fall air. Then, in a month or so, the light goes out of the countryside, the edge of coolness is lost in a general chill, and the look and feel of Exeter dulls. But after Christmas, if it is one of the good old-fashioned winters, a still, dry cold crackles around the school, and the ground is clamped beneath a congealed crust covering a foot or more of snow. At night the outside lamps shine on a white, silent world of cold elegance. The narrow white houses with their green shutters belong in this frozen landscape, the small windows letting little of the inner warmth escape outdoors.

When spring breaks out, after such a winter, it is a plain miracle, and it sweeps a whole new way of life into the school. Canoes nose up the winding Exeter River between revived woods; adventures take place after supper in the small park that lies beside the lower, tidewater river; windows are opened everywhere at last.

These sharp changes which nature brings help keep the mind alert through nine months of forced mental growth. If what goes on indoors is sometimes a monotonous repetition, it's a relief to have a swiftly changing world visible through the windows.

Exeter has reached out to bring variety to the school from all parts of the country. And although the curriculum changes only slowly, and the philosophy of education not at all, the surroundings fluctuate unendingly, and the boys, varied to begin with, continue in their individual ways to be varied and changing. Exeter's role is to make the changes rich and permanent.

A REMEMBRANCE OF THINGS PAST

The following article was written twenty-five years after the publication of *A Separate Peace*. Knowles reveals that his purpose in writing the novel was to tell a story of growth through tragedy which he believes was the key to the book's popularity because it allowed young people who had not attended elite prep schools to respond to the characters regardless of their background or gender. Therefore, the theme of *A Separate Peace* lifted it above its setting and specific place in time.

FROM JOHN KNOWLES, "MY SEPARATE PEACE"
(*Esquire*, March 1985)

What I set out to do in the novel was to unscramble, plumb, and explain what had happened during a very peculiar summer at Phillips Exeter Academy in New Hampshire, where I was a sixteen-year-old summer-session student in 1943. It was just as World War II was turning in our favor, and were we boys going to be in it or not? And what was war, and what was aggression, and what were loyalty and rivalry, what were goodness and hate and fear and idealism, all of them swirling around us during that peculiar summer?

I wrote the book to dramatize and work through those questions.

The story itself was certainly not the usual kind of material for a best seller. The narrator, Gene Forrester, bright and athletic, and his roommate, the extraordinary schoolboy athlete Phineas, are taking an accelerated course through the Devon School in New Hampshire so as to get into World War II before it ends. Beneath their great friendship in these idyllic countryfied surroundings there is a lurking rivalry, hostility, and destructiveness. During a dangerous game of jumping from high tree into the river, Phineas is gravely injured.

Gene is suspected of having provoked this "accident" out of buried resentment, and sometimes he thinks so himself. One of their group meanwhile goes off to the military service and soon after creeps back to Devon, "psycho." And then the students stage a mock trial to try Gene, and the book moves on to its climax. It is a schoolboy story and it is also an allegory about the sources of war.

I based the narrator, Gene Forrester, on myself; Phineas on my friend, the exceptional student athlete David Hackett. We were in school together for only one summer, at Exeter Academy; his athletic career was

First Academic Building, Phillips Exeter Academy. (Author's photo)

conducted at Milton Academy outside Boston and at McGill University in Montreal. There he excelled in many sports, preeminently in hockey, qualifying for the U.S. Olympic Ice Hockey Team in 1948.

Dave was not crippled by a fall from a tree in 1943, but I reversed matters while writing *A Separate Peace* and turned a real, not very serious accident to me into a fateful fictional one for him. This reversal made it possible to show the darker streaks of human nature. If I were going to make my point, then the Phineas character would have to be the victim.

David went on to work for his lifelong friend Robert Kennedy in the Justice Department in Washington, to marry happily and have five children, and to view with some bemusement the short, legendary, and tragic life of Phineas, a character he inspired and very much resembled, up to a point.

Some of the other characters in the novel were loosely based on other students: Brinker Hadley on [author] Gore Vidal, for instance. People react in a singular way when they find you have constructed a fictional character with them in mind. Gore feels that the muses intended *A Separate Peace* for his pen and that only some inexplicable blunder on Mount Helicon caused it to descend upon me.

A British reviewer remarked that one would think, on reading *A Separate Peace*, that the author "had never heard of J. D. Salinger." His novel about a preparatory schoolboy had been published several years before I sat down to write mine and had been very widely read and discussed and admired. When I was about a third of the way into my book I ran across a copy of *The Catcher in the Rye*. Always having meant to read it, I started in. Oh my God, I said to myself on about page 10, a teenage boy! In a prep school! This thing could *influence* me, if I let it. I closed the book and only returned to it when mine was in galleys. Then I read and admired it very much. They are very different books. His is a 360-degree circumambulating of one fascinating character. Mine is linear, a narrative involving two and then four interrelating characters.

Isn't such a success with your first book, people ask, a kind of curse, since everything that follows will be compared unfavorably to it? No, because first of all, it freed me from having to teach school or be a journalist, enabling me to devote myself entirely to fiction writing. And it gave me a public identity.

The one limiting result of this success is that my later work was expected to resemble *A Separate Peace*. My readers wanted my books to be set in schools. They loved *Peace Breaks Out*, which is a "companion novel" to *A Separate Peace*. They also approved of *The Paragon* and of my most recent novel, *A Stolen Past*, about a Russian princess and her son, set mostly at Yale. Other books, if they were not set in schools, got a cooler reception. They weren't really Knowles novels.

A different kind of unsettling experience occurred when the novel was made into a movie. Paramount released *A Separate Peace* in 1972, and I went to see it in fear and trepidation. But it was very different from what I anticipated. They had certainly not vulgarized the work; in fact, the movie was almost painfully faithful to the book. It had been gorgeously photographed at Exeter Academy, and they had created and solved great difficulties by shooting there during each of the four seasons, shutting down production in the intervals. John Heyl and Parker Stevenson, neither of whom had dreamed of being an actor, turned in effective and genuine performances under the direction of Larry Peerce.

What was hard to bear were the emotions embodied by those young actors filmed in the very place where the original events transpired. Revealing emotion didn't bother me in words, in a book, but on that great big screen it all seemed too painful, too personal.

The book is autobiographical. By no means did all the incidents happen as portrayed, but the emotional truth of it comes to life. "You have to strip yourself naked," Scott Fitzgerald wrote. Thornton Wilder, discarding an early attempt at a novel by me, wrote in a letter: "Everything in this novel lacks intensity. . . . Find a subject which you are absorbed in. . . . Select your next subject from the compelling elements in your life. . . . It is from our most vital subjectivity that we write. . . ." Well, *A Separate Peace* really should have been dedicated to Thornton.

All of this is essentially literary gossip, and what counts, in the long run, is what the book has meant to readers, so many millions of readers, and why.

A Separate Peace is one long and abject confession, a mea culpa, a tale of crime—if a crime had been committed—and of no punishment, or only interior punishment. It is a story of growth through tragedy. Young people, on their deepest emotional level, respond to that. It makes not the slightest difference that the story's externals may be totally foreign to them. In the novel there is not a girl in sight; that means nothing—women of all ages and every background treat it as central to their view of life. It takes place among some privileged kids in a first-class preparatory school: that doesn't mean anything either. One of the most moving letters I ever got was from the teenage participants in a drug treatment program in the Bedford-Stuyvesant section of Brooklyn. Another was from a group of paraplegic veterans of the Vietnam War. Co-eds in Finland, old ladies in Italy, a murderer on death row in Utah—all have communicated their depth of feeling about the book.

These responses, of course, are the greatest reward *A Separate Peace* can bring or ever will bring to me. The book has affected millions of lives, influenced them deeply, modified what they saw and felt in the world about them. The ultimate importance of *A Separate Peace* is that it has reached out to the readers who need it.

Knowles went back to the Exeter campus in 1972, while the movie based on the novel was being filmed. During that time he granted several interviews to the editors of the school newspaper, from which the following item is taken.

FROM JOHN KNOWLES, "REFLECTIONS OF JOHN KNOWLES
ABOUT HIS NOVEL"
(*The Exonian*, November 1, 1972)

All the faculty here were between fifty and seventy years old when I first entered Exeter in the fall of 1942. I had a young French teacher and one other young teacher but they had left for the war by mid-year. All of the faculty on the campus were so much older than we were, that we had no connection with them. They just were too old, too tired, and too busy. One of the reasons that Gene and Finny develop this intensely close friendship is that they had no one to relate to; no older person to pattern themselves on, to look and talk things over with, they only had each other. All the students really had to relate to each.

I was happy to be on the swimming team and Dan Fowler was the only faculty man I could begin to think I had any connection with as far as rapport. A faculty member might drop in once a term to a club or organization meeting, but that was rare. The master of Sleeper House was inaccessible. I was in Peabody with Mr. Galt and Mr. Bissell. This situation of the faculty explains a lot about the book. The students were thrown back upon themselves. One faculty member I mentioned in the book is a reference to a real person. I wrote about old Mr. Wittman, Doc Wittman, as Mr. Patchwithers. He is the very old professor who gives the party in the book. I think Doc Wittman is no longer living.

Also the school minister in the book was George Carhart. Mr. Carhart was in the English department, but I liked the sound of the name.

Mr. Galt might be construed as having said the remark, "Is it raining in your part of town?" in the book.

It is true that I put part of myself into all four main characters in *A Separate Peace*: Phineas, Gene, Leper, and Brinker. In addition to using someone for Brinker, and myself for Gene, I had to, as most novelists do, draw from myself for everyone in the book. David Hackett never went through all the experiences of Finny, and I had never spoken to Gore Vidal. So that is what a novelist has to be: someone with many facets.

I did OK here at Exeter academically. I was not a really good student. I was not Gene Forrester in that department. I do think I could have been, but I wasn't interested in studying. All I wanted to do was to get through. I didn't want any trouble from my family, the Dean, or anybody. There were certain things I was interested in. I really liked French and other languages. I enjoyed English. I was the only person in my senior year English course. They made a special class for me.

The character of Brinker in the book is based on Gore Vidal. I know Gore quite well now, but I didn't know him when I was at Exeter. I think I did rather a good job on Gore. I was a lower-middler and Gore was a senior as I observed him. He made an impression on me and I said, "Now that's a very unusual and thriving person." And when I had to write about that kind of person, I used what I imagined Gore to be like. Years later he is quite a good friend of mine and he is very much like that.

David Hackett was a full-time Milton student but was my model for Phineas. But he was here at Exeter. He came here in the summer of 1943 for the six weeks that the book is really based on. That was when we had the Super Suicide Society of The Summer Session. Hackett wasn't my roommate. Since there were so few students in the summer session everyone had their own room. Hackett lived across the hall. In effect, though, he was my roommate.

David Hackett did recently see the film before it opened in New York. He lives in Washington and was very close to the Kennedys. I had invited David to several private showings, but he chickened out every time. I think he was afraid to face the film for complex reasons which I understand. One night Ethel Kennedy said, "And now we are going to see the latest Jerry Lewis movie." The guests, including David, went to the projection room at Hickory Hill and they walked in and there was *A Separate Peace*. I think David Hackett liked it very much.

John Heyl and David Hackett do not resemble each other physically on the screen, but they are the same type.

There was a boy who died while I was here, Bob Tait. He died on the operating table. The PEAN [the school yearbook] was dedicated to him. I knew him but I wasn't using him as a model. It is a question of the subconscious. Gore reminded me of Tait, a wonderful human being who died on the operating table during his senior year on Christmas day. I never knew what he was being operated on for. So, maybe I did subconsciously remember him, but I never thought of him directly when I was writing the book. Tait died when the morrow escaped from his broken leg. I might have known that, but I never remembered until Gore Vidal reminded me.

Actually, I didn't have anyone in mind specifically for Leper. I just knew there was a Leper somewhere, although I put him together from different impressions. Let's face it, there are Lepers in the world, so I felt I didn't need a model for that character.

I never went through old PEANs to write *A Separate Peace*. It was an uncalculated, subconscious creative process.

"A FEW TRUE THINGS"

The following is a follow-up on an earlier article that the *Exeter Bulletin* ran to observe the fiftieth anniversary of the publication of *A Separate Peace*. Here Knowles explains further how some of the episodes in the novel grew out of events that took place during the summer school session of 1943—for example, the accelerated academic program to graduate boys before they reached the draft age, the volunteer labor details to help with the war effort, and the sense of isolation the class of 1943 felt due to the wartime situation.

FROM JOHN KNOWLES, "WE REALLY DID HAVE A CLUB"
(Exeter Bulletin, Summer 1995)

We really did have a club whose members jumped from the branch of a very high tree into the river as initiation. The only elements in *A Separate Peace* which were not in that summer were anger, envy, violence, and hatred. There was only friendship, athleticism, and loyalty.

It was that summer that I realized I had fallen in love with Exeter. Most students don't experience summer there: I did so for two consecutive summers, 1943 and 1944. In other words, I was almost continuously at Exeter from September 1942 through August 1944, when I graduated. We're talking total Exeter immersion here.

The great trees, the thick clinging ivy, the expanses of playing fields, the winding black-water river, the pure air all began to sort of intoxicate me. Classroom windows were open; the aroma of flowers and shrubbery floated in. We were in shirt sleeves; the masters were relaxed. Studies now were easy for me. The summer of 1943 at Exeter was as happy a time as I ever had in my life.

Everything fit. There was a lively, congenial group of students in Peabody Hall that summer, many of them from other schools, accelerating like me. One was David Hackett from Milton Academy, on whom I later modeled Phineas in *A Separate Peace*. A great friend of Bobby Kennedy's, he later served under Bobby in the Justice Department.

Returning to Exeter for the fall term of 1943, I found that a charged, driven time had come to the school. I remember how virtually all the younger masters disappeared one by one, and old men became our only teachers. Too old to be in any way companions to us, they forced the class of 1943 to be reliant very much on itself, isolated. Maybe that made us stronger in a certain way. There was apple-harvesting "for the war," railroad-yard clearance "for the war," numerous collection drives "for the war," and all those patriotic movies in the gym with Spencer Tracy, or Van Johnson, of someone heroically bombing Tokyo. The massively crowded trains, hopelessly behind schedule, we had to take to try to get home for holidays. Nobody in a basic industry with special allowances. All those maps of heretofore strange parts of the world with strange names like Anzio and Guadalcanal and Saipan.

Looking back, I think we were all quite mature, surprisingly responsible. In earlier wars, boys of our age had just gone off to raise hell or enlist or both, but we stayed dutifully at our desks doing tomorrow's homework. Tomorrow, they felt in 1862 or 1917, you died perchance, so discipline went by the board, and they cut loose. We didn't; I don't know why not. Was it that our war was so overwhelmingly vast, the first truly world war, that it overawed us into being dutiful, responsible, approaching it one step at a time?

I know that I studied diligently. I took both Latin I and Latin II with Mr. Galbraith. A finer, more inspiring teacher I never encountered. By the time he was through with me, I thoroughly understood the nature and structure of a language, and he had crucially influenced both my thinking and the way I expressed it in words. I am the writer I am because of him.

In fact, despite the giant holes in the faculty caused by the war, the best teaching ever experienced was at Exeter. Yale was a distinct let-down afterward. The teachers there either read their year-in-year-out lectures to us in large auditoriums, or, meeting us in small groups, seemed preoccupied with their extramural careers or reputations of whatever. They did not seem to be there primarily for us. It was Exeter which taught me how to approach new material, organize it, and express it.

Exeter, in those emergency years, also managed to keep a full athletic program going, and I know very many of us are grateful for that. I arrived at Exeter quite sure that I was a good swimmer, and it came as quite a shock when my buddy down the hall, Pleninger, beat me in the first time try-outs with Dan Fowler '45, and proceeded to be faster than I was ever after, and deservedly became the captain of the varsity team.

Swimming isn't the most thrilling sport in the world, far from it; it's a damn bore most of the time, but it does make you healthy and gives you a good body. I finished first as the anchor man in the final, decisive relay against Andover, to become an athletic mini-hero for about 15 minutes.

You can see by now how I admire the school and love it and therefore *A Separate Peace* has one peculiarity for a school novel: It never attacks the place; it isn't an exposé; it doesn't show sadistic masters or depraved students, or use any of the other school-novel sensationalistic clichés. That's because I didn't experience things like that there. I found there a gorgeous world prepared to shape me up, and I tried to present and dramatize that.

TOPICS FOR DISCUSSION AND RESEARCH

1. To what extent does Devon School in *A Separate Peace* resemble actual preparatory schools?

2. How much does Knowles have in common with the narrator of *A Separate Peace?*

3. The novel describes various cliques among students. What subgroups comprise the student body in your school?

4. Why does Knowles fictionalize his experiences, altering them to serve an artistic purpose in *A Separate Peace?*

5. How closely do the descriptions of prep schools as elitist, exclusive, and snobbish institutions correspond with your impressions of Knowles's fictional Devon School?

TOPICS FOR FURTHER EXPLORATION

1. After reading *A Separate Peace* examine some of the following novels for a comparative analysis of the way that prep school life is described in fiction: J. D. Salinger's *The Catcher in the Rye*, Richard Yates's *A Good School*, Robert Anderson's *Tea and Sympathy*, John McPhee's *The Headmaster*, F. Scott Fitzgerald's *This Side of Paradise*, Evelyn Waugh's *Decline and Fall*, Muriel Spark's *The Prime of Miss Jean Brodie*, John Irving's *The World According to Garp*, and John Cheever's *Lawrenceville Stories*.

2. Many modern writers, including Knowles, John Cheever, J. D. Salinger, and Fitzgerald, used actual incidents from their own school experiences. Does it enhance or limit your enjoyment of a novel to know that the plot or characters were not entirely created from the author's imagination? Is it better in some cases not to know all the facts? Explain your answer.

3. Note some of the features of the landscape and campus of the Devon School as described in *A Separate Peace*, and compare them with the actual geography of Phillips Exeter by referring to a map of the school grounds found in *A Separate Peace: The War Within* (19).

SUGGESTED READINGS AND WORKS CITED

Aldrich, Nelson. "Preppies: The Last Upper Class?" *Atlantic* (January 1979): 56–66.

Baltzell, E. Digby. *Philadelphia Gentlemen—The Making of a National Upper Class*. Chicago: Quadrangle Books, 1958.

Birmingham, Stephen. *The Right People: A Portrait of the American Social Establishment*. Boston: Little, Brown, 1968.

Birnbach, Lisa, ed. *The Official Preppy Handbook*. New York: Workman, 1980.

Coles, Robert. *Children of Privilege*. Boston: Little, Brown, 1977.

Cookson, Peter W., and Caroline Hodges Persell. *Preparing for Power: America's Elite Boarding Schools*. New York: Basic Books, 1985.

Gathorne-Hardy, Jonathan. *The Old School Tie*. New York: Viking, 1978.

Halberstam, David. *The Best and the Brightest*. New York: Random House, 1969.

Knowles, John. "The Young Writer's Real Friends." *The Writer* 75 (July 1962): 13–18.

McLachlan, James. *American Boarding Schools: A Historical Study*. New York: Scribner, 1970.

Nichols, Acosta. *Forty Years More: A History of Groton School*. Groton, Mass.: The Groton Trustees, 1976.

Nora, M. "A Comparison of the Actual and Symbolic Landscape in *A Separate Peace*." *Discourse* 11 (1968): 356–62.

Prescott, Peter S. *A World of Our Own: Notes on Life and Learning in a Boys' Preparatory School*. New York: Coward-McCann, 1970.

Ravitch, Diane. *The Great School Wars*. New York: Basic Books, 1974.

Wakeford, John. *The Cloistered Elite*. New York: Praeger, 1969.

3

America's Prep Schools in Wartime

The selections in this chapter from the records of some preparatory schools reveal how these institutions were forced to adapt and change their routines and traditions in the face of the emergency measures that the war brought to the home front. Although no bombs ever fell on the United States during World War II, there was the fear that they might and also the feeling that everyone should support the war effort.

After the shock of the Japanese surprise attack on U.S. naval and air forces on December 7, 1941, at Pearl Harbor, the nation was sent into a state of deep shock and was convulsed with fears of further attacks on the mainland of the United States. Although the country had been drifting toward war with Japan and Germany, many were totally surprised when it did come. Many Americans were committed to a policy of isolationism and had no heart for fighting foreign wars. It was assumed that the Atlantic and Pacific oceans, which were guarded by U.S. naval fleets, would be an impossible moat for any other nation bent on harm to cross. Nevertheless, America was in the process of preparing for war in 1940. Congress passed the first peacetime draft act, and the U.S. Army, which then numbered 167,000 regular soldiers, was being expanded by the draftees drawn from the ranks of all physically qualified single men between the ages of twenty-one and thirty-five.

Despite the fact that America had plenty of manpower to fill the draft calls, the military was woefully ill prepared to fight a modern war. The Great Depression of the 1930s had cut military spending to the bone, and regular army and naval forces were equipped largely with World War I surplus guns, tanks, and ships.

The feeling of security stemming from geographic distance from the fighting in Asia and Europe was shattered by the Japanese sneak attack on Pearl Harbor. Most of the U.S. fleet was sunk, and suddenly Americans felt vulnerable to attack. It seemed possible that Japanese carriers might appear at any moment off the coasts of California and Oregon. The mood of panic was heightened by the fact that Germany and Italy declared war on the United States a few days later, leaving the country facing enemies on both shores.

The nation's attitude toward the war changed completely as Americans were outraged by these acts of aggression and President Roosevelt now had public opinion for waging war totally with him. Although the country was united, it was not ready for war, and the early months of 1942 saw mostly defeats for badly outnumbered U.S. troops at Bataan, Guam, Wake Island, and other Pacific outposts that the Japanese overran. The Germans operating "wolf packs" of U-boats were sinking ships with impunity off the eastern seaboard and the Gulf of Mexico. In the light of these threats, it is no wonder the country was jittery with what was called "war nerves." Whole cities enacted blackouts: all lights were extinguished so that enemy bombers could not locate targets. Such a mood of panic prevailed that during the early months of the war, there were many false alarms, and rumors ran rampant. In Los Angeles, it was believed that the Japanese fleet was offshore and that the city was going to be bombed, a panic that later inspired the 1979 movie by Steven Spielberg, *1941*.

In November 1942 there was an actual bombing raid on American soil. The Japanese launched a seaplane from a submarine off the Oregon coast, and the pilot dropped his bombs on the forests, hoping to set off fires that would consume the entire West Coast. Although the Japanese flew two missions and dropped incendiary bombs, no forest fires were started (it was the rainy season) (Lingeman, 48).

In order to counter the possibility of more air raids, the government set up the Civilian Defense Volunteer Office, whose ranks provided air raid wardens and the Ground Observer Corps of "aircraft spotters," as they were more usually called. The function of the wardens was primarily to enforce blackout regulations and to conduct people to air raid shelters where any existed. The purpose of the Observer Corps was to staff observation posts and search the skies with field glasses for enemy airplanes. These posts were staffed by people from all walks of life, even prison inmates, but mostly school boys, women, and senior citizens; at its peak involvement in the war effort, the observers totaled over 600,000 volunteers (Lingeman, 52). Although the observers never spotted any enemy planes, they did help put an end to the false reports of enemy airplanes that had set off numerous alerts during the first months of 1942, which were triggered by friendly planes' being mistaken for Japanese or German bombers.

The only deaths caused to American civilians during the war came from explosive devices attached to some 6,000 balloons that the Japanese released in 1944 to drift across the Pacific carried by the jet stream and land in the northwestern United States and start fires. Only a few of these balloon bombs reached their target, and though they started no fires, they did kill six people in Oregon who were curious about these objects and came too close just as the timing device set off explosions (Lingerman, 56). More dangerous than fire balloons and air raids by single seaplanes were the submarines that prowled the American coastlines. German U-boats operating in the Atlantic sank 120 ships just off the shores of the United States. Many were sunk close enough to land for the fires and explosions to be witnessed by people living near the ocean. The beaches were littered with oil stains, flotsam, and debris from the wrecks of tankers and freighters attacked by the U-boats; even more gruesome, bodies of merchant seaman who lost their lives were washed up by the tides. In addition to creating a menace to all shipping, the U-boats planted mines in the harbors of a few American port cities and landed the only German invaders to reach U.S. shores. On June 13, 1942, a submarine put teams of saboteurs ashore on a Long Island beach and another group near Jacksonville, Florida. Their mission was to spread terror and destruction by blowing up war plants, railroads, bridges, and air bases. All the saboteurs were fluent in English and had lived in the United States prior to the war; they were extensively trained in spying, secret radio signals, and explosives. This mission, called "Operation Pastorius" by the German, was a serious threat to national security.

The German secret agents were detected by a Coast Guardsman

who was patrolling the beach just as the first team of saboteurs was coming ashore in rubber boats. Their story that they were survivors of a sinking fishing boat aroused his suspicion; however, they were allowed to go about their business, and they would have likely gone on to carry out their deadly mission but for one of the German commandos' suddenly having some compunction about his role as a terrorist; he was married to an American and had even served a few years in the prewar U.S. Army. He called the FBI and turned in all of his co-conspirators. They were quickly rounded up, tried, and executed as spies. Had it not been for the German turncoat's providing the information that led to the arrests there would probably have been more attempts to land saboteurs by submarine on U.S. shores, but the lack of success of Operation Pastorius discouraged the German high command. No more commando missions were attempted.

Japanese submarines also constituted a threat on the Pacific coast. On June 21, 1942, an attack on Fort Stevens, Oregon, was launched by a Japanese submarine, which fired seventeen shells at shore installations, marking the first bombardment of the American mainland since the British shelled Fort McHenry in 1812, inspiring Francis Scott Key to write "The Star-Spangled Banner." Another Japanese Navy submarine opened fire on the beachfront oil wells south of Los Angeles, but neither of these attacks did more than minor damage. The main result in both cases was to create a lot more public alarm than the threat warranted.

World War II had a traumatic effect on the United States. The shock waves were felt the strongest during 1942–43, the years in which the main plot events of *A Separate Peace* take place. It is obvious from what Knowles writes that the war had a significant impact on the students and faculty of boarding schools. As the following selections show, what happened in the Devon School was not unusual and was, in fact, rather typical. For example, at the Hotchkiss School in Lakeville, Connecticut, all outside athletic contests were eliminated due to gas rationing, and students' engaged in planting and harvesting "victory gardens." The younger faculty were taken into military service and replaced by older men, making for the graying of the staff virtually overnight (James R. Chandler, Hotchkiss class of 1953, letter of July 17, 1999). In the case of the Groton School, Douglas Brown, the school archivist, writes that many of the school's customs were modified during the war years; restrictions on fuel and certain foods respectively changed the athletic programs and menus. The demand for labor in war plants meant that many housekeeping janitorial services were suspended; the students cleaned their own rooms, took out trash, and waited on tables. Also, as Acosta Nichols reveals in his book *Forty Years More*, the students provided work parties of "snow squads" and "maintenance squads" to help fill in for the labor shortages caused by the war (similar to the tasks depicted on the novel). Other casualties of the war were described by Hubert C. Fortmiller, associate head of the Middlesex School in Concord, Massachusetts, who writes that over thirty graduates of the school lost their lives in World War II and that during the war years there was a considerable reduction in the size of the student body due to enlistments. Of the forty-one boys who graduated in 1944, many joined the Marines together, trained together, and served together. Fortmiller points out that "discipline, self-sacrifice, and commitment to public service" are very much a part of the character-building goals of schools like Middlesex and explains why the participation of its students in World War II was so energetic" (letter of July 28, 1999). The impact of the war was similar at the Choate School. Ted Ayres, the school's alumni director, class of 1946, remembers that Choate ran accelerated courses for seniors, so that they could earn diplomas before they reached the draft age of eighteen, and that courses on aeronautics, navigation, meteorology, mechanics, map reading, first aid, and advanced mathematics were introduced into the curriculum and called "War Courses." As at other prep schools the boys helped to harvest local crops and planted victory gardens on the school grounds. In addition, Choate students took courses given by the Army in airplane spotting and acted as air raid wardens at night. Like all other students during the war years, they were encouraged to buy war stamps and war bonds to help finance the war effort. Because of gas rationing, normal school functions, both social and athletic, were cancelled, and Thanksgiving holidays were suspended for the duration of the war. The main sacrifice made by Choate students was in the loss of life among those who served in the military during the war; some one hundred died in service (Lee Sylvester, archivist at Choate, letter of July 19, 1999). As the following documents demonstrate, life at America's exclusive preparatory schools was suddenly and in some ways permanently changed by the war. As Gene Forrester says in *A Separate Peace*, this moment in history put its stamp on him permanently. The same could be said of the generations that came of age in this period of national crisis.

EXETER DURING THE WORLD WAR II YEARS

The following three selections that appeared in the *Exeter Bulletin* during the war years illustrated the way life changed at Exeter during World War II. From the perspective of the administration, it was a question of how the school could support the war effort in some meaningful way without changing the nature and the purpose of the school too radically. The military did not give the school authorities much direction on how they could make a contribution to the war effort. Each selection describes how Exeter tried to accommodate the school's curriculum and academic schedules to the special circumstances created by the war.

FROM M. R. WILLIAMS, "LIFE AT THE ACADEMY DURING WORLD
WAR II"
(*Exeter Bulletin*, July 1942)

Ever since the attack on Pearl Harbor, members of the Academy faculty have considered the paramount problem of the year to be what this school could do to help in the national emergency. Investigations and discussions to this end have been the concern of the Principal, various departments, and individual teachers for uncounted hours. As was to be expected of all true citizens at such a time, realities were the only things considered. Gestures essentially futile, no matter how photogenic, seemed too wasteful for words. But the realities were not easy to discover. Almost all generalizations on the Second World War have agreed on one point—its vast difference from any other war that man has known. It is the war in which "never before have so many owed so much to so few." It is a war for sheer survival, "the war nobody wanted." It is not only a soldiers' and a sailors' war but a war of scientists and mathematicians, even a combination of all four, a war of the air forces. Largely because of the unexampled nature of what had been happening so swiftly, schools and colleges received at first from the government only what seemed like general advice.

At the outset, it was clear enough that certain measures encouraged in previous wars were not being recommended this time, such as student corps, close-order drill, maneuvers, or trench digging. Soon it became evident, too, that neither the Army nor the Navy was much interested in well-intentioned efforts of layman to give pre-service courses in the various branches of military or naval science. Selective service would attend to all that later on, doubtless rearranging many premature plans and preparation of individuals. In the meantime the question of what to offer to boys of 16 to 19 years of age who wished to be doing something that really counted found no convincing official answer.

The answer, to be sure, was given by both the Army and the Navy at the conference of independent boys' schools at Pawling on December 19 and 20 [1941], only a little more than a week after Pearl Harbor. Although it may have seemed not quite like a revelation to some Academy students to whom it was repeated, mainly because it sounded remarkably like what had already been told them in the schoolroom, it has been reiterated by the same sources and appears now to be accepted by the majority of students below the draft age. At the meeting, Lt. Col. B. W. Venable, U.S.A., explained the impracticality of an ROTC [Reserve Officers Training Corps] or an SATC [Special Army Training Corps] in schools at the present time and expressed the opinion that good schooling of mind and body is a source of strength in any field of army activity. He advised that schools continue their programs with as little disruption as possible. At the same meeting, even more specific recommendations came from Lt. Commander Burton Davis, U.S.N., who stressed the Navy's need for thousands of well-trained men, and he especially deplored the present deficient training in mathematics. Hundreds of men who would make good officers, he said, must be turned down because the Navy does not have time to teach them the mathematics which they should have learned in school or college. Commander Davis suggested the following fields of instruction to contribute to preparation for naval service. Morse code: plane trigonometry, solid geometry, quadratics, physics, chemistry, shop mathematics, vocational training, elementary navigation, principles of radio, elements of telephone and radio communication. He also emphasized the need for more thorough inculcation of obedience and self-discipline. Subsequently recommendations almost identical were made by the National Council of Chief State Officers at Nashville, Tenn., on May 10–14 [1942], and officially endorsed by the Departments of War and Navy and by the United States Office of Education. Only today, the writer received from the Navy Department a release for the press and radio entitled "Navy to be Represented at National Education Association," to be held at Denver, June 22 to July 2. In it are found these sentences: "The educators are to be asked, as one contribution by them toward the war efforts, to place greater stress in secondary schools on mathematics and physics so that pupils on completing their studies will be better equipped to take part in the Navy program, without facing the necessity of taking refresher courses in these subjects. . . . The least possible disturbance of the educational program of secondary schools, other than the renewal of emphasis on mathematics and physics as basic requirements for success both in the Navy and in industrial life, will be the keynote of the Navy's message to the convention. Previously at educational meetings Navy officials have stated the Navy's educational policy as one that calls for men who have sound instruction in the basic studies such as English, mathematics, and the physical sciences, with emphasis being placed on physical conditioning." The breadth and wisdom of this program is apparent in its provision for service both in war and in the subsequent peace, and for the training of both mind and body.

Meantime the faculty had come to much the same conclusion. A careful reappraisal of the curriculum—especially with cognizance of the changes adopted for 1942–43, the growing trend toward more and more courses in mathematics and science, and the popularity of the special study groups in the Morse code, navigation, radio, etc.—demonstrated that few alterations, if any, were necessary to comply with the wishes of the Army and the Navy. Some of the factors which led to this conclusion were these. All graduates of the Academy have a thorough grounding in algebra and plane geometry. In 1941–42 the number of students completing algebra and plane geometry was 206, and of these the majority will go on to trigonometry, solid geometry, and college algebra. The number taking Mathematics 4 (trigonometry, solid geometry, and college algebra) was 195; Mathematics 5 (the calculus), 32. In the middle of the year, 22 students enrolled in a special course which completed trigonometry by the end of the year. Thus the total completing elementary mathematics was 206; the total having at least trigonometry (over 90% having more) was also 206. The total Academy enrollment in 1941–42 was 744; of the Senior class, 211.

Last year registration in science courses was as follows: Biology, 43; Chemistry, 187; Physics, 171; Physical Sciences (Chemistry and Physics), 63. Of this number, those completing college preparatory work in either Chemistry or Physics or both were Chemistry, 102; Physics, 105; Physical Sciences, 35.

Enrollment in these courses, naturally took place before this country entered the war. Next year, with the inducements plain, enrollment in Physics and Advanced Mathematics will undoubtedly be high, although at this time it is not possible to give exact figure. In addition, the special course in trigonometry will be continued, and there has been added a course in elementary aeronautics under an instructor who is a licensed pilot and open only to students who have taken or are taking Mathematics 3 and a major course in Physics. The voluntary groups for study and practice which have been run for the past five or six years will continue in meteorology, marksmanship, medicine, First Aid, navigation, Morse code, and communication, radio, and conversation in modern languages. Unpaid volunteer groups of students will work on Academy grounds next year as they have this year, and next year the care of dormitory rooms will be entrusted to students.

Lest it be feared that the Academy has turned into a concentration camp for mathematics and the sciences, last year's enrollment by departments may be reassuring: Art, 50; Bible, 14; Business, 22; English, 731; French, 572; Geology, 12; German, 87; Greek, 47; History, 246; Latin, 411; Mathematics, 666; Mechanical Drawing, 32; Music, 23; Biology, 43; Chemistry, 187; Physics, 171; Physical Sciences, 63; Social Studies, 14; Spanish, 60.

The broad and flexible athletic program of the Academy also seems singularly well adapted to the purposes outlined by the War and Navy Departments. Variety enables each boy to choose the sport which fits him best, and in that sport to develop the competitive spirit, the sense of cooperation and team play, good sportsmanship, and the will to win which has for centuries traditionally made the good soldier. There is no better conditioning for the rigors of combat flying than such contact athletics as are found in football, lacrosse, hockey, or basketball. Coordination, control, and precision are developed in such sports as baseball, tennis, squash, or golf. Endurance as well as coordination comes in rowing. So on through the list, each sport has a practical value of its own. And other extra curriculum interests of the student teach practical lessons in co-operative effort and democracy, as well as reveal abilities not always called upon in classroom or athletic field. In short, the elements and qualities which the experience of years has demonstrated to be the best basis for the education of youth between the ages of fourteen and nineteen years seem to hold good for war as well as for peace: accuracy, thoroughness, honesty, manliness—each in the fullest possible human conception of the word.

If much of this sounds unoriginal, one has only to turn to the sort of questionnaire sent out by the Navy seeking confidential information about candidates for commissions. Here ratings are requested on a person's Adaptability, Determination, Thoroughness, Resourcefulness, Tact, Accuracy, Self-reliance, Judgment, Executive Ability, Aggressiveness, Co-operation, Leadership Ability, and Temperament. Questions are asked about his health, discretion, outside activities, associates, and educational background. These are not subjects which can be taught in a cramming school. These and such other aspects of education as awareness of the world about one, whatever is changing nature may be, and a sense of responsibility to play one's part in it are the business of education, as any teacher worthy of the name well knows. Bargains, mark-down sales, remnants, notions, and patent medicines have no more justification in secondary education in war than they have in peace.

At the same time, one would be far astray to conclude that the Academy is untouched and unmoved, or unwilling to be moved, by the war. For over a year the same winds that have been blowing through the outside world have swept through the school, leaving many changes behind them. Some would have come, war or no war. Some were already made before war was declared. Some are clearly by-products of the war. The most important developments in the past year, arranged more or less chronologically, are as follows:

1. 20 members of the staff have entered or about to enter government—service military, navel, or scientific.
2. Over 800 graduates have been reported in service, and the list is far from complete.
3. The Academy curriculum was revised to permit more flexibility of choice. American History was made a required subject.
4. Classes in First Aid were conducted by the Athletic Department.
5. Fraternities were abolished.
6. A group of student volunteers for work on Academy grounds was organized. Student care of dormitory rooms arranged for next year.
7. A bureau for student summer employment on farms and at camps was set up.
8. A series of conferences for vocational guidance was begun, to be continued next year.
9. Special courses in trigonometry and elementary aeronautics are offered for 1942–43.
10. Since last spring, the school has contributed to funds for a United Nations X-ray unit and an ambulance and for the Christian Fraternity budget over $6000.

FROM "THE ANTICIPATORY PROGRAM: CHANGES MADE AT
EXETER TO MEET THE SPECIAL CIRCUMSTANCES CAUSED BY
THE DRAFT"
(*Exeter Bulletin*, February 1943)

Development of the Selective Service Act made it necessary for the Academy to consider plans for those boys in school who would reach their eighteenth birthdays before their normal date of graduation. Investigation by a committee of the faculty, known as the Committee on the War Program, showed that there were in school last fall 78 boys who reached or would reach their eighteenth birthdays by December 31, 1942. Of these, 68 were Seniors. Under the existing interpretation of the Service Act, it seemed likely that most, if not all, of these boys would be permitted to complete their school year. In addition, however, there were 180 boys whose eighteenth birthdays would fall in 1943; 207 who would be 18 in

1944. Eliminating Seniors and lower classmen who could graduate before they were 18 (either through promotions within the year or by attending the Summer Session), the committee reported that some 167 students now in school might profit by a new and specially arranged program. It then proposed what was called "The Anticipatory Program," to go into effect in June 1943. This was accepted by the faculty on December 1, 1942.

The committee saw no reason to suggest any changes in dates of graduation or much in the usual functions of the regular or of the Summer Session. The Summer Session would go on very much as it had done for the past twenty-four years (July 13 to September 3, seven and one half weeks, fee $300). Already the faculty had granted permission for students to complete requirements for the diploma in the Summer Session; and for the duration, the Summer Session is now offering new or advanced work in a wider range of subjects than formerly. In addition, the faculty accepted the recommendation of the committee that during the emergency, the requirements for the diploma should be reduced from 17 to 16 major courses. Within this freer framework of the curriculum, it seemed that the great majority of students should be able to get their full secondary education, their diplomas, and their admission to college before they became eighteen.

The Anticipatory Program was devised to meet the special needs of the 167 lower class students mentioned above, not sufficiently advanced to finish school before reaching the draft age. Doubtless, too, some boys in other schools similarly situated might be interested in a scheme like this. For students availing themselves of this plan, the Senior year is to begin on June 28 and to end February 5. It will be divided into two semesters (June 28 to September 4, and September 15 to February 5). During the summer term a boy will normally take the first half of four studies which will meet six times a week, in periods of 55 minutes each. In the fall term his class will meet the usual four or five times a week, in periods of 50 minutes each, completing the second half year of studies begun in the summer. In the summer term a student may take a minimum of three subjects, if his needs will be met by this number. On February 5, 1944, students in the Anticipatory Program will receive their diplomas and enter college. Inasmuch as the actual work of the school year will not be materially shortened, the Senior year being merely moved ahead half a year, "Anticipatory" seemed a better descriptive term than "accelerated," the one used by the colleges. It is merely a question of whether one thinks in units of space or of time.

Students eligible for the Anticipatory Program are those who meet the usual Academy requirements of maturity and scholastic ability, who are far enough advanced in their schooling to graduate in a single school year; and who, in all probability, would be drafted before they could graduate in their regular course. In short, it is a program for the Senior year only. Students from other schools who wish to attend the summer term only will be accepted for that term on the recommendation of their schools, if a satisfactory cooperative plan of study can be worked out with these schools. Again, only with the approval of their schools, students from other schools may take their full Senior year at the Academy in the Anticipatory Program and receive the Academy diploma in February.

The subjects offered under the Anticipatory Program are primarily mathematics, physics, English, and history courses recommended by the armed services. The following subjects will be definitely in the program: third year mathematics (algebra and geometry); fourth year mathematics (plane trigonometry and solid geometry); some spherical trigonometry and college algebra; fourth year English, third and fourth year French; third year German; American history; physics; and chemistry. Other courses necessary to enable the students to meet requirements for graduation may be added.

The fee for the Anticipatory Program is the same as for the regular school year, $1050. The established system of grants and scholarships will apply to Exeter students who enroll for the full program. For boys from other schools who attend the summer term only, the fee will be $400. Grants or scholarships will not be available for these students. The charge covers everything except books, laundry, athletic equipment, and unusual medical expenses.

Application for admission to the Anticipatory Program should be made as early as possible, in any event before May 15, 1943. Application forms and detailed arrangements of programs for individual students can be secured by addressing Philip E. Hulburd, Director of the Anticipatory Program, Phillips Exeter Academy, Exeter, N. H. Information concerning the Summer Session can be obtained from H. Darcy Curwen, Director of the Summer Session.

FROM HENRY PHILLIPS, "HOW EXETER RESPONDED TO THE
COMING OF WORLD WAR II: PREPARATIONS FOR THE DEFENSE
OF EXETER"
(*Exeter Bulletin*, February 1943)

When possessions of the United States were attacked and war with the aggressors was declared early in December, the town of Exeter and consequently the Academy began to intensify the preparations already begun which identify us in New Hampshire with many other communities in the land. Whether or not the lightning will strike is an academic question; all of us, townspeople as well as faculty, students, and employees of Phillips Exeter, are united in a common enterprise of protection.

Because the local chapter is served by many ladies of the Academy, a word about the Red Cross is in order here. It was at the request of Polish residents of Exeter in the fall of 1939 that the chapter began to do more than conduct the annual Roll Call and engage in its peacetime pursuits. This chapter was the first in New Hampshire to commence production of articles for the relief of the stricken in Poland and alter those of other countries. In January of 1941 a Motor Corps was organized and shortly afterward a number of ladies of the town and faculty began learning things about their cars. They were to be seen in the Academy gym and cage, hearing lectures and changing tires. They took a first aid course and a home nursing course, and the Motor Corps is now the best organized of our defense groups. In all of the activities of the Red Cross members of the Academy have played a large part.

The next group to prepare itself for the government's call was an Aircraft Observation Post, composed again of townspeople and faculty members. The Army authorities at Mitchell Field called this post to twenty-four hour duty immediately upon the declaration of war. Observers are located in the tower of the Robinson Seminary and on Shaw's Hill in Kensington.

The New Hampshire Council of Defense appointed a defense chairman for the town in July 1941. By this time the state had started to lay general plans for defense along the lines pursued in Massachusetts. Our neighboring state had appropriated a large sum of money and was training its organization long before our authorities in Concord [the New Hampshire state capital] had begun to consider the matter. During the latter part of the summer in Exeter, the town chairman appointed his committees, and sent out a call for wardens for each sector of the town. There was a certain amount of the "It Can't Happen Here" spirit going around, but we gradually and at least "on paper" made up the complement of the committees.

It is unnecessary to dwell on the apparatus of a local defense committee. There are representatives of vital services: light, gas, water, telephone; fire department, police. There are wardens, deputy wardens, demolition and decontamination squads; committees on blackouts, on receiving persons from damaged places.

The part which the Academy itself plays in this scheme, in addition to distributing the help of its personnel among the general activities of the town, will be described. Immediately upon the declaration of war, the faculty unanimously passed a resolution, framed in the wording of a similar statement of April 1917, stating that "The Faculty of the Phillips Exeter Academy offers to the town of Exeter, the State of New Hampshire and to the Nation whatever service it may be able to render." Soon a committee of the faculty known as the War Activities Committee was appointed by Dr. Perry. It is made up of the heads of departments and representatives of the business office.

The first concern of this committee has been to prepare the Academy buildings for taking part in the practice blackouts which the town, in common with other communities in the country, will order. Although blacking out the school would seem to be a simple matter, a good deal of organizing must be done, a good deal of talking in meeting and considerable work on paper. The Academy community itself numbers almost a thousand souls. Everyone's safety has to be thought about. Now it is impossible and unnecessary to darken all of the thousands of windows in the dormitories and houses. Instead, each dormitory constitutes a committee, under the leadership of the resident teachers and certain boys, to arrange to darken certain rooms where the members may gather during a blackout, and to see that boys are gathered there at the proper time. Everything has been done to insure the success of the blackout, no matter at what time it is required. In addition, certain members of the Academy's staff are being instructed in more specific duties. As soon as local citizens could receive the basic training necessary for them to become instructors in the duties of wardens, fire fighting volunteers, and the rest, classes were established in Exeter to train volunteers for these jobs. Many of the wives of our faculty had already received training by the Red Cross in its various branches. Faculty members themselves and other men employed in the buildings and on the grounds are now receiving instruction in first aid, handling incendiaries—in short, going through the regular course of training for wardens.

From the first part of the school year, great interest was shown among the students for participating in defense efforts where they could properly serve. With the coming of war, Dr. Perry felt that the enthusiasm should be turned into practical uses. Accordingly, in the classrooms and dormitories many boys have been assigned to positions of responsibility. They will assist in measures taken for emptying the class buildings, and for preparing dormitories for blackouts. Their numbers will make light work of the Academy's part in the town's defense plans.

Besides these duties, boys have volunteered for the spotting post at suitable hours. A few of those best equipped in radio are developing a mechanical detector to be located at this post, and—what may be most important—a system of radio transceivers to supplant the telephone services in an emergency. This last would enable wardens to communicate with the Report Center, and for orders to be issued thence to the different emergency services.

In case of a disaster in a nearby town, Exeter will be prepared to offer help. The Academy will be able to set up beds in Alumni Hall or the contagious ward of the Lamont Infirmary, and our kitchens are able to feed those received.

The impression should not be gained, from this resumé of war activities of the Academy as part of the town, that our regular work is not proceeding as nearly on a normal basis as possible. In fact, it will be the aim of the Academy during this war to show, as Mr. Benton [one of the junior faculty] put it in a talk to the school recently, that "the training which the Academy gives in individuality and freedom also fits us for regimentation and intelligent subordination to the needs of the present crisis."

In the course of filming *A Separate Peace*, several people who had known what life at Exeter was like during World War II were consulted for background facts.

FROM HOWARD T. EASTON, "EXETER IN THE FORTIES: A
FACULTY PERSPECTIVE"
(*The Exonian*, November 1, 1972)

To get the "feel" of the time of *A Separate Peace* at Exeter, it is necessary to remember that it was war time. We all had to adapt to unusual circumstances, some of them quite trying. Many of the regular faculty members were in the service; substitutes had to be trained in the way of the school in the classroom, dormitories, and on the athletic and social scene. Faculty leaves were out for the duration. Classes were larger, and boys had to work harder, especially the seniors who wanted to get their diplomas before the age of enlistment or the draft. John Knowles himself gained his diploma by taking two math courses and French in the summer of 1944. Gas rationing curtailed travel by automobiles; food stamps limited what could be bought in the stores or served in the dining rooms. In lieu of sports, boys could elect to pick apples in the fall, or in winter shovel snow for the Boston and Maine [Railroad].

As far as possible, however, the Academy tried to maintain a normal program: chapel was held every morning and church on Sunday, a practice which helped to keep the morale of the school high. Sadness could not be avoided as word of the loss of Exonians in the war was reported in the Bulletin and EXONIAN. The two-year Latin requirement for a diploma was still in effect; college board exams were taken; graduation exercises were held in February and August as well as in June to accommodate the Anticipatory Program graduates. THE EXONIAN issues of the period show that athletic contests in football, soccer, basketball, lacrosse, baseball, and tennis were very much in the news—even riflery served as a non-letter sport in the newly constructed range in the Academy Building. The literary and other special groups maintained a nearly normal existence.

Dr. Lewis Perry [a senior instructor] at the trustees' request continued beyond the time of a richly earned retirement; Dean Wells Kerr and Treasurer Corning Benton carried the heavy load of day-to-day existence with their usual skill and devotion; department heads and faculty worked without stint in dormitories, classrooms, and on the playing fields to insure that the students have as proper a learning and living experience as the tense times would allow.

We were an enclave living as best we could in a stormy world which could not help but disturb our separate peace.

James Hitt's *It Never Rains after Three O'Clock* gives the story of a southern preparatory school for boys from its inception in 1893 to 1968. The chapter on how the school adjusted to wartime conditions provides a different perspective on the way World War II changed conditions of secondary education in other parts of the country.

FROM JAMES E. HITT, *IT NEVER RAINS AFTER THREE O'CLOCK: A HISTORY OF THE BAYLOR SCHOOL, 1893–1968*
(Chattanooga, Tenn.: Baylor School Press, 1971)

THE WAR YEARS

As the United States mustered men and materials for the titanic effort of World War II, Baylor in Chattanooga, Tennessee, was approaching its 50th-anniversary year, which began in the fall of 1942. That school year was a momentous one in the history of Baylor.

Baylor was operating its military program under a 55-C [civilian–military school] classification. The schedule was much the same as that for R.O.T.C. [Reserve Officers Training Corps] units save that Baylor was required to furnish its own officers. The stepped-up program differed from that of the past in that the cadet corps drilled four days a week instead of three, and on the fifth day the boys attended classes in military science and tactics, meteorology, aviation, or radio. A physical education program was conducted under military supervision and included calisthenics and runs on the obstacle course. All the boys, save those who were physically disabled, were required to take military. They met formations and marched to drill, chapel, and meals; but they were permitted to go to and from classes without marching. All boys saluted and were saluted in return before addressing teachers, whether or not the teachers were on the military staff; and all classes came to attention when teachers entered classes or were ready to begin. One cadet in each class was assigned to report the absentees to the teacher.

Incidentally, the sloppy salutes the boys received from non-military teachers caused Colonel R. B. Bayle, commandant for two years at Baylor, to discontinue the practice of boys' saluting strictly academic teachers in the fall of 1944, when he took charge of the military.

Three days after the Japanese attack on Pearl Harbor, the administration at Baylor decided that one of the best contributions the school could make to the cause of victory would be to grow as nearly as possible its own food supply; so in the spring of 1942 the school entered upon a somewhat ambitious experiment in farming. October of 1942 Headmaster Barks, in an interview with local newsman Springer Gibson, explained that the school's reason for starting the experiment was threefold: first, by farming, the school would be cooperating with the government in helping to avoid a food shortage; second, the project would result in a saving of money the school could pass on to its patrons, since the school would not have to raise tuition prices to offset higher food prices; and, third, farming would provide a constructive activity for the school's Victory Corps. Mr. Barks explained the Victory Corps in this wise:

"Our government has done something for every group except the high school boy. College boys enlist in reserve corps of one of the branches of service and go on to finish their education or get as much of it as possible. Civilians can and do participate in civilian defense. But there is no help for the high school boy—the boy of 16 or 17 years of age. And he's the one who has the most pressure on him. He can get no satisfaction unless he quits school and enlists."

The Victory Corps, planned on a national scale, is, I believe, a move to take care of that. The government wants boys in the Victory Corps to work at such things as mechanics, radio, that will help in the war effort. We can't do that; our machine shop isn't big enough. What we plan to do is let boys who volunteer for our Victory Corps work on the farm project here. In that way, they'll be helping the food program—and then it'll teach them what a day's work really is.

The farm program transformed most of the golf course and much of the regular campus into a pasture for some fifty head of white-faced cattle and a herd of sheep. In the barn area, under the great oaks at the southeast corner of the main campus, turkeys and chickens were raised on wire flooring off the ground. A herd of hogs waxed fat on the grounds across the lake. And crops of hay and corn and gardens of vegetables were planted in every available space. For example, the small area where the campfire site for summer camp is now located, between the river inlet and the old creek channel from lake to river, was for years the school's potato patch; and the vegetable garden was located where the tennis courts are now situated.

Farmer Heywood was particularly proud of the school's luck in raising turkeys, since turkeys are notoriously difficult to raise because of high susceptibility to certain diseases and stupid tendency to drown themselves if allowed to stay out in the rain. "We've raised forty-six out of fifty," Humpy boasted, displaying his expertise to Springer Gibson. "They're not so hard to raise if you keep them on wire—off the ground—

keep them warm when it gets cold, inoculate them, and keep them out of the rain. Nothing to it."

The man who supervised the school's farming project and provided the agricultural knowledge that made it succeed, of course, was Humpy's right-hand man, Armeda Belcher, who succeeded his brother-in-law, Amos King, as caretaker and maintenance man in 1937. Mr. Belcher was another of those Baylor employees who came to stay. In 1968 he was still on the scene as superintendent of buildings and grounds, he and Mrs. Belcher having resided in the little white cottage at the southeast corner of the original lease for approximately thirty-five years.

During its first year the Victory Corps farming project was so successful that it attracted national attention. In early April of 1943 W. G. Foster, editor of the *News-Free Press*, heard over the radio a program in which Baylor School was praised by a national network out of New York as having the outstanding school Victory Corps in the United States. So he made a visit to Baylor to see for himself. What he saw provided the substance for a newspaper article which was published on April 8, 1943. A portion of that article is quoted below:

> They battle to make the "farm" team out of a Baylor! Coach Humphrey Heywood directs the football team in the fall and the "farm" team in the spring, summer, and early September. The boys have to take a certain course specified by the Government and they have to made a "C" grade or better in everything as specified by Headmaster Herbert Barks. And competition is keen for the honor of working on the Baylor farm. . . .
>
> What I saw [at Baylor] literally amazed me beyond expression. A large part of the school property of 160 acres has been given over to the farming industry, 186 acres have been rented from an adjoining farm, and 33 acres have been rented from Radio Station WDOD, which has a transmitter station just south of the school property.
>
> Using Coach Heywood as a "guide," I viewed 3,000 chickens of various stages of development, 65 pigs and hogs, a herd of purebred beef cattle, a herd of sheep already producing food for the Baylor table, a large garden, where various vegetables already are peeping above the surface, fields dedicated to the growing of sweet potatoes, Irish potatoes, corn and hay. The Baylor dining table thus groans under beef and pork steaks and roasts, with sausage, "chitlins" and all the trimmings, fresh from the slaughter pen; eggs laid by chickens whose dainty feet never touch the ground; broilers, fryers, and baked chickens that never have been in cold storage; mutton fattened to the delicious stage; vegetables fresh, with none of their

vitamins lost in shipping; "roasting ears" by the hundreds and everything that goes to make flesh, muscles, and brain cells. . . .

The years of the Victory Corps were the war years, of course, with
maximum student participation in the farm work occurring in the years
of 1942–1943 and 1943–1944. In the latter year membership in the Victory Corps numbered approximately 250 boys. Under the Baylor plan,
each member was expected to work on the farm about once a month.
The plan was highly satisfactory both to the boys and to the school. The
school's interest in farming, however, did not extend beyond the war
years much longer than it took for gradually disposing of livestock and
farm equipment. Incidentally, the golf course was never reclaimed from
pasture. During the war the golf team trained on the links at the Mea-
dowlake Golf Club, and after the war it continued to do so for a number
of years and then shifted its practices to the course at the Signal Mountain
Golf Club.

The following excerpt is from a history of the Groton School. It is
a continuation of the record of school life at this famous prep
school that was given by Frank Ashburn in *Fifty Years On* (1934).
It is especially informative about the changes brought on by World
War II to institutions like Groton.

FROM ACOSTA NICHOLS, "WAR AND A NEW ADMINISTRATION,
1940–1946," *FORTY YEARS MORE: A HISTORY OF GROTON
SCHOOL, 1934–1974*
(Groton, Mass.: The Groton Trustees, 1976)

Problems were magnified by certain wartime conditions. The huge expansion of Fort Devens quickly drained off all the available labor in the
Nashoba area. People promptly commented that under the Rector [Mr.
Peabody] the lawns had been beautifully trimmed, but now the grass was
unkempt. Similarly, the boys on Sunday had always previously appeared
in neat blue suits, but the demands of the Navy for uniform cloth suddenly made such material unavailable, so that boys in Chapel began appearing in assorted suits. Or, in the early days of student waiting on table,
there was necessarily a good deal of chaotic confusion, which was at once
contrasted with the smooth efficiency of the waitresses of earlier days.
Surely, some people argued, all of these things indicate that Groton is
falling to pieces, and it must be the Headmaster's fault!

During the Winter Term three innovations, all of which were to be
continued later, were instituted. Groton played its first regularly sched-
uled hockey game against another school, setting a happy tradition by

beating Brooks 6–1. The Food Store began its career in the cellar of the Schoolhouse. Its original purpose was to raise money for the Missionary Society by selling candy, cookies, and other foods on Wednesday and Saturday afternoons. By the '60s and '70s, however, its operations were to expand greatly, and its principal function came to be to supply mid-morning snacks to boys who had preferred sleep to breakfast. And, speaking of sleep, the third innovation of the term was Mr. Crocker's [the headmaster] decision to have Sunday morning breakfast much later than it had hitherto been. The change made it impossible for the maids to take care of the dormitories and still get to church on time, so on Sundays alone boys were required to make their own beds—a practice that was shortly to be extended to the other six days of the week as well.

It was during the Winter Term, too, that the Aircraft Reporting Center on the Schoolhouse roof had its first trial run. Since Fort Devens was at the time the home of the only combat-ready division in the United States, it was thought to be a likely target for Nazi air raids in the event of war. So the Schoolhouse tower became a spotting station, equipped with a telephone connected directly to Army Air Force Headquarters. From February 1941 until December, this post was activated for occasional drills; from the night of Pearl Harbor until late in the war it was manned around the clock. (In all honesty, it must be observed that few of those who gave conscientious service in the station had any idea of the type, speed, altitude, or flight direction of the planes on whose presumptive attack they were supposed to give a detailed and accurate report!)

The First Division, quartered at Fort Devens, happened to have a good many Groton alumni in its ranks, including Brigadier General Theodore Roosevelt '06, whose wife took up residence in Parents' House. Many of these alumni were frequent visitors to the school until they went overseas a year later, thus beginning an association with the Fort that was to become increasingly intimate.

Even at this early stage of the war, there were many collections of money for various war-related causes. From time to time, members of the faculty have put on a show for the entertainment of the boys. Probably the most elaborate of these ever to be staged was a performance for the benefit of British War Relief, in April, featuring a question-and-answer show based on the then popular "Information, Please," but including dances, songs, and numerous skits. The participants were flattered that most of the boys in the audience, who had originally paid cash for tickets, came back afterward with an additional $5 or $10 contribution as a tribute to the quality of the show.

Since the war affected school life in many different ways with ever deepening impact, it can perhaps be better discussed topically than chronologically.

Changes in faculty personnel were extensive. Two masters left shortly after Pearl Harbor, and nine more by the start of the next academic year. In all, seventeen were to enter the armed services, only three of whom (More, Satterthwaite, and Nichols) were to return to the faculty afterward. Moreover, several of those who remained had periods of uncertainty as to whether they might be drafted. Necessarily, the loss of many experienced teachers could not help but be disruptive. Between June and September 1942, for example, there was a 100% turnover in the Science Department.

The quality of the replacement faculty was uneven. Fortunately from the school's standpoint though not the nation's, diminished enrollment in colleges freed many college teachers for other employment, and Groton thus gained some splendid additions to the faculty, notably Messrs. Hawkes, Wickens, Mommsen, Foster, and Pick. There were some, however, who would probably not have been engaged under normal circumstances.

If uncertainty about forthcoming military services was hard on the masters, it was undoubtedly worse for the boys. Morale was seriously affected, and it is surprising that it did not disintegate. For contradictory official announcements and rumors came with bewildering rapidity: that high school and secondary school students would be able to finish their school careers, that they would have to enter the armed services on their eighteenth birthdays (or their seventeenth, or at the age of seventeen and a half), that they would be allowed to complete the half-year (or full year) after their seventeenth birthdays but no more, etc. Who could blame a boy of, let's say, seventeen years and nine months who was starting to write a long term paper and who had just heard an announcement that all over the age of seventeen and a half were to be inducted immediately, if he ceased all research for the paper? In any case, the teenagers of the early 1940s knew that virtually all of them would shortly be on active duty, and that, as in all wars, they, as the youngest combatants, would probably bear the heaviest share of casualties. The impossibility of planning for college, let alone for the longer future, was another depressant of morale.

Much thought was given to the question of the sort of diploma or certificate that would be awarded to boys drafted before completing the regular school course. The final arrangement was that, if a boy had to leave at the end of the first half of the Sixth Form year, he might do extra work during the preceding summer, and then receive a "War Diploma," equivalent in all respects to the regular one. If he had to depart before the start of Sixth Form year, he might get a "War Certificate," simply stating that he had attended Groton School in good standing for a certain number of years.

Word came constantly of alumni actively in the war. By September 1942, 369 were known to be in uniform, and a year later well over 700 of a then living alumni body of about 1300. Thirty-one gave their lives, ranging from President Franklin D. Roosevelt '00 and Brigadier General Theodore Roosevelt '06 to Stephen B. Curtis '43. From time to time graduates on home leave came to the school and told of activities in their theater of operation.

There was much discussion as to whether a curriculum such as Groton's that is basically humanistic was appropriate in time of war. The conclusion, endorsed by governmental authorities, was that the liberal arts were just as vital as ever in the interest of the postwar society, but that certain courses aimed at preparing for armed services might be added. Accordingly, new classes in navigation, radio, and auto mechanics were instituted, and the emphasis on mathematics was increased. Additionally, virtually all members of the school community received instruction in first aid. Perhaps strangely, the military authorities said that there was no point in attempting drilling or similar military activities, but they did urge a physical toughening program. So special calisthenics and other hardening exercises were introduced, and a very rugged commando obstacle course was set up.

On the day of Pearl Harbor, the aircraft spotting station on the Schoolhouse roof to which reference has already been made was activated. After a few days in which the school supplied the spotters around the clock, an agreement was made with the local American Legion post whereby its members would man the station by night and the school would do so by day. This arrangement continued for a couple of years. So did the sale of saving stamps and defense bonds, which had begun as early as September 1941. Like all Schools, Groton was required to hold periodic air raid and blackout drills. Mr. Beasley was appointed Air Raid Warden, and appropriate areas were designated as shelters. Scrap collection drives were pursued vigorously. The school woodworking shop made very precise models of planes that were to be used by the Navy in training lookouts in aircraft recognition.

Needless to say, wartime restrictions and shortages made themselves felt. Ration books had to be turned in to the Dining Hall, and the limited supply of gasoline hit hard, though with varying impacts at different times. For example, for a while there was no gas available for the crew coaching lunches, some athletic trips had to be canceled, picnics at Lake Baddacook or mountain climbing expeditions became rare events, and groups sometimes had to take strange roundabout routes to reach their destinations. In October 1942, for instance, the football squad managed to get to the Harvard-Princeton game by going on foot to Ayer, and thence taking the train to Cambridge. Or on another occasion the football team, heading for its game with Milton, had to walk to Ayer and go by train to Boston, then taking the subway to Ashmont and having final trek on foot to Milton. One wonders that they could have been ready to play a game upon arrival. A painful deprivation to those who loved the game was the virtual impossibility of getting five balls [English football], for the one factory that made them suffered a direct hit in the Nazi blitz.

Undoubtedly the aspect of wartime that most directly affected the boys in school and that had the most profound lasting influence was the temporary or permanent assumption of many sorts of jobs around the place by students. Prior to 1941 maids or janitors had made all beds, done all sweeping and cleaning as well as all serving and waiting at table, and the outside force had done all the work around the grounds (except in such extreme emergencies as the 1938 hurricane). As the demand for labor in defense and related industries soared after 1940, domestic servants began to disappear from private houses, and many began to question if it was wise for boys to be waited on at school in a way that they could not be at home, even if the school were able to find people to provide the service. After Pearl Harbor, much of the school's labor force disappeared, and boys and masters of necessity had to begin doing many jobs that others had performed. Early in 1942 it was announced that, effective at the start of the next academic year, boys would henceforth make their own beds, sweep their dormitories, and wait on tables. This was to be a permanent change. No doubt this development would have soon come about in any case, but wartime conditions hastened its arrival. By 1944, the indoor domestic duties had been extended to cleaning studies, washing dishes and silver, and mopping the kitchen and pantry.

Even before Pearl Harbor, many boys had taken summer jobs on neighboring farms, and had helped to harvest apples in nearby orchards. This work continued. "Snow squads" of older boys and masters were created to shovel out drives and walks when necessary and to clear the entrances to buildings. These squads continued to be employed on occasion until the early 1960s, when extensive mechanized equipment rendered them unnecessary. By 1943 the "snow squads" expanded into "maintenance squads," in which all boys in the Upper School were enrolled in groups of eight, of which as many as required could be called out when needed for urgent work, being excused from classes and afternoon appointments to do so. Additionally, many boys were allowed to elect service on afternoon "work squads" in place of the normal sports. These last groups performed such labors as caring for tennis courts, raking leaves, cultivating "victory gardens," or helping local farmers on a regular rather than occasional basis.

One accomplishment which these "work squads" carried out especially creditably was an anti-termite project, wherein the termite-infected foundation beams of Hundred House were removed and concrete supporting walls substituted.

The shortage of labor resulted in one permanent and regrettable loss—

the school golf course. In the late 1930s a good deal of money had been spent to get the course into good shape, and it had become a source of much pleasure to the resident community and to visiting alumni and parents. With the other demands of the war years, however, its maintenance was too much of a job to undertake. Five years of neglect caused the course to revert to nature to such an extent that its restoration proved to be prohibitively expensive. It is now a forest area, and only a few old-timers can recognize flat areas or depressions in the woods as the tees or sand traps that they used to be.

Easily the most onerous of wartime jobs, and the only one that was cordially detested by masters and boys alike, was coal shoveling. Transportation problems caused the authorities to inform the school that there could not be regular deliveries of coal (which the Power House then burned instead of the later oil), and that it would be necessary to get a year's supply at a time. This was done, and a mountain of coal arose in the field behind the Power House, exactly where the Scott Hockey Rink was to be later. Groups drafted on a rotating schedule had to shovel the coal each day into the school truck, which then carried it to the Power House. Since in cold weather four or five truckloads a day were necessary to furnish light and heat for the buildings, this was no small job. If the coal was frozen in sleet or ice, it was truly arduous. And in any season it was filthy.

Inevitably, there was a good deal of confusion in the early days of work done by boys. Unquestionably, beds were less neatly made than heretofore, and dormitories and studies became less clean. A great many problems had to be worked out by the trial and error method before service in the Dining Room became reasonably smooth and civilized. Endless questions arose: Should waiters wear a special jacket? Should they attempt to eat with the other diners, jumping up as necessary to clear the table and get new supplies, or should they dine separately at a different hour? If different, should their meal be before or after the rest of the school dined? How long a time did they require? etc., etc. Ultimately, all of these questions were resolved, but at first there was considerable chaos.

The disappearance of domestic servants in private houses as well as in institutions had one effect that was long-lasting. Older alumni will recall not only the lavish tea parties that were held daily at the Peabodys' [the Rector] house, but the frequent entertainments in faculty homes. These were easy to handle if there was somebody in the kitchen to cook and to wash the dishes, and before the war such service was not only available but, in those pretax and pre-inflation days, affordable even on a schoolmaster's salary. Without such help, however, a faculty wife who had to put the children to bed or to prepare her husband's supper before he went to some school duty could not entertain a dozen hungry boys at 5:30 P.M. Understandably, if regrettably, boys were to be seen much less in faculty homes than heretofore.

At the end of the war there was a good deal of debate about the extent to which students should continue to do work that had in earlier days been done by employees. On grounds of principle as well as economics the school felt committed to have the boys do some work of this kind, yet there is no question but that the full program of labor undertaken in the war years had cut seriously into academic time. How could the program best be modified to reduce the amount of time expended? The final decision was that boys would continue to wait on table, make their beds, and clean their dormitories, but that other work would be done by employees. This arrangement, with minor adjustments from time to time, has continued ever since.

TOPICS FOR DISCUSSION AND RESEARCH

1. The young people of America were told by the nation's leaders during World War II that they were vitally important to winning the war. How does this view differ from the way society looks at teenagers now?

2. The war changed not only the academic traditions and calendars of schools that operated year round on accelerated schedules, but it altered morale and manners. Examine the way students' attitudes were affected by the sense of emergency the war created.

3. During World War II young people were instructed to save and not to spend money to conserve and not to waste anything. They were encouraged to contribute at least 10 percent of any money they made for buying stamps for war bonds. How do you think young people now would react to making sacrifices and being denied luxuries and nonessentials?

4. Given what has been written in school histories concerning what the war did to change the routines at eastern preparatory schools, how faithful was Knowles in *A Separate Peace* to the actual facts about life at Phillips Exeter during the period from 1942 to 1944.

5. Using the information provided by Zook about the military's takeover of college campuses, devise a curriculum that you think a soldier or sailor should follow.

6. Do some research on the false alarms and panics set off by "war nerves" during the first months of the war. Try to find a video of Spielberg's 1979 movie *1941* to see how these events were treated comically.

7. Investigate the extent of the U-boat menace to American merchant shipping on the Gulf and Atlantic seaboard and show how it was finally defeated by the U.S. Navy.

8. Study the activities of spies in the United States during the war and the measures that the FBI took to uncover their operations.

9. Examine the posters that were created during the war to generate public support for the war effort and devise drawings of your own to encourage enlistment in the services, volunteering for defense work, or conserving essential war materials.

10. Research the impact the war had on school and professional sports programs.

SUGGESTED READINGS AND WORKS CITED

Adams, Henry H. *1942: The Year That Doomed the Axis*. New York: McKay, 1967.

Bailey, Ronald H. *The Home Front U.S.A.* New York: Time-Life Books, 1978.

Dupuy, R. Ernest. *Civilian Defense of United States.* New York: Farrar and Rinehart, 1942.

Herge, Henry C. *Wartime College Training Programs of the Armed Services.* Washington, D.C.: American Council on Education, 1948.

Hinshaw, David. *The Home Front.* New York: G. P. Putnam's Sons, 1943.

Hitt, James E. *It Never Rains after Three O'Clock: A History of the Baylor School.* Chattanooga, Tenn.: Baylor School Press, 1971.

Hoehling, A. A. *Home Front U.S.A.* New York: Crowell, 1966.

Lingeman, Richard R. *Don't You Know There's a War On? The American Home Front, 1941–1945.* New York: G. P. Putman's Sons, 1970.

Nichols, Acosta. *Forty Years More: A History of Groton School, 1934–1974.* Groton, Mass.: The Groton Trustees, 1976.

Zook, George F. "How the Colleges Went to War." *American Academy of Political and Social Science* (January 1944): 1–7.

4

"Gone For a Soldier"

There was much support for the war just after the attack on Pearl Harbor, which outraged most Americans because it was a sneak attack and also because it was carried out on a Sunday. But as *A Separate Peace* reveals, this sort of enthusiasm was not always felt by those who were of an age to be drafted, especially not after the war had been going on for several years. Young men like the boys in the novel had nothing to look forward to upon graduating from school except going into the service and possibly getting killed. They had very little control over their futures; their destiny was controlled by world events. And although the destruction and the actual fighting were in remote and distant foreign places, Knowles's novel reveals how the war was becoming an increasingly real prospect for eighteen-year-old boys.

The generation gap that existed between the older generation that had enthusiastically fought in World War I and the younger generation that would unwillingly have to fight World War II is illustrated at several points in *A Separate Peace*. Toward the end of the novel when Gene and his class are about to graduate and face induction into the military, a classmate's father advises Gene to join the marines or paratroops so he can see a lot of action and amass a glorious war record that will serve him well in later life (assuming he survived). Gene is offended by the man's attitude and astonishes the parent by telling him that he has decided to join the navy because it poses the lowest risk; he confesses that he has no desire to serve in the infantry because it is the most dangerous branch (191). The point is that Gene and his friends are willing to go to war but they are not especially patriotic about it. The World War II generation's cynicism was not as widespread as the antiwar sentiment that was so strong during the Vietnam War era, but there was little of the fanfare and war fever that had attended America's entry into World War I. In fact, if Japan had not bombed Pearl Harbor and Hitler had not declared war on the United States three days later, America would have probably remained neutral for much longer than it did. The patriotic fervor following the declaration of war against the Axis powers was soon tempered by a series of crushing defeats at the hands of Japanese in the Pacific, which continued until the tide finally turned after the Battle of Midway in 1942. Meanwhile, in North Africa, the war against the Germans went badly at first. The green U.S. troops were mauled by the experienced Afrika Korps commanded by the wily "desert fox," General Erwin Rommel. By the middle of 1942, it was obvious to most Americans that the war was going to be a long, hard struggle, and many sacrifices would have to be made.

After the rush of volunteers who flocked to enlist began to abate, the majority of the 12 million Americans who would be in uniform came into service through the draft (Flynn, 53). In 1942 all men between the ages of eighteen and thirty-five, including married men and fathers who had been exempt from service in the 1940 Draft Act, were registered and eligible to become draftees. The most comprehensive form of conscription in American history was headed by General Lewis B. Hershey, who was appointed director of selective service, a position he would hold until the Vietnam era. Those who were selected to serve were picked by local draft boards, composed of men over draft age who lived in the same districts as those of the men called up. It was therefore not unfounded humor to say that when the "greetings" letter from the draft board arrived in the mail of those who had been classified 1-A (available for military duty), it read, "Your local draft board composed of your friends and neighbors hereby notifies you that you have been selected for training and service in the U.S. Army." At first only the army used draftees to fill its ranks, while the Navy and Marines depended on volunteers, but as casualties mounted, the Navy and Marines also had to rely on draftees.

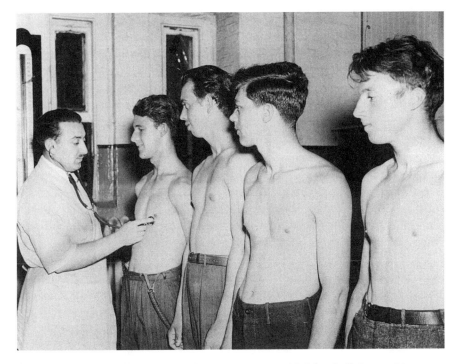

Examination of draftees at the induction center at 39 Whitehall Street, New York City, 1942. (U.S. Army Military History Institute)

In very few cases were deferments granted to those who were drafted. Unlike the situation during the Korean and Vietnam wars, being in college was not a way to avoid the draft; there were practically no 2-S deferments in World War II. The only way to escape military service was to be classified 4-F (physically or mentally or morally unfit for service) or else to be doing essential war work or be a conscientious objectors. "COs," by reason of religion or moral principles, rejected killing, but even they had to enter the military as medics or noncombatants.

Yet out of nearly 50 million Americans registered, there were few attempts to evade the draft. No one burned a draft card in protest as many did in the 1960s during the unpopular Vietnam War, nor did anyone flee the country to sit out the war in a neutral country.

There were, however, many who were rejected and avoided the war for legitimate reasons. Over 5 million Americans were classified as 4-F because they could not meet the minimum standards set by the army. In order to be rated 1-A and fit for military duty, a man had to be at least five feet tall, weigh 105 pounds, and have correctable vision. Those who had flat feet, hernias, or a venereal disease were rejected. But the main reason for rejection by the military was mental. Nearly a half-million men were turned away due to illiteracy, but as the war dragged on and the Army's need for manpower increased, the ban on illiterates was removed, for those men could be used in the infantry. In its desperation, the army created grammar schools to bring these troops up to the fourth-grade level (Bailey, 45).

Another reason for rejection of inductees was emotional instability; over 3 million men were classified 4-F. The high rate of men suffering from psychological problems was a concern for the secretary of war, who appointed Dr. Edward Strecker to try to discover the causes for so many mental disorders among men of draft age. The mothers of America, he concluded, were to blame for not "weaning their offspring emotionally as well as physically" (Bailey, 45). The writer Philip Wylie came to the same conclusion in his book *Generation of Vipers* and labeled this overprotectiveness of mothers "momism." The exact reasons for the high percentages of mentally troubled youths have never been fully explained, but it seems unfair to place all the blame on women for child rearing when the anxieties of the Great Depression and the world at war must have contributed to the emotional instability of that generation.

Another group of undesirables who were weeded out during the psychiatric screening process were homosexuals. The question often asked by an army psychiatrist was, "Do you like girls?" Some men were excluded if they appeared or acted effeminate, because they would be detrimental to unit cohesion. Many gay men concealed their sexuality, however, because they wanted to serve.

Those who were not turned down by the service and entered the military found themselves entering a strange new life. After arriving at training camp, the new recruits were processed at a "reception center," a name that implies a welcome, but it was usually not a cordial greeting. Men who were drafted in the Northeast were most likely receive basic training at Fort Dix, New Jersey; those from the South went to Fort Benning, Georgia; and those from the West went to Fort Meade, California, but there were dozens of other "forts" and "camps" where the new recruits were sent to learn how to be soldiers.

In the first few days, the new soldiers were jabbed in both arms by medics with long needles, giving the first of a long series of shots that the troops received depending on where they were to be stationed. They were also given GI haircuts at the regulation half-inch length and issued uniforms that rarely fit, handed a rifle that was never to be called "a gun," and assigned a serial number that was stamped on their identity or "dog tags," as they were called, and stenciled on all other items the soldier owned. It was an unpardonable military crime to forget one's serial number, and troops were expected to recite it along with their name and rank whenever they were addressed by noncommissioned officer (NCO) or an officer. It was a part of the army's process of stripping away the recruit's civilian identity and converting him into a cog in the military machine.

What many of these young soldiers went through as they made the transition from civilian life has been described by John Keegan as "culture shock"—exposure to a system of subordination and autocracy entirely alien to American values (Keegan, 54). On top of the boredom and inefficiency that was a part of army life, there was another element—a complaint that goes beyond normal over-crowding, bad food, lack of respect for individuality, and lack of privacy. It refers to a form of minor sadism that makes military life worse than it needs to be. It is the petty harassment by those in authority over those below them in the chain of command. It is a sergeant putting a private on kitchen police (KP) duty because he saw the soldier reading a volume of poetry or because a bright college boy asked a question at drill the sergeant could not answer. It is any kind of petty harassment that is small-minded and trivial, Fussell points out, such as the military obsession with haircuts, shining brass, and polishing leather. Also falling into the category are frequent inspections of barracks, weapons, and equipment, all done for the sake of "generating the maximum anxiety over matters of minimum significance" (*Wartime*, 81). As Robert Lowry says in his study of World War II novels, "The view that the military is a quasi-fascistic organization is attested to in fiction like Joseph Heller's *Catch-22*, Norman Mailer's *The Naked and the Dead* and Irwin Shaw's *The Young Lions*." All three of these authors were World War II veterans and so spoke from the perspective of personal experience.

Army life was especially hard on men who had the benefit of some education in prep schools or colleges. Some would be selected for the Army Special Training Program or Officer Candidate School and be given training to prepare them as specialists or officers, but many would remain in the ranks as enlisted men and endure all the debasement and humiliation that went with being a soldier. Living in the barracks was an ordeal at best, and it was not intended to be a comfortable place. A typical barracks was a two-story wooden frame building that housed a platoon, a unit of approximately thirty-six men that included four squads. There would be a row of nine double-decker bunks on each floor of the barracks; first and second squads were downstairs and third and fourth upstairs. The living arrangements were totally communal, the men sleeping so close to each other that the bunks were set up for sleeping head to toe to keep down the spread of colds and flu. The showers and toilets were entirely open, with no partitions. For a man who was at all modest, bathing and answering the calls of nature were embarrassments. In the army there was no place for any refinements among the enlisted men. But for some men whose lives had been devastated by the Depression, the army offered three hot meals a day and a bed.

Thus, for soldiers from the social and economic underclass, adaptation was somewhat easier. As Lee Kennett points out, in the America of the 1940s, one home in three did not have running water or electricity or central heat, whereas the army barracks, for all their bareness, had these basic comforts (40). Soldiers from middle-class homes or college campuses had more difficulty adjusting to the lack of privacy, the constant country music on the radio, and the crude barracks language. In such an environment, anyone who read something more refined than pulp fiction or comic books was considered a snob by the others and regarded with suspicion by the NCOs, who scorned college boys. A corporal or sergeant could make a soldier's life miserable. The treatment could be humiliation by a "chewing out," extra guard duty or kitchen duty, or ever physical assault. Although NCOs were technically not supposed to strike the men, they often did with the tacit consent of the superior officers.

America's citizen-soldiers resented the mindless regimentation, and all lived for a two-day pass or a furlough home. But as the article written by Lin Zinberg shows, going home was often a frustrating experience for a soldier, who now found himself lacking rapport with his family. This fact is also illustrated vividly by the situation that Leper faces in *A Separate Peace* when he goes home without leave and finds his mother cannot comprehend what he experienced during basic training that caused him to snap. Leper was facing a common dilemma for soldiers: military life was literally driving him crazy, and he could not step back into the civilian world.

Boys like Leper who did not fit in with the others were known in the army as a "sad sack"—a soldier who was inept, eccentric, and unable to do things the "army way." He was victimized by his fellow soldiers and NCOs who singled out men whose behavior was erratic. Life in the barracks could become unbearable for those who did not fit in. As a Walter Reed study on the Department of Troops showed, the first step to surviving was getting oneself accepted, concluding that "the soldier's sanity and very life depended on it" (Kennett, 63).

Leper could not cope with the realities of army life, which were far removed from his idealized conceptions of the military that he had seen in recruitment films for the ski troops shown at school. So he deserted and left the post without leave, making his own sort of an insane separate peace.

Psychological casualties were high during World War II. There were men who could not make the transition from civilian to military life—recruits like Leper who were used to the comforts of family and home or school and friends and could not stand the strain of living in the crude environment of the barracks. The army showed little compassion or understanding for those who could not cope and thus broke down. The breakdown rate was even worse when men who were shaky were sent into combat. The mental attrition for men who were in combat for twenty-eight days straight was as high as 90 percent. Paul Fussell, the author of several books on war, points out that it was not just the weak or sensitive troops or the cowardly soldiers who broke down. "Inevitably all men will break down if in combat long enough. . . . There is no such thing as getting used to combat. . . . Men will break down in direct relation to the intensity and duration of their experience" (*Wartime*, 281).

Psychiatric casualties of war have been depicted in fiction, such as the collapse of the brave B-17 squadron commander at the end of Lay and Bartlett's *Twelve O'Clock High* and the insanity of Yossarian in Joseph Heller's *Catch-22*, where the "sane" people are those who have rebelled against the absurd violence of war and declared themselves insane. Only the ironic "catch-22" prevents them from escaping the war because a man who realizes that war is insane is actually sane. Thus, there was a growing realization that there was no way out and that, given the odds, one was either going to be wounded or killed or go completely crazy. But just going crazy was often not enough. Giving into fear was considered reprehensible by the military; soldiers were supposed to be afraid but never give into it. In the movie *Patton*, the general encounters a soldier in the hospital suffering from a mental condition euphemistically called "combat fatigue." When he discovers the nature of the man's problem, he flies into a fury, calling the man a yellow coward and threatening to shoot him on the spot. In fact, one American soldier, Private Slovak, was shot by a firing squad for cowardice in the face of the enemy. During the Battle of the Bulge in Europe from 1944 to 1945, the army doctors were ordered to "recondition" men who had snapped under the stress of combat and send them back into battle as soon as possible as the best cure for their nerves, which was the official justification for putting crippled men into harm's way. Actually, the army's losses of over 19,000 killed during the first ten days of the battle necessitated using anyone who could be put into the front lines, including clerks, cooks, and the walking wounded.

General Patton's attitude toward those who broke down was not unique. In *A Separate Peace* Leper's fellow students are disappointed and angry when they hear that he has cracked up and gone AWOL. His behavior brings dishonor and shame on the student body for having been thrown out of the service with a Section 8 dishonorable discharge, given to those who were classified as crazy, criminal, or homosexual and thereby unsuited to serve.

The military attitude toward soldiers with mental or sexual identity problems was unsympathetic. Army commanders would only admit that stress could cause physical but not psychological damage to soldiers. Men who seemed to be suffering from nervous exhaustion were regarded as cowards and shirkers. Homosexuals were discharged with dispatch. General Patton encouraged his troops to make fun of or shun those soldiers who were "sissies" or had psychological problems. Most officers scorned the diagnosis of army psychiatrists who tried to get commanders to understand neurotic behavior as a disease and denied the reality of such breakdowns.

To the men, however, neuropsychiatric collapses were very real indeed. The main sign was a certain expression—a vacant look or stare, as well as a robotic kind of movement. Other symptoms of combat fatigue were uncontrollable tremors ("the shakes"), verbal repetition, infantile behavior, and inappropriately crying, laughing, or yelling (Loutry, 355).

Soldiers who experienced breakdowns often spoke of not being able to get disturbing memories or images out of their minds, and they could not rid themselves of their nightmares, whether awake or sleeping. In *A Separate Peace* Leper tells Gene that he has experienced distorted visions that he can't shake off. On another occasion he hallucinates that a soldier is sweeping out the barracks with a man's amputated leg rather than a broom. Young men like Leper had to deal with their traumas or risk being destroyed by them. Many would never be able to forget the feelings of strangeness and alienation or excise the anguish they felt during their experiences in the service.

SUGAR-COATING THE DRAFT

As the world situation grew more dangerous with war raging in Europe and Asia, it was apparent to the Roosevelt administration that America could be drawn into the conflict and that preparations for war should be made in the event the nation was attacked.

America had been at peace since World War I ended in 1918, and during the next two decades, the size of the army and navy had shrunken so small that the New York City Police Department had more people than the U.S. Marine Corps. The ranks of all the services were filled entirely by volunteers, and most of those men who joined were those who were down and out and had no chance of making it in civilian life. Military life, at least for those in the enlisted ranks, was considered as a last resort to jail or starvation. For the officer class, it meant low pay and slow promotion in the years between the wars.

Until 1940 the United States was one of the few nations without a program of compulsory military training, something that was considered by most Americans as a European tradition that was definitely undemocratic and anti-American. But as the war clouds became darker, Congress approved the Selective Training and Service Act in September 1940. It was a highly controversial bill and passed by only a few votes after a long and hot debate between the isolationists who wanted to keep America neutral and those who saw it as the moral mission of the United State to side with England and Russia, the only two major European nations still unconquered by the Axis powers. The new law was America's first step toward getting ready for a war that it did not want to fight. On October 16, all men between the ages of twenty-one and thirty-five would register with their local draft boards. With over 16 million eligible, the men who would be selected for induction were chosen by lottery and picked by their draft number in the interest of fairness.

As men were called up and reported for duty, the U.S. Army printed thousands of informational pamphlets intended to help the men make the transition from civilian to military life. The following document, "You're in the Army Now," was put out by the U.S. government to try to help those who were drafted come to terms with military life. The information provided was very detailed and practical, telling the new soldier what he needed to pack on his trip to the induction center, what to expect when he arrived, what sort of food and physical and mental tests he would have, and what would lie ahead during his year of active service. The tone is very upbeat and reassuring, attempting to persuade the new recruit that "military training is hell . . . if you enter into it in the right spirit, it can be lots of fun," as the author of this pamphlet writes.

FROM J. A. POWER, "YOU'RE IN THE ARMY NOW"
(U.S. Government Pamphlet, 1940)

On a day that you will never forget your notice from the Local Draft Board will arrive at your home, telling you when to report for Induction, which means your transfer from civilian to military status.

Failure to report promptly at the hour and on the day named is a grave military offense for which you may be tried by court martial. Willful failure to report with an intent to evade military service constitutes desertion, which, in time of war, is a capital offense.

Upon reporting to your local board, you will not need, and you should not bring with you, anything except hand baggage. You will not be permitted to take trunks or boxes with you on the train. You should take only the following articles: A pair of strong comfortable shoes; not to exceed four extra suits of underclothing; not to exceed six extra pairs of socks; four face and two bath towels; a comb, a brush, a toothbrush, soap, tooth powder, razor, and shaving soap. It will add to your comfort to bring one woolen blanket, preferably of dark or neutral color. This blanket should be tightly rolled, the ends of the roll should be securely bound together and the loop of the blanket roll thus formed slung from your left shoulder to your right hip.

You should wear rough strong clothing and a flannel shirt, preferably an olive-drab shirt of the kind issued to soldiers.

On the day you leave home you go to your local Draft Board, where other conscripts are waiting. You are put into groups of eight men. The Board picks out one man as leader, and another as assistant leader for each group.

During the next two or three days before you leave for your Training Center, you are given three different tests: A complete physical examination, an intelligence test, and an interview.

If the Army Doctors find you're not fit, you're sent back home at Government expense.

The purpose of the Intelligence Test and the Interview is to find out what job in the Army suits you best. You don't have to be a College

graduate to rate high in them. This new citizens' army is a vast, complicated machine that requires a lot of brain and a lot of brawn to run.
When they finish at the Reception Center, many of the rookies will be
sent to special schools, or given specialized training, depending on their
ability and capacity to learn. That will come in handy when they've finished their year's training and return to civilian life.

When the Intelligence Test is over the recruit has to face a sharp eyed,
sharper-minded Interviewer for about ten minutes. It's the job of this
Interviewer to fit the rookie into that part of the Army where he will be
most useful.

The Interviewer has the questionnaire the rookie filled out for his Local
Draft Board, showing his background and history. Before him is a "Qualification Card," which he fills out as the rookie supplies the answers.
When the questioning is over the Interviewer makes an estimate of the
recruit's possibilities, based on his age, his experience, the kind of job
he held in civilian life, previous military training, his ability to lead, and
his intelligence.

On the Soldier's Qualification Card the Interviewer jots down his recommendation for the new soldier to fit into:

1. A specialist's job in the Army

2. A combat soldier

On the next four pages are printed the qualification card that is filled
out by the Interviewer. Read it so you can be ready to answer the questions. When your year's training is over each of you will have a M.O.S.
[military occupation specialty].

You are now in camp. It may be Camp Dix in New Jersey or Camp
McClellan in Alabama, but no matter where you are sent the procedure
you will follow will be about the same.

And this being your first day in camp—your initial experience with
military life—it is one you're likely never to forget. A new life lies ahead
of you and it is natural that you will be filled with curiosity.

You remember all the stories you've read, the movies you've seen, and
wonder how all that measures up to the realities of the life you're about
to face.

In civilian life everything was centered about you as an individual. But
here, you realize, you are part of a vast machine. You're going to need a
new point of view, a new way of looking at things.

A thousand questions race through your mind. Will the food be good?
Can I stand the gaff of a ten mile march? How often do I get leave of
absence? Suppose I get sick, who looks after me? Suddenly, the whole
business seems confusing and for a minute or two you feel panicky.

Well, take it easy! And let's start at the beginning and see what it is
that goes to make a good soldier.

An old West Pointer puts it this way:

"A soldier is part of the country's fighting machine. Above everything else, he's got to be the sort of man who can be depended upon in a pinch. The dependable soldier, therefore, is a man of character. He must be steady, loyal and reliable. Any man who considers himself too smart for the Army is gong to have a tough time of it. But a willingness to do his duty—and sound common sense—will carry him a long way."

But what about the idea that a soldier is supposed to be a super-tough, rip-snorting guy who's ready to tear 'em apart at the drop of a hat? Isn't war hell, as Sherman said? Sure it is, but nowhere in the world will you find less bloodthirstiness than you will in the Army. All that tough stuff belongs in the movies and in novels.

Like most Americans, you have a more or less sober, intelligent notion of what all the shouting is about in Europe. You've seen great liberty-loving countries go under the heels of the dictators. You value the American way of living—the right to belong to any church you choose, the right to a free press, free speech and so on.

The Army is the protector of those rights, no matter what political party is in power.

The Army says that war may be hell, but if you want to avoid it, you've got to be prepared to resist. Certainly *military training* isn't hell. What's more, if you enter into the thing in the right spirit, it can be lots of fun.

A Colonel in the Regular Army put his finger on the Army viewpoint when he said: "Professional soldiers don't like war any more than doctors like epidemics."

Procedure will vary at different camps and in different branches of the Service. With hundreds of thousands of new trainees reporting to duty, and with the plans of the Army changing to meet the new conditions, no hard and fast rules can be outlined in advance. However, there are certain facts that you must know.

First, you are sworn in as a soldier.

Along with a group of other men you are lined up to take the oath of enlistment. An officer will be in charge. He makes a short talk. He tells you that you are to enter into a contract with the United States Army.

Then he'll deal with a very practical matter: The rates of pay in the Army.

The officer will recommend that you think about the Government's life insurance plan which is cheap and worth looking into. He'll suggest that if you have made any false statements on your draft papers about your citizenship, marriage, criminal record, etc., you'd better speak up now.

Then he calls the names of the men in the group and reads the oath of enlistment, and you and your fellow trainees will raise right hands, and say, "I do."

You're in the Army now. And things begin to happen.

TELLING IT LIKE IT IS

The following article, written by Dale Kramer for *The New Republic* appeared during the height of America's military buildup for World War II. From this insider's perspective, we are able to see how one young man perceived the shift from civilian life to the army. His purpose in writing about his experience as a serviceman is to tell it like it is. Private Kramer is not able to tell his readers the unvarnished truth, however, because editorial conventions of that time were much stricter than now. In talking about army language, he cannot reproduce the profanity and obscenity that made up so much of the military vocabulary. The author wants to get across the point that there is nothing glamorous or heroic about being in uniform and that real soldiers resent Hollywood efforts to make it seem so. He also tries to explain the caste system that military ranks create, and that while rank has its privileges, civilian-soldiers of the U.S. Army do not put their noncommissioned and commissioned officers on a pedestal as would be the case in armies without democratic traditions.

FROM DALE KRAMER, "WHAT IT'S LIKE IN THE ARMY"
(*The New Republic*, December 1943)

From ten to fifteen million men—perhaps more—will serve in the armed forces of the United States during this war. If not the largest body of fighting men ever mustered by a single nation, it will have been the most swiftly mobilized. Englishmen were trained for the sea; conscription in France was traditional; and every Russian youth had been taught to revere a place in the Red Army. As for the Axis powers, deification of the warrior—from Mussolini's insane "live dangerously" advice to Japanese hara-kiri after defeat—is of course a leading doctrine. Not only were Americans physically untrained for combat, but the thought of ever participating in war was foreign to the two generations fighting or preparing to fight.

Consequently the shift from civilian existence to life in barracks, on ship, and in bivouac tents was ten times more difficult than for the soldiers of any other nation. Many doubted that it could be accomplished, and no one has been more amazed than civilians-become-soldiers that it has been accomplished. Army regulations do not require that a soldier enjoy Army life; high officers who during tours of inspection inquire of a man how he likes Army life do not appear displeased at forthright negative responses. In the pressing need for forging a powerful fighting instrument in the shadow of the enemy the recruit's body is battered, his soul tried, his ego crushed; and he realizes that his powers of physical and mental recuperation are beyond his wildest expectations.

It is doubtful if the civilian, no matter how many war novels he has read or how careful his digestion of newspapers and magazines, ever gets much of an idea of life in the Army. The soldier writing home to his parents, his wife, his girl, or his children makes a few attempts at placing the whole complex situation—his feelings, the new and strange things about him—down on paper, and then he gives it up and confines himself to a few routine details before getting to intimate things. It would probably always be so; a man can bridge the gap from civilian to the soldier's life, but he will never be able to explain adequately what he sees and feels after he gets there. Soldiers are well aware of the fact. We had read everything, yet from the day of induction we were in a foreign climate. I do not entertain any hope of suddenly clearing the atmosphere. It is only that the national experience—the men going, their close ones seeing them go—is so tremendous that every soldier, in a letter, in a moment to a friend, or in print, feels the necessity for making his small attempt.

Each day at induction stations for more than two years now the nation has been cut down the middle and its cross sections exposed. In the rural areas the county-seat lawyer, his office closed for the duration, lines up with the farmhand, the college boy with the lad who left high school to go to work in the garage. At Governor's Island, where New York men were inducted prior to the opening of Grand Central Palace, I saw a Wall Street man, resplendent in carnation and Homburg, sharing a bench with a Bowery bum who was sleeping off a jag. Zoot-suited youths mingled with muscular, open-shirted longshoremen. At that time men up to forty-five years were being called, and the two generations of the recruits were more discernible than ever. A solid, conservatively dressed man stood near a bareheaded Princeton student—shift the scene, and the picture might be that of a father visiting his son on the campus. The dividing line between these generations falls at about twenty-nine or thirty years. Above this are the men who have some memory of the last war, who were jolted by the depression as they came of age, and who at last were becoming to some degree settled in their way of life. Below the line are the younger men—the large majority—who have greater stamina, are gayer, and on the whole are more adaptable.

At the induction center there begins a lesson in the prime essential of Army life—patience. The prospective soldier is made acquainted with the waiting line. A corporal or a sergeant tries to put him into it, and he moves reluctantly, as in the civilian world. Naturally infuriated, the noncommissioned officer gives a sort of preview of what may be expected should tardiness be shown in the future. For the soldier will stand in line when he wants to eat, to be paid, to board a bus from camp—in short, whenever he wants to do anything that more than a dozen others are intent upon doing. In time he will lie motionless for hours in his foxhole or other concealment or cover. Now he waits for his turn to be measured, weighed, tapped, questioned, and judged. In the mind of all is one question: "Shall I be accepted?" In a room at the end of the line total strangers inquire of each other: "Did they take you?" Men stuff red-stamped "rejection" papers into their pockets and stand aside, dressing slowly, their thoughts their own. Some cannot hide a feeling of satisfaction; others are clearly depressed. (A frail lawyer who was placed in charge of my group from the draft board was turned down. Two weeks later at Camp Upton, the reception center, he bobbed up in uniform; he had demanded reexamination and this time had gained entrance.) Final touches are put to papers, and those accepted raise their right hands and become soldiers of the United States. We poured off the dark ferryboat into lower Manhattan's streets, notices of time and place to report in our pockets, to swallow a last concentrated capsule of civilian life.

In this war the passage of men into the Army is without much public fanfare. "The Rotary Club gives each man a candy bar and he gets on the bus and that's the end of it," a small-town veteran of Belleau Wood told me. Probably the fact that the men are taking a bus has something to do with it—somehow it would be more fitting to take a brass band to the railway station. In more worldly New York City an American Legion post gave each of us a pack of cigarettes and a booklet containing hints on how to get along in the Army. We shuffled down the subway steps, and to the homebound commuters rushing into Pennsylvania Station we were another of the endless lines of men waiting for troop trains. Once we were aboard, the wooden benches replacing cushioned seats reminded us of the Legion's humorous offshoot, "Forty and Eight," so named for French railway cars' capacity of forty men and eight horses. At dusk the train rolled through Yaphank, and again there stirred in us vague recollections—this time of Irving Berlin's "Yip, Yip, Yaphank," and another generation of soldiers who sang it.

The swiftness with which America has mobilized its vast manpower became clear to us for the first time at the reception center. In the innocence of our civilian pasts we had believed that we should be put to bed until, fresh and clear-minded, we were aroused for aptitude tests, and, in good time, fitted for uniforms. "You will be pushed around here," a lieutenant told several hundred of us gathered in a long warehouse. We were split up according to initials of our last names; I have since seen not a single one of six acquaintances who were with me, and of the four I have heard from no two are in the same branch of service. We K's [soldiers whose names begin with "K"] set our traveling bags and our

overnight cases and our brown-paper bundles in the barracks streets assigned to us, marched into our first mess hall, and marched out again to
the testing buildings. After some hours of forcing brains fatigued by
sending-away celebrations to cope with strange aptitude problems, we
retrieved our civilian relics and crept to bunks assigned us—to be up a
couple of hours before dawn.

The general details of a soldier's classification by the Army are now
pretty well known. He is interviewed and his employment record, his
schooling, his grades on aptitude tests, and other more or less intimate
facts of his life are noted down on a card which accompanies him
wherever he goes; from this information he is classified for the best niche
he can fill in the Army. Confusing himself slightly with Sergeant Quirt [an
amorous character from the anti-war play *What Price Glory?*], he is taken
to a movie on sex hygiene [to avoid the dangers of venereal diseases]—
where ushers are stationed about to carry him out in case he faints. In
due time he stuffs a barracks bag with shoes, hats, half a dozen assorted
uniforms, overcoat, raincoat, leggings, etc., which, due to an intricate
system of sizings, fit him remarkably well. (Few soldiers keep their civilian
shapes for very long.) As the line approaches the inoculation section,
veterans of half a day's longer service call out in frightening tones, "Watch
the hook, watch out for the hook." (This phrase appears to be a collo-
quialism peculiar to the East, but everywhere there are men who double
with laughter upon warning recruits of the supposed terrors of the nee-
dle.)

Less than twenty-four hours after entering the reception center we had
boxed our civilian clothes and sent them home. We caught such glimpses
of our uniformed figures as we could in the latrine mirrors; and if we
did not look to ourselves much like soldiers, the Army thought that we
came close enough; for since reception centers depend largely on recruits
for roustabout labor we were wanted at once for duty. Thus on the second day of their Army careers men found themselves on kitchen police.
For my part, after being interviewed, uniformed, and inoculated, I was
induced to plod to a warehouse for an eight-hour hitch unpacking boxes
and counting barracks bags. None of us doubted that we had entered
upon a new life.

A soldier never speaks of himself, unless he is an officer or has been
in the service long enough to be given special missions, as being "sent"
anywhere. He is shipped. When noncommissioned officers came through
barracks calling out names of men wanted for shipment I assumed that
they were to go to the warehouse, as I had, to load our unload equipment
or foodstuffs. It developed that once a man has been classified and out-
fitted he waits until his name appears on the typed shipping list, a copy
of which is posted on the bulletin board in the barracks in which he has
been sleeping. At 4 A.M. he is asked by a noncommissioned officer—who,
unless he has a powerful and penetrating voice, has just blown a whis-

tle—to arise and look at the list. If his name is on it—usually it is there within one to three days—he distributes his new belongings between his two barracks bags, and, hanging them in balance over his shoulders, he joins a new line. Because some men fail to see their names on the lists, causing noncommissioned officers to go through the barracks and the streets shouting for them, and because of the time taken in checking equipment, it is usually evening before the station is reached.

When the soldier rides back into Pennsylvania Station two, three, perhaps four days after his departure, a unit in the endless line of men with barracks bags and awkward in new uniforms, he already feels himself a long way from the civilian world. For a million men those moments in Penn Station will remain vivid and poignant no matter what their later experiences. All about are the hurrying figures of men in mufti going home, the flashing silk stockings and the clicking high heels of women. He shifts scenes in his mind: his memory of himself in the civilian throng noting the duffel-bag-laden soldiers; himself now in that line gazing upon the civilians. Lonely, unaware of his destination or even the branch of service to which he is going, he grips the iron handholds of the train and swings himself and his barracks bags silently aboard.

Strangers destined to live side by side are not long in beginning to feel one another out in preparation for adjustment one to the other. The task among new soldiers is complicated by the fact that the conventional knobs by which to get hold of a man's personality are lacking. Men cannot be judged by clothing, since it is new and strange to them, nor by the manner in which they wear it, since for a while they will certainly wear it badly. Even facial expressions are not the normal ones. The chances are that tired men will curl up on the seats or—if slated for a very long trip—in their berths and sleep while the train speeds out across the country, direction unknown.

The first meal helps more than anything else to break down the barriers. In an express or freight car the cooks have set up a long low range, banked earth about it, and stoked it with lengths of firewood. The stovepipe hung from the roof and passed out the door is only fairly adequate, and the cooks and the KP's work half-naked in the smoke and steam. But the food, washed down with hot coffee, works miracles. Names, occupations, home towns, streets, and hundreds of other bits of information are exchanged. Men who a few hours before were heartily sick of one another's faces have started friendships which will blossom in the months—perhaps years—ahead. A few poker games are started. But the major pastime is that of guessing the destination. Terrain is analyzed, and the names of a few towns and cities are noted. Some men draw maps of the nation and attempt, from their sketchy information, to establish their position on it. Pools are organized, each man choosing a camp according to his best judgment. At last the outskirts of the actual camp are reached and the men adjust themselves to the knowledge that they are to be in the Air Corps, the Engineers, Infantry, the MP's, Signal Corps, Chemical Warfare, mechanized outfits. Barracks bags riding their shoulders, they climb down from the train under the scrutiny of officers and non-commissioned officers assigned to train them—officers and non-coms anxious to see what manner of potential soldiers they have drawn. After a hot meal in the mess hall and assignment to barracks each man seizes pencil and paper to spread news of his whereabouts.

The standard barracks is a roomy, two-storey structure, usually painted white, with two small rooms at either end but with the majority of the floor space devoted to single or double-decker iron cots. In the rooms dwell sergeants and sometimes cooks whose early rising would disturb the greater room. A wide stairway enters the building at the side near one end and ascends to the secondary storey. At this end, and a few feet lower than the first floor, is the soldier's combination drawing-room, meeting hall, and information center—the latrine. Here originate the latrine rumors, which account for about one-half the soldier's conversation, and here the recruit is taught the magic results of Government Issue (GI) brushes and soap applied vigorously to white porcelain. Here, and on the familiar boards of the barrack rooms floors, he masters the Army's valuable precision tool, the mop. He rails at scoundrels from other barracks who steal his mops; and finally utterly unscrupulous himself, he crawls out in dead of night to steal others. On a mopless morning, the breath of the inspecting officer hot on their necks, sergeants themselves go wheedling to sergeant friends in other barracks, and find those friends false.

The sanctity of a man's home is well established in jurisprudence, and likewise by Army law and tradition is the soldier's bunk his castle. It must of course be made correctly, the floor about it swept and mopped every day, and clothes and personal belongings arranged on shelves and in the trunklike foot lockers according to regulations. But round his bunk the soldier raises substantial if invisible walls inside which he retires as the king to his intimate chambers. With the men about him he eventually establishes the neighborly relations of a farmer. When he rises early for KP a neighbor makes his bed; should he fall ill someone steals extra oranges from the mess hall or carries ice cream from the Post Exchange. Having established his home to his liking, the humblest private becomes a lion before a sergeant trying to move him to another barracks or even to a point a few bunks distant.

By the settling of strangers, of widely varying temperaments, of different backgrounds, into anything like a peaceful communal life is not easy. Men of my own outfit came about equally from New York and from the South, and in the early days there was some tendency toward clannishness. The Southerners, more homesick than the others, stayed close together, in leisure hours leaning moodily on their breast-high, double-decker bunks. Occasionally there would come a snatch or two of a hill ballad.

> "I stayed awake last night;
> and walked the floor,"

one man sang dolefully and repeatedly. He expected to confine himself to a single line, he said, until letters arrived from home. Subsequent lines, it turned out, had more cheer in them. For a while officers and non-coms referred to "the Southerners" and "the New York men," but this became less common as personalities and abilities began to emerge.

Nor do differences in ages cause much difficulty. It is true that younger men, particularly if of gregarious nature, find adjustment easier—perhaps little harder than at college or a summer camp. Older men have had a considerably more difficult time of it and, particularly in basic training, where men of forty-five have undergone the same rigorous training as youths of twenty, many have suffered greatly. For lawyers, teachers, business men, and the like it has been, psychologically, as if everything had gone to smash and they were reduced to the honorable but unfamiliar occupation of digging ditches. They do however have the advantage of a generally larger perspective, which helps them to overcome physical handicaps. Since heroics are rare and unpopular—men like to joke about the "board of friends and neighbors," who according to draft notices, "selected" them for service—younger men have concluded that their elders are not well suited for the hard life of soldiers and consequently no stigma is attached to over-age men who seek to be discharged.

The rough edges which have to be worn off result, in the main, from the wide variance in men's temperaments. The great cleavage is over the matter of noise in barracks. Some men indubitably like noise; take it away and they suffer. Their opponents, members of the quiet camp, are at a disadvantage for the obvious reason and quiet disturbs the noisemaker for only the time it takes to shout, scream, sing, whistle, or turn on his radio. Unfortunately the American custom of allowing the radio to go full blast, no matter what the program, is carried into the barracks. The noise lover has another advantage in that, lacking sensitivity to what goes on about him, he may disturb a score of men without even knowing it; while each of the others hesitates to complain for fear of getting a reputation as a grouch.

Some men do not care much about the noise either way, preferring at first to withdraw within themselves, living as far as possible in the past. They are the letter writers. They sit obscurely on foot lockers during the daytime, when they must keep off their bunks, and they sit or lie on their bunks before lights-out. In their laps, serving as desks, are stationery boxes or writing folders, and they scribble endlessly. Sometimes they achieve an almost terrifying efficiency. One man who lived near the top of the stairs worked out a system which permitted him to write letters even during the morning barracks-cleaning periods. By his bunk stood a gallon tin can which served as a receptable for cigarette butts. When he heard the approach of the sergeant from downstairs (which was easy, for the sergeant was always shouting orders behind him) he would seize the butt can and patter down to the latrine, ostensibly to empty the can. This procedure was repeated several times each morning. The sergeant never caught on, and the man's neighbors, somehow recognizing that he had a problem to work out with himself, did not complain.

In time a sort of armistice is worked out between the noise lovers and the quiet men. Gradually the noise lovers come to realize that they are not alone in the barracks; and of course the step from theft of mops to sabotage of radios is relatively short. One soldier, disturbed by two men who conversed long after lights-out, grew tired of asking them to be quiet. He awakened them an hour before reveille one morning—their favorite hour of rest—and insisted on chatting until the bugle sounded. The cold logic of his action impressed them; they had not been able to realize that others wanted to sleep when they did not.

Magazines filled up their pages with what has been palmed off on editors as picturesque Army slang. It is a waste of paper. A few common expressions are used—for example, a loafer is sometimes referred to, mostly by recruits, as a goldbricker; soldiers who draw menial details are occasionally referred to as yardbirds; meals are commonly called chow; a bad report or a mild bawling out is a gig. Officers have originated a term for other officers who at unexpected moments appear to check their work. They call them submarines, and criticism on some point or another is torpedoing. "I was submarined three times to-day and torpedoed twice," one officer will report half dejectedly, half jokingly to another. But the real Army language will never be known to good folks. It is unprintable and unrepeatable in polite circles, though wondrously rich and varied. Much of it comes from the old Army, while regional terms are constantly being woven into the pattern. The tone of the average soldier's language goes down about thirty per cent during his early days in the service, and then it mounts toward the normal, without ever quite reaching it. Only a limited number have the memory, the imagination, and the desire really to master the Army vocabulary.

The point at which a man ceases to think of himself as a recruit cannot be placed exactly, but in most cases it comes with the firing of the small weapons toward the end of his basic training. By that time the original aches and pains have vanished. His muscles are hard and he has spring in his step. He has gained a little weight or lost a great deal. He feels right, even jaunty, in his uniform. He knows his duties and, if he performs them adequately, his fear of noncoms and officers has evaporated. It is the firing of the actual weapons of war however that permits him to feel that he is at last on the way to becoming a soldier. Only a few have fired heavy-caliber rifles and side-arms in civilian life, and the percentage who have never even had a gun in their hands is high. It is found that the kick of the gun is not so overwhelming as had been expected; bull's-eyes are hit at surprising distances. Mastery of machine guns, artillery, planes, and other weapons or tools of whatever branch they are assigned to lies ahead. Farther away is the greatest experience of all—going into battle. But each is well aware that he is not the same man who reported to the induction station on the day which seems to him a long time ago.

PSYCHING UP THE SOLDIERS

In 1944 the War Department issued the following pamphlet, which was intended to persuade new soldiers of the moral purpose of the war they were being asked to fight. The army realized that something was needed to boost the morale of men who had just been uprooted from their normal lives and were now faced with adjusting physically and emotionally to a strange way of life. The writers of this tract are trying to "psyche-up" the new soldier by reminding the recruit why he has been called on to make personal sacrifices, especially since no bombs are falling on America, whose shores seem safe from invasion. The pamphlet's purpose is to convince the new soldier of the dire threat posed by Nazi Germany and imperial Japan and how necessary it is for Americans to stand up to these aggressors. Thus, the soldier is asked to give up some of his civilian freedoms while he serves in the army in order to preserve the larger freedoms that a democratic nation cherishes. Such morale boosting was not enough in some cases, however; many new soldiers cracked under the stresses of the military way of life.

FROM WAR DEPARTMENT PAMPHLET #20–13
(Washington, D.C.: U.S. Army Publication, 1944)

You are now a soldier, helping America to defend herself against aggression. The world's future now depends in part upon you.

Probably you have conditioned your mind to self-sacrifice. Yet—at this moment you—may feel merely lost. You know that you are sharing common experiences with millions of other men, many of them much like yourself; yet—right now—your impressions of the soldier's life and work are probably confused.

This is natural. Meeting your Army face-to-face is an experience full of surprises and nervous strains.

You are not only confused; you are curious. You know that all these things have happened before—but they haven't happened to you before! You find yourself accepting advice and information—from those who know and from those who don't.

KNOW-HOW IS A HELP. Will you accept one more bit of advice? It is this: There is more mental comfort, more personal satisfaction, in knowing your place and your part in this Army than in any other single thing

G.I. on KP (kitchen police), U.S. Army Reception Center, Fort McPherson, Georgia, 1942. (U.S. Army Military History Institute)

you can now do for yourself. Be selfish about it, if you like; learn your job because knowing how to handle yourself will make you.

MAKE YOUR OWN MORALE. When a soldier thinks about himself, he may say that he feels pretty good or that he likes his job; when anyone else thinks about him, the word "morale" is sure to come up. Let's dispose of that confusing word once and for all.

According to one humorous book on Army life, soldiers' morale is something civilians talk about. Certainly soldiers talk less about it. They know what it is and they know how good it is; they don't have to talk. Perhaps the soldier with the best morale of all was the one who said, "The hell with this morale—let's get the war won!"

New soldiers soon learn that morale isn't just made of girls to dance with at the USO [United Service Organization], nor of uniforms that fit, nor even of letters from home. All these things which remind soldiers that they have the respect, concern, and best efforts of the folks at home and of Army authority are but one side of the picture.

Morale is also the product of just being a good soldier. As you share experiences and hardships with other soldiers, you earn a right to that quiet pride which is part of every fighting man's personal strength. This is a pride which comes of having gotten through, when the going was tough. You feel it when you realize that you are sacrificing a great deal emotionally in becoming a soldier, and perhaps just as much materially. You show it by making that sacrifice in good spirit.

There is more to morale. It is knowing that you are in an Army which has never lost a war. It is belonging to the company with the squarest commanding officer who ever lived; to the platoon with the drill award to its credit; to the squad with the greatest guys in the world.

Morale is knowing that what you are doing is worth while. It is studying the manuals when your time is your own; staying in formation when your every muscle aches; going up into the lines when your every instinct says, "Go back!" Morale isn't just feeling good; it's what you learn the hard way.

Morale is confidence—in your training, in your weapons, in your leaders. It is knowing that you know your job thoroughly and that you are a better fighting man than your enemy.

Morale is contagious. When you have it, your buddies have it. It keeps them working and training as you do; it keeps them fighting at your side—when your life depends upon them. When you know that you and Jack and Harry will face death together and won't let each other down— then, soldier, you've got morale! Then nobody needs to say any more about it.

FACE THE FACTS OF WAR. As you read this, you may be wondering why all this has to happen to you. Why do you have to kiss your family good-bye for months, maybe years—maybe for good? What's in it for you?

British or Russian or Chinese soldiers won't worry about those questions. They're fighting for their lives, and they know it. So are we—but lots of us don't know it or don't always remember it. We would if our home towns had been bombed and our folks carried off to slave in enemy fields and factories.

Luckily, we have been spared such a first-hand taste of war at home. Unluckily, human nature is such that we can't imagine what these things are like unless they actually happen to us.

Yet, unless you know why you're going to fight, you won't be able to stand the gaff. When a man is in a foxhole, one thing keeps him steady. That's knowing why he's there.

Having it all make sense is something no one else can do for you. In a matter as important as this, a man sticks to his job when it may cost him his life has got to be as much a part of him as his trigger finger.

While you have time, think what freedom means. America wasn't and isn't Heaven on earth. The streets weren't paved with gold, and some of our people were in the gutter. But the road ran straighter than any other that mankind has ever built, and a man got as far along it as his work and brains would take him. Some of us spun along that road in limousines, while others humped along in jalopies—but if we didn't injure our fellow citizens or block the traffic, there was no one to tell us we had to stop.

Look at the other side of the picture. Hitler says in "Mein Kampf" that "democracy is like garbage—something to be dumped into the sewer." The Japs say: "The individual man is less than dirt. All that matters is the Emperor, who is our God."

A lot of us didn't believe at first that these people meant what they said when they vowed out loud that they would rule the world—including us. But, little by little and then a lot faster, they started showing us that unless we fought back, they would be in our own back yard. These enemies did their worst to the Czechs, the Poles, the French, the Chinese, the Dutch. They started on us at Pearl Harbor. Suddenly, Americans in Omaha and Dallas and Chicago, deep inside our borders, realized that no place on earth is more than 60 hours' flying time from any other. America's freedom was attacked.

That's why we're in this war. That's why you're in this Army.

Maybe the Army seems like a strange place to talk about freedom. Actually, there couldn't be a better place. Certainly—you give up many things, take orders and learn to knock people down instead of building them up. But as soldiers we have freedom of speech, freedom of religion, freedom from want, freedom from fear. Because of us, the people at home will always have them, too.

Perhaps the thing you're fighting for doesn't go by any fancy name. It may be a few acres of good, fertile land. It may be a blonde or a redhead. It may be your kid brother's college education or what your folks told you about coming over from the old country in the steerage. It may be something you just don't want to talk about.

Whatever it is, burn that reason way deep in your mind. When the order comes for you to risk your life on a beach-head or to guard a water tank where nobody ever passes by or to sit at a desk in a depot—you'll do the job. You'll do it because you'll know the reason why.

The Road ahead. You are now taking your first steps on the road to victory. The road is long, and you will find this one rough in spots. Nobody knows just how long it is, nor how rough it may be. In this Army, though, there are no doubts about where it leads. Men who know that they can always take care of the next few yards ahead know that eventually they will cover every mile.

You're on the way, soldier. Good luck. Go ahead an easy step at a time, don't fret too much about what's too far ahead to be seen, and you'll make it all right.

SHIPPING OUT

Gene Forrester at one point in *A Separate Peace* takes a train to Vermont to see his friend Leper who has gone AWOL from the army. He says of this experience, "That night I made for the first time the kind of journey which later became the monotonous routine of my life . . . This became the dominant activity of my army career. . . . Journeys through unknown parts of America became my chief war memory" (130–31). The experience that many soldiers had of being shuttled around the United States from one military base to another that Gene describes is reflected in the following letter written by Thomas Brush to his mother. Private Brush, who had recently been inducted into the U.S. Army, was a former prep school boy who had attended the Loomis School in Connecticut and had recently finished his sophomore year at Yale when he was called up for military service by his local draft board. His letter reveals his wry observations about his fellow soldiers and shows the culture shock and confusion that were in store for young men of his background who were entering the armed forces.

FROM "LETTER FROM PRIVATE THOMAS BRUSH"
(Military History Archives, September 5, 1943)

Camp Upton, September 5, 1943. (—my fourth day in the Army). Dear Kay:
We were awakened early this morning. Men shipping out are always awakened early (generally around 4:00 A.M.) but we were wakened especially early this time, as was the whole barracks. A new shipping list had come down from the office and had to be read and digested by everyone. There was little more sleep for any of the shipping boys that night, least of all for me. I rose and washed and dressed, putting on my suntans, which are our best uniforms, those khaki officer-like uniforms you see about. But to mark me as one about to be shipped, instead of the overseas cap that is ordinarily regulation with that uniform, I was required to wear on my head that pot-like fiber helmet thing issued us, a horrid thing, of no beauty, with a most uninviting chin strap. Packed all my equipment carefully—although, as I later discovered to my dismay, evidently not carefully enough—and slinging the two canvas bags over my shoulder I stomped out of the barracks at 4:45 and with the other fellows of Shipment I, assembled in front of Barracks G, where we milled

about for half an hour, being lined up in columns of twos, counted, recounted, checked, roll-called, moved, and lined up again.

It rapidly became apparent that the rumor that had run through the camp the day before of a huge shipment that day, Wednesday, the 8th, was no idle talk. I do not know how many men Camp Upton holds; they never told us and it is a military secret anyway. But I can say this: that the camp is divided into five receiving areas (not including the permanent camp, a basic training outfit for infantry) and that each receiving area works separately. There must have been 800 men from my unit alone. If the others contributed as many, four thousand men left there that day. There were seven shipments in all, combining men from the different areas, and a whole line of kitchen cars that had been collecting there (and for which I cleaned pans) had suddenly vanished that morning.

Eventually, when we had been all lined up and checked in, we were marched a short distance to a sort of yard where after much delay we each checked our own equipment. I discovered I was short one pair of socks. What happened to it, I cannot imagine. When I get to my new camp, I shall have to have it replaced, but that will not cost too much, I don't suppose. We were then permitted to fall out, charge up to the messhall, and get chow. While I was eating it the entire unshipped membership of my barracks moved by, and I said one more goodbye to them. John Liscaulocos, Clark Burghley, "Buzz" (the rest of whose name I never did get), Joe Rizzo the fat guinea, who inducted the day before his 38th birthday, a mad wag of whom I had been rather afraid my first day there, but who I learned to like. They were from Brooklyn, all those men; everyone I have come into contact with is from Brooklyn or the neighboring vicinity of Long Island. They were tough people of the working class, skilled mechanics, factory workers, a type I have never come in contact with before. With the exception of Buzz, who was only temporarily in New York, taught English and dabbled in amateur theatricals, not a man of them had ever been to college. Most of them had had no more than one year high school. I was afraid, at first, that they might hold my two years at Yale against me, and the fact (never divulged by me directly, but in evidence whenever I spoke English or told anything about myself, no matter how toned down) that I was moderately in the chips; but they did not seem to. They accepted it calmly, the way they accepted the fact that they were Italian, or Polish, or Lithuanian, or Russian, or German, or Jewish. They were not ashamed of that, so eventually I ceased to be ashamed of my better fortune. I remain careful, however, not to flaunt it. So on the whole, I have learned a thing or two at Upton: a little something about people, and a little something about the correct way to mop a floor.

Back to the yard, where we were checked and counted again. Shipment

No. 2 went first, and shipment No. 5 was told to fall out and report back at eleven. They were cautioned against telephoning their families, with the object lesson of the two bad train wrecks of the previous few days held up before them. We remained, talking among ourselves and walking around. It was quite cold, and so I dug into my pack and produced my field jacket, a very handsome article that everyone in the Army loves. "It's real classy," seems to be the attitude about it, although I never heard the words used. They express it in discussions of what it would cost if they were to try to buy one like in the civilian life.

Finally we were to pick up our two bags, tied together at the net and slung over the right shoulder, and whatever else we had—I had a small canvas handbag, very cheap, which I had purchased days ago at the PX, and in which I kept my various small articles that are so difficult to find in a big bag: toilet articles, neckties, letterpaper, and the like; and march down to the station, if such that freight house can be called. Here we were lined up again, checked and counted and told to sit down on our packs. We were moved two or three times, each of which movements entailed the same process of checking. Finally in single, alphabetical file we passed before a lieutenant who checked our names off against the master list, while a sergeant checked to be sure our papers were in one of the boxes that were to go with us to our destination—last name, to which we responded with our first and with the last our serial numbers. (At present the number of everyone at Upton begins with 3299). Thus when I arrived, between Brosso and Busche, he said: "Brush" to which I replied, "Thomas, 8154," and passed on. We all lined up then for a short-arm inspection. No one being rejected by this, the substitutes, wretched fellows who had gone through everything up to now on the chance that some of the regulars would for one reason or another be disqualified or absent, were sent back to their barracks, to unpack their bags, and go about the regular business of the day, and wait hopefully for the next time.

One of the chaplains then spoke to us briefly; I discovered afterwards to my amazement that it was the Jewish one. The three, Protestant, Catholic and Jewish, take turns at this job, evidently. An officer then addressed us, telling us not to misbehave on the train, and wishing us the best of luck. He did not, however, tell us either our destination or the length of our journey. He did say that any mail that arrived for us would be forwarded and would probably arrive at our new camp before we did, which was a hint that the trip might well be long.

On to the train, where another indication of a long trip appeared: we were told to change into our fatigue clothes. The train was an ancient affair. It was composed of old day-coaches of the Pennsy railroad. The seats were covered with soot, the reason for which rapidly became apparent. There was no air-conditioning on the car and everyone opened the windows. Everyone settled down for a long trip, and at 11:45 A.M. it began.

As I say, no one told us where we were going. No one ever did, and we did not know where we were till we had arrived and asked someone. Furthermore few if any of us knew to which branch of the service we were assigned. As you may imagine, it was a situation ripe for rumors. They began before the train started to move, and continued till we arrived, each and every one reinforced by cogent arguments. For example, the first one that proved to be wrong was that it was to be a very short trip. "The long trips start at night." Everyone in the train seemed to have a different opinion of what state we were going to and what branch of the service we would end up in. Some suggested California, others Colorado, Louisiana, or Massachusetts. We arrived at Penn Station after about 2½ hours, in other words about 2:15. It was there that we learned the wonderful news about Italy's surrender. An eager soldier dashed through the train from one end to another, holding up before him a copy of the Journal-American with the glorious headline. We could hear a cheer approaching down the length of the train, and when he entered our car we all cheered too. I was sorry to see that it all produced a fine spirit of optimism among everyone. They all seemed to think the war would be over by the middle of the next summer, Japan and all. I did my best to discourage this, but to little avail, so I desisted.

I was sorry to be in New York so close to you, and yet not able to phone you. We were not allowed at any time to leave the train, from the beginning of the trip till its end, in fact, we were not even allowed to leave our car (number 3561, long shall I remember and execrate it), except at mealtimes, of which more later. As a matter of fact, even had I been able to telephone you, there would have been nothing I could have told you, for we had all been strictly advised against this sort of thing.

We left Penn Station at 2:35, and as soon as we emerged into the light of day in New Jersey, it was obvious that we were not going to New England or New York anywhere.

Around 5:30 P.M., they fed us for the second time, a tedious process. It was the intention of the powers that be to work some exercise for us into the process of going into the kitchen car for our food. So we would go from our car, through the kitchen car (there were two, merely oven-and-pot-equipped baggage cars) where we collected paper plates, on through the rest of the train to the very end and back. This was the only exercise we got.

I will pass over the lengthy afternoon and evening. I had brought a Pocket Book mystery the day before at the PX. I finished it before dinnertime, and gave it to a Negro soldier who was passing in the chow parade through our car. I had nothing else to read on the train except old magazines, a newspaper, and my copy of the Soldiers Handbook, dull reading. At 3:45 we arrived at Altoona, Penna., where urchins sold bottles of Coca-Cola through the windows, making exorbitant profits.

Shortly after this we began to try to sleep, a discouraging procedure in that sooty daycoach. I got some sleep and then woke up with a stiff neck to find us hustling through Ohio. Wondered if perhaps we would go through Salem, for the main Pennsy Line, as you know, runs through there. But I had been asleep when we went through, it soon became apparent, for we arrived at a station that eventually turned out to be Columbus. Guesses had ranged from Pittsburgh to Indianapolis. I had guessed Cincinnati myself.

To sleep again and spent a very restless and uncomfortable night. I am not used to sleeping upright or with my hat on, and the corporal in command of our car took the other half of my seat, so I was not able to sprawl out. Furthermore it grew very cold and endless soot came through the window.

Woke up at 5:45 coming into Richmond, Indiana. Lousy breakfast. Lengthy and suffocating dull morning. About this time the rumor began that Oklahoma was to be our destination. Where the rumor came from no one could say, but soon everyone was saying it. I held out for Colorado. Some people felt that California was the destination. Many thought that it would be New Mexico; but the majority thought it would be Oklahoma, as it turned out to be.

Lunch, as poor as usual, and as little of it as usual. Around 2:45 we arrived at St. Louis, foolish-looking town, with an enormous railroad yard. Spent a half hour there, full of gossip and rumor. In the middle of the afternoon we arrived at the little town of Moberly, Mo., a tiny little town which many soldiers will long remember. The citizens of Moberly evidently have a lot of boys in the service, for they treat well the ones that pass through. Ready and waiting for us at the station was a little group of girls with cookies, doughnuts, magazines, and cigarettes, which they passed up to us in the windows. It really felt good. Most of us were pretty low, partly because of the long, dirty, cramping, journey, and because of the nervous suspense, never knowing where we were going nor what we were heading into, and because of the shortage of chow, and curt treatment. We felt forgotten, spurned and despised, and it was really wonderful to find out that there were some people who thought soldiers were human. It was particularly appropriate just then, because a station or two before that we were pointedly ignored by everyone in the station. We all were calling out, trying to find out where we were, and not one person replied although many stared at us. It eventually dawned upon us that in our unshaven condition, fatigue suits, and in that ancient train, we must be looking pretty disreputable. In fact, I think it very likely that they thought us convicts, for not one person ever answered a question or even smiled at us while we were there, which fortunately was not long.

I could go on and on with the recital of the dreary day, but I shall spare you that, at least. It was endless and boring. We dropped a huge Negro contingent off on the way, bickered among ourselves as to our probable destination, etc. Don Freeman, not as youthful a man as the vigor or his style of drawing would indicate, in fact a paunchy fellow with glasses, drew sketches of many of the people in his car, an honor for the most part unappreciated, as few seemed to have heard of him. There were endless gambling games, in which (in spite of my study of Jacoby on Poker) I took no part whatever. I have found out that, so far, there is always a poker game going on somewhere, but it is nowhere near as universal as I had imagined, and if you don't want to play you don't have to. One youth, aged 19, who had never played poker before, sat in with all the ingenuous enthusiasm of the beginner, and after an hour or two had $1.20 left in his pocket, which will have to last him till the first of next month unless he sends home for more. I only mention this commonplace story because he and I got fairly well acquainted.

Kansas City, Missouri and Kansas. Lengthy arguments with soldiers in another train, rookies like us (in fact I later learned that they came here the way we did, and some of them are in this very barracks) but what a difference in accommodations! They had a fine long train, all Pullman, one man to each lower and upper, two to a compartment, and a whole car of individual roomettes. They had porters, and dining-car with waiters, and cheering crowds; and all we had was dust.

After Kansas City we set to sleeping again. This time there was much sliding around and pulling apart of seats. We bunched up three to a double seat (capacity four) and passed a wretched night, the train bucking like a steer, and the man across from me snorting like a calliope.

Up at 5:30, angry and filthy dirty. (I forgot to mention that the lights in the car gave forth only the feeblest of illumination; the generator was functioning improperly. Also my particular window was jammed and could not be opened. Leaving me forced to borrow breaths of other people's air). Breakfast, where they gave us more than usual, a sign that the journey was nearing its end. Then they told us to change out of our fatigues back into suntans—a sure sign.

(This letter-journal will be continued in the next installment)

> All my love
> Tommy.

YOU CAN'T GO HOME AGAIN

The following story was written by an enlisted man, Private First Class (PFC) Lin Zinberg, who was trying to convey through fiction how his six months of army life had estranged him from his old life as a civilian. Rather than finding his two weeks' leave a welcome respite from barracks life, he is ill at ease and uncomfortable back at home with his parents. Zinberg's story shows that his military experiences are not understandable to the people on the home front. He has been coarsened and inwardly changed and has to disguise the fact that he is not the same nice boy that his parents sent off to war only half a year before. In the same way, Leper had great difficulty in trying to make Gene understand what he had been through during his ordeal in basic training. As one veteran said, "No matter how much we can try we can never give the folks at home an idea of what it's really like." The emotional connection that once existed between parents and their sons was altered, if not sundered, by the army experience. The ingenuousness of civilians rankled soldiers, who resented the unrealistic views that Americans on the home front held about military duty.

FROM: P.F.C. LIN ZINBERG, "HOME IS WHERE . . . ?"
(*The New Republic*, October 25, 1943)

After six months he had a ten-day leave and as soon as he hit town, he was sorry he came home. His mother sobbed, my boy! when he opened the door and fell on him. His father just stood there, hands on his little round belly, beaming as he said over and over, "Albert, Albert, and look at the corporal stripes!"

It was the first time he had been called Albert in months—it seemed to start the restlessness. He kissed his mother and held her while she wet his face with kisses, than he put his arm around his father and said, "Hello, Pop," quietly.

All during supper they stared at him, asking endless questions, excited . . . and he couldn't tell them it was really nothing, he had finished basic and took part in two long problems—what was that? What was there to fuss and talk about?

It was worse after supper, he sat in the parlor and tried to smile as his mother asked the same questions over again, as friends came and gushed, "Why look at Albert, a corporal—a man!"

An aunt asked, "Albert, you don't think there's any chance of your going over?"

Al lit a butt and said, "No, hardly any," and knew he would be taking the boat ride in a few weeks. But how could you explain the desire to see action? It was something beside the question of right or wrong; you wanted to see the result of your training, to find out if you really were a soldier, to put your skill and gun to the final test.

The girl next door said, "Golly Albert, you seem . . . well, as if you were older than twenty. You are bigger."

"Can't you call me Al?" he asked, his voice so sharp she backed away. He wondered how he had ever been fond of this silly kid. He laughed and pushed his little finger into her stomach. "I feel like an old man," he said.

She giggled.

And when his father took out a bottle and he took a quick drink, his mother got red in the face and asked, "Why, Albert, do you drink a lot?"

"No, not a lot, just a shot now and then," he said, feeling the warm glow of the rye in his guts. Good stuff, he thought.

The mother was still worried. "The way you took that long drink . . ."

"I take a drink now and then," he repeated. Nor could he explain the boredom of small Southern towns where a shot on Saturday night was something to look forward to. Not that he ever became very drunk—it took the edge off things.

For a while he answered questions and tried to think of a way of getting out of the house and when he saw there wasn't any escape he said he was tired and went upstairs to his room. The room looked comfortable.

He went to bed and smoked and knew his mother would come in soon. He was sure of one thing, it would be impossible to spend the rest of the seven days at home.

After the noises downstairs had died out and he was finishing his third butt, his mother came in—outlined by the hall light—looking fat and sloppy in her thin nightgown; he had never noticed that before.

She said, "Smoking in bed? Albert, you'll have to be careful or . . ."

"I'm careful."

She sat on the bed and held his hand. "Now tell me all about it," she said happily.

"About what?"

"About camp . . . and things. Remember how I'd come in here and you'd tell me all about the high school dances?"

"That's right, I remember. Only this isn't a dance."

She hesitated, then asked softly, "Did you meet nice girls?"

"Yes, very nice girls," he said, thinking of the few whores he had known, the older women you met in bars, the "good" girls at the USO and "Y" dances, the lively factory girls dancing in the juke joints, the fourteen-year-old kids walking the streets in some cities in the South.

"I hope you didn't . . . well . . . become involved with any of them? A boy has to be careful. . . ."

"I'm very careful. They give us lectures on that."

"What?"

"Lectures on—girls."

"You mean they . . ."

He said, "I was careful not to become involved."

She said I'm glad and squeezed his hand. They were silent for a while and he was embarrassed—he felt sorry for his mother, felt sorry without knowing why. She asked, "What about the camp? Tell me all about it."

"It's the same every day; get up early, exercises, chow, drill, chow, more drill . . . sometimes we go on the range, or have a problem—a hike."

"It must be terribly hard. I hope you weren't sick."

"It isn't too hard. In a way I enjoyed it. Maybe that's why they made me a two-striper."

"Albert, you've changed. You used to be so lively and full of fun. Now you're serious, and so quiet."

"I'm tired."

"So full of jokes and . . ."

He thought, I have to tell her something funny. Al the funny boy. He said, "This is funny. I was helping in the supply room and one of the new ninety-day wonders was getting ready to give the boys the manual of arms. He thought no one was watching him as he stood behind the supply house and went through the manual—brushing up on it. I was watching him from the window. When he finished, he came to right shoulder arms and marched across the road, counting cadence for himself. Just then a private turned into the road and saluted the looie [lieutenant]. The looie was rattled, standing there with a gun on his shoulders. So what does he do, he comes to *present arms!* Christ, the private almost dropped, he was so astonished." Al laughed at the memory of it.

The mother sat there and he knew her face was puzzled, even though he couldn't see her. She was waiting to laugh.

Al said, "It was funny, the looie coming to present arms for the dogface." It sounded crazy in the quiet darkness of the room.

She laughed a little. Al was sorry he'd started. He said, "That's an army joke, I guess."

They were silent again and he wished he could say something to make her laugh. Finally he said, "Guess I'll go to sleep now."

"Of course, the train ride was tiring. I'll wake you early and . . ."

"No, I'd rather sleep late."

"I thought you'd want to be up early, so you can start visiting everybody—so many people want to see you."

Al said, "I'll start in the afternoon. Sleep late and do some washing when I get up."

"Washing?"

"Yeh, my underwear and sox."

"Why, Albert, I thought you sent that to the laundry."

"There was no laundry."

"That's awful. The girl will be in tomorrow, she can wash."

"Take me a second."

"She has to wash anyway and . . ."

"All right." He sat up and kissed his mother, trying to really kiss her and not just peck at her cheek. "Good-night, Ma."

"Good-night dear." She stood up and opened the door and stopped—looking unreal and ghostlike in the dim light. "Do you love me, Albert?"

"Of course, Mother. Sure I do."

She kissed him again and went out.

He lit a cigarette and wondered if he did love her. Yes, I do love them, he thought, maybe more than before, but in a different way. Jesus, if they would only stop treating me like a kid—I'll go nuts spending a week here. Maybe I can send myself a phony telegram, spend a few days in Chicago.

He blew a smoke ring into the darkness. He felt a long way from home . . . he didn't know where his home was.

FITTING IN THE RANKS

The army was well aware that the American democratic spirit did not lend itself to an easy subordination of the individual to a class system based on military rank. Therefore, the military designed a basic training program that was intended to shock new soldiers into compliance by exhausting, bewildering, and intimidating them. This process of erasing individuality was referred to as "knocking the civilian" out of the men. As the following article by a professional sociologist shows, the essential thing from the U.S. Army's point of view was that group solidarity be achieved and that unit harmony was put above any individual behavior. As far as the army was concerned, personal attitudes had to be subordinated to a collective mind-set that was defined by the military. The reactions of men to their introduction to the army was in large part deter-mined by their civilian backgrounds. Young men who came from farms or blue-collar jobs where hard labor was customary found military life relatively easy, and living conditions were in many cases an improvement over what they were used to. Soldiers who came from comfortable middle-class homes or straight from col-lege were frequently disoriented and depressed upon being in-ducted into the service. As this article reveals, soldiers devised various ways of coping with military circumstances. Some of these strategies for getting along included becoming "gold bricks," or malingers, becoming "gung-ho," or eager to please, acting like a "screw-up," who never gets anything right, or trying to "get lost," by becoming as inconspicuous or anonymous as possible. Some soldiers appear overly confident and loud, while others become aloof. Those who become well adjusted, however, mold their be-havior to a group level. Successful soldiers are those who get rid of self-consciousness, introspection, and depression. Given these expectations, it becomes obvious why a loner like Leper was such an abject failure as a soldier.

The following selection examines the dilemmas facing soldiers who are mentally disturbed or psychoneurotic. In civilian life, such people can maintain some stability and manage to function, but in a military environment without the support of the family group, a family doctor, or sympathetic friends, the person with a psychoneurotic disorder has no one to help him solve his problems and is likely to become dysfunctional. The ability to perform limited duty that would be useful to the army can be determined by short psychotherapeutic sessions and encouragement from commanders, but such efforts are problematic, and in most cases soldiers with psychological problems are an impediment to the war effort. This article illustrates the point that young men like Leper in *A Separate Peace* should have been screened better and never should have been allowed to join the army because they were obviously unfit for military service.

FROM MAJOR NICHOLAS MICHAEL, "THE PSYCHONEUROTIC IN
THE ARMED FORCES"
(U.S. Government Publication, 1946)

A psychoneurosis maybe defined as a defense mechanism through which the patient protects himself against difficult environmental stresses. It is a necessary, adaptive reaction that springs into activity at the time of need. It may be called a subconscious device enabling the patient to explain to his conscious self (through the guise of a disease) his inability to meet certain life situations in a normal way. A psychoneurosis is not a conscious effort to deceive, avoid danger, or attract attention, nor does it arise at the will of the individual. It is not a volitional act.

Apparently the co-mingling of various etiological factors brings about the symptoms, for no single factor can be considered as the cause of psychoneurosis. All the causation theories have their proper place but in time of war the activation of the self-preservation instinct plays the most important role. Since the danger is real, there is no reason to assume that sexual life plays an essential part. It seems more likely that the instinct of race-preservation is underdeveloped, because the patient is subconsciously unwilling to endanger his life for the benefit of the future race.

The psychoneurotic finds it difficult to live in any environment since he is constitutionally poorly equipped to meet the every-day issues of life. In civilian life, however, he has greater leeway to protect and defend himself against danger. He can side-track or avoid threatening experiences, change his environment, work part time or rest if necessary. The psychiatrist, family physician, and sympathetic relative are always on hand to help solve his problems. Thus with a minimum effort he is able to maintain a place for himself in society. This ability in civilian life does not necessarily mean that he will be able to do the same in the army. Here he must either become a concrete member of the team or fail. The danger, stress, discipline and necessity of facing the issue increases his anxiety and symptoms. It is so unlike his previous life that, instead of sympathy and understanding, he may be caused embarrassment and receive ridicule.

In spite of the screening done by examining boards and induction stations, the number of psychoneurotics inducted is too large. This is partly due to the fact that it is impossible for the psychiatrist to devote more than a few minutes to each selectee. In such a brief time it is difficult to decide about questionable cases, for there is always the fear, among some examiners, that the patient is malingering. Thus, in many instances, only obvious, clear cut cases who demonstrate hysterical or anxiety state during the examination are eliminated.

Experienced psychiatrists are essential in induction stations. They understand the personality make-up and know the capabilities of a psychoneurotic. The evaluation and determination of mental fitness for military service require good judgment and good judgment comes mainly through experience. Such examiners easily recognize personality disorders. The facial expression and attitude are informative. A few pertinent questions may decide how much time to spend with each individual. The main thing to be borne in mind is that personal feelings must never be permitted to interfere with good common sense.

The opinion and recommendation of the personal physician should be carefully considered. More than anyone else, he has observed and treated the patient over a long period of time. He knows his limitations, failures and successes in his own environment. Unfortunately, most physicians hesitate to express their views, leaving disposition and judgment entirely to the induction board. They hope the patient will in some way adjust.

J. W., age 24, gave a history of being a sickly and protected child. Soon after graduation from high school at the age of 19, he began to complain of fullness in the stomach, nausea, shortness of breath, headaches and a feeling of weakness. His only employment was helping in a grocery store during weekends. He never went out with a girl.

J. W. is inadequate, asthenic [weak or ectomorphic, that is, of slight body build], apprehensive, hypochondriacal and markedly self-centered. He answered sick call the first day after induction and was admitted to the station hospital within seven days. After two periods of hospitalization he was given a medical discharge.

A short history from the family physician would have prevented J. W.'s induction.

Members of the family are sometimes anxious and willing to see the patient inducted. This not only relieves them of the responsibility but arouses their hope that he will now be forced to live his own life and possibly learn to get along without them. An unselfish mother who was visiting her son, suffering from hysterical aphonia [loss of voice], said, "I wanted him to go into the service for he was becoming too attached to me. I as afraid something like this would happen." A dissatisfied wife wrote, "My husband will complain of stomach trouble and nervousness. His doctors tell me that he is physically well. I believe he is just lazy and should be inducted." Both histories revealed lack of adjustment.

Physicians not psychiatrically minded consider psychoneurotics more or less malingerers. They do not try to differentiate between the two and are frequently hostile to individuals who have no physical basis for their complaints. They insist that such persons should be forced to stay and, if necessary, be punished. The following expression is not unusual. "I hate to see such men get out. They just don't want to stay in the army, and if you let them go home others will get the same idea." They do not realize that individuals whose personality make-up is considered normal cannot successfully simulate the symptoms of psychoneurosis.

The term malingerer is usually applied to those who consciously try to deceive by imitating the symptoms of illness. Close observation of suspected malingerers revealed personality disorders and maladjustment in civilian life. Pure, unalloyed malingering does not exist for there is something fundamentally wrong with the individual who uses such means to evade the army. The number who are likely to malinger are so few, their services so poor, that it is best to do without them. No amount of punishment will make them good soldiers. Three patients were suspected of being malingerers but after months of effort to set them right, it was necessary to send them back to civilian life. The following case is an example.

E. L., age 29, was a cook for an infantry regiment and seemingly did satisfactory work for over a year. He contracted vascular syphilis and was transferred to a rifle platoon. He immediately complained of nervousness and urinary incontinence. The syphilis was adequately treated and repeated physical examinations including spinal fluid were negative. He refused duty, was voluntarily incontinent, and seemed satisfied to stay in bed all day long. Every effort to reason, argue or shame him back to duty failed. E. L. was given up as hopeless after repeated periods of hospitalization over a period of six months and was discharged.

This patient changed jobs frequently in civilian life and just "got along." He was quiet, surly, irritating and did not have much to say to the other patients. His condition resembled that of a psychopathic personality more than a malingerer.

The psychoneurotic in the field answers sick call repeatedly. The medical officer for a while makes every effort to encourage and assure him that he is in good physical condition. This, in addition to a mild sedative, may temporarily keep him on duty. Gradually he will be told that he is not sick, that it is all in his mind, and to stop answering sick call. A strict company commander will insist that he continue in the field; a more understanding one will assign him to duty around the company area. He will fall out on conditioning marches, complain of his inability to continue with a field problem and be among the first to be evacuated to the rear during maneuvers.

M. L., age 24, was a highly restless, fearful and apprehensive individual. He did not join the other soldiers in social activities around camp and rarely went to town. He frequently complained of a painful left knee joint and repeated admissions to the station hospital did not help. He insisted that something was wrong and begged the surgeon to operate on his knee to prove he was right.

The patient was returned to civilian life after seven months and placed in the hands of a psychiatrist.

A few psychoneurotics can be kept in the army in time of peace and be forced to serve out their year. Observation will reveal that they are usually assigned to duties requiring a minimum effort and considered unnecessary. Investigation of such individuals in an infantry regiment revealed that all but one were eliminated prior to departure for overseas duty.

F. M., aged 25, a competent, reserved and somewhat shy platoon sergeant had an excellent record with over a year of service prior to an auto accident while on leave in the north during the winter. While driving back home during the night, his car left the road. He was found unconscious eight hours later and taken to the local hospital where he regained consciousness. He was unable to recognize members of his immediate family and could not recall events prior to and after the accident. Repeated physical examination were negative. He gradually cleared mentally but was still somewhat perplexed a month later. By means of suggestion he cleared entirely within a few days after admission to the station hospital and was sent to duty.

This case did not show any evidence of previous attacks or maladjustment. He was very devoted to his mother and deferred his marriage on account of her.

A few psychoneurotics are retained on limited duty and apparently do good work, but it requires the constant encouragement of the organization commander and an understanding medical officer. A short psychotherapeutic session will sometimes improve and encourage the patient especially since the element of danger has been eliminated.

M. W., age 28, a promising musician, was first assigned to the band of an engineer regiment. He attended sick call frequently and after two admissions to the station hospital did not feel any better. He was apprehensive, anxious, complained of vertigo, dizziness, unsteady gait, feeling of weakness and fear of death. He was in love with a girl and wanted to get married but kept putting his marriage off because of his condition. His talents as a musician brought him a transfer to an organization in the station complement with considerable improvement. He has only been hospitalized once in the last three months. M. W. is doing useful and necessary work. He visits the psychiatrist from time to time. His organization commander valued his services so much that he promoted him to a staff sergeant.

The ability to continue successfully even on limited duty is the exception rather than the rule.

T. Z., age 23, had a cerebral concussion two years prior to enlistment. He began to complain of dizziness, headaches and inability to wear a steel helmet. He went to the Canal Zone, was hospitalized there, then sent to a general hospital on the continent, placed on limited duty, and admitted to the station hospital. He was somewhat inadequate, self-centered, and constantly complained of headaches.

This patient could not adjust on limited duty and after a period of hospitalization of over eight months he was discharged.

Hospitalization of the patient will often bring relief of symptoms. The protective environment, relief from responsibility and danger will encourage him to return to duty. His complaints may cease when placed for the first time in the enclosed, fenced-in neuropsychiatric section and he may feign good health until release from the hospital. This pretense will be temporary.

CONCLUSION

The psychoneurotic is mentally and constitutionally unsuitable for army life. His use on limited service is questionable. He can contribute much more to the war effort by remaining in civilian life.

TOO SOFT FOR SERVICE

The problem of the high number of men who were rejected or discharged finally reached the highest-ranking general in the U.S. Army, George Marshall. The difference of opinion relating to the rejection rate for psychiatric reasons between medical and line officers is due to doctors' seeing such men as sick and commanders seeing them as slackers. From the tone of General Marshall's memorandum, which follows, it appears that he thinks a lot of men in mental hospitals are faking, but the potential of such people to make soldiers is so small the army is better off without them. The reason for the widespread cases of psychologically disturbed young men, as General Marshall sees it, is the most interesting aspect of the argument. He concludes that American culture has led young people to expect luxuries, and a paternalistic government has taught them to expect something for nothing.

FROM GENERAL GEORGE MARSHALL, "REJECTIONS OF
INDUCTEES FOR MILITARY SERVICE FOR REASONS RELATING
TO PSYCHONEUROTICS," *NEUROPSYCHIATRY IN WORLD WAR II*
(Washington, D.C.: Department of the Army, 1946)

[The following is General Marshall's rough draft:]

The War Department has just completed, under the direction of the Inspector General, whose principal assistant, Maj. Gen. Howard McC. Snyder, is a medical officer, a comprehensive survey of induction and discharge processes in continental United States relating to physical rejections of inductees and discharges from the service for similar reasons. One hundred and thirty-seven stations or installations were inspected so as to assure a nationwide cross-section of the situation. As a result of this survey, new instructions have been issued which it is believed will materially reduce the number of rejections.

However, one problem that is extremely difficult of solution. It pertains to the fact that between 25 and 35 percent of all rejections and discharges for physical reasons related to psychoneurotics. While in the opinion of the several high ranking and experienced medical officers participating in this inquiry, the doctors concerned, Army, Navy, and civilian, on duty at induction stations are performing their duties in a manner which precludes any thought of predilection or partiality, this does not mean that the line officers on duty at induction stations always agree with the medical officers or that the doctors do not at times disagree among themselves. Nevertheless, it appears that all are doing their utmost to fill required quotas with the best material available.

The greatest differences of opinion relate to rejections for psychiatric reasons. Most physical defects can be seen and measured and therefore quite accurately diagnosed and appraised. Psychiatric disorders, however, are for the most part invisible, and their detection rests with professional ability and experience of neuropsychiatrists. These specialists at times have appeared either over-enthusiastic or over-cautious. In other instances, it is evident that medical personnel have been too limited in numbers or too inexperienced in training properly to diagnose the large groups of men which must pass rapidly through induction stations. As a consequence, many psychoneurotics have been inducted into the Armed Forces, with the consequent complications of a later discharge.

It is this question of psychoneurotics which is least understood and is most difficult to handle. Functional nervous diseases are recognized as entities by neurophychiatrists but these disorders cannot as a rule be definitely measured nor confirmed by laboratory tests or objective findings. For this reason, there is a greater divergence of opinion regarding these cases than in any others. To the specialists, the psychoneurotic is a hospital patient. To the average line officer, he is a malingerer. Actually, he is a man who is either *unwilling*, unable, or slow to adjust himself to some or all phases of military life, and in consequence, he develops an imaginary ailment which in time becomes so fixed in his mind as to bring about mental pain and sickness. In a sense, this might be considered as shirking, yet among the thousands of psychiatric cases in the Army no record exists of any psychoneurotic ever having been convicted for malingering. This is because no doctor is either willing or able to state under oath that the pain complained of by the psychoneurotic is nonexistent. The doctor may believe there is no pain. He may even say so—off the record—but he cannot swear to it. For this reason, the laymen or uninitiated line officers incline to the belief that a medical officer's diagnosis of psychoneurosis is either wrong or else that the doctor is influenced by a hyperconsiderate professional attitude.

This view is emphasized in the light of certain happenings with which line officers in time become familiar. For example, at one general hospital during the course of his recent inquiry, there were approximately 85 psychoneurotic patients. Most of these were walking about, performing light duties, and appearing quite content with their lot, and with the prospect of an early discharge for physical disability. Shortly after representatives of The Inspector General arrived, rumors spread through the hospital that discharges for physical disability, insofar as psychoneurotic disorders were concerned, had been discontinued. Immediately, practically all the psychoneurotics became confined to their beds, too sick, by their own testimony, even to get up and go to meals.

A further example has been handed down from the last World War when on the publication of the Armistice some 8,000 of 10,000 shell-shocked patients were reported to have made an instantaneous recovery.

The fact remains that thousands of hospital beds are being occupied by soldiers under observation and treatment for psychoneurosis who require the services of cooks, nurses, doctors, ward attendants, and so forth, all a burden on the Army and manpower generally. Whether or not the diagnosis in their cases is correct does not appear to be half so important as does the fact that the men are occupying hospital beds and taking up valuable time of limited medical personnel. Furthermore, in most cases, the primary reason for these men being in hospitals is not because doctors made patients of them but because line officers were unable to make soldiers out of them.

The desire of commanders to be rid of below-average soldiers is understandable, particularly so when those commanders are necessarily held to rigid training schedules and the accomplishment of objectives according to a time schedule. In addition, there is no established method by which psychoneurotics can be adjusted more slowly to military service than are normal soldiers. They all must of necessity, in a huge Army, receive virtually the same treatment and undergo similar training. The standards set for all men are more or less alike, but are based on what is to be expected of the average man. However, the true psychoneurotic is not average; he cannot keep up nor assimilate military life as do the others, whereupon, as a defense measure he discovers some ailment to which he attributes the reason for his inadequacy and immediately begins to go on sick report. This latter action is quite frequently condoned, if not actually encouraged, by the officers and noncommissioned officers who have become weary of waging a losing struggle to keep the men up to the standard of other soldiers. We find some instances that the line officers have importuned medical officers to help rid them of the burden of these particular cases, meaning of course by the method of disability discharge. As one doctor stated: "Conducting sick call is a game of wits; these man says he has it and the doctor says he hasn't." In some cases, it appears that the men are smarter than the doctors, especially the inexperienced medical officers; on the other hand, the doctors do not care to disregard the possibility that the psychoneurotic does have some organic ailment. In any event, the psychoneurotic eventually gets into the hospital. Once there, the man's potential value to the service is either destroyed or seriously impaired. There, he exchanges information regarding his ailment with other patients and from them he learns the symptoms most likely to perplex the doctors. He is recognized and treated as a sick man. He wears the clothes of an invalid. His food is bought to him. He is catered to by "gray ladies," and above all, he escapes from those duties which he seeks to evade. He cannot be punished for malingering; therefore, the worst that can happen is to be sent back to his organization where he can and will start the same process all over again. In the meantime, he enjoys a life of leisure with one great goal ahead; to wit, a discharge for physical disability, a comparatively high paid job as a civilian, a discharge bonus, and eventually a pension from the Veterans Administration Bureau.

Perhaps the most important factor contributing to the spread of psychoneurotics in our Army has been the Nation's educational program and environmental background since 1920. While our enemies were teaching their youths to endure hardships, contribute to the national welfare, and to prepare for war, our young people were led to expect luxuries, to depend upon a paternal government for assistance in making a livelihood, and to look upon soldiers and war as unnecessary and hateful. The efforts to change these teachings in a few short years have left millions of our people unconvinced. The burden of changing the minds of such people who are being inducted into the Army has fallen primarily upon the hard working young platoon leaders and company commanders of our great war Army, and the indications at present are that the problem is not yet being satisfactorily met. This is manifested by the ever-increasing number of psychoneurotic patients crowding into our hospitals. A determined effort is being made throughout the Army to better this situation. It is admittedly difficult, and also it is important that there be a general public understanding of the problem.

TOPICS FOR FURTHER EXPLORATION

1. Research the positions of certain religious sects like the Seventh Day Adventists, the Amish, or Quakers on military service. Incorporate these arguments in a debate on the pros and cons of the draft.

2. Read Erich Maria Remarque's *All Quiet on the Western Front* and Irwin Shaw's *The Young Lions*, and write a report on the difference in the way that young German and American recruits were treated during their basic training in each army.

3. What explains the fact that there was so little resistance to the draft during World War II? There was also resentment at men of draft age who were not in uniform. Why?

4. Army life is intended to mold men into disciplined units that will respond to orders without question. The American army has always had problems with getting its troops to behave like soldiers in European armies. What about U.S. history or society would explain this fact?

5. The generation that was asked to fight World War II has been called the greatest that America has ever produced. Can you discover from contemporary sources such as magazines or newspapers any evidence that people in the war years saw themselves in such a heroic light?

6. Compare the experience of someone you know who has served in the new coed American army, which has relaxed discipline and physical demands, with that of an older person who served in the old army of World War II to see how much the military reflects the changes in society in last fifty years.

7. The utter subordination that the military tried to impose on individuals came as a nasty shock to young men who came from sheltered backgrounds. How do you think you would have coped with army life? Would you resist or submit to martial discipline? Write a mock-journal entry describing the experience.

8. In World War II, the military's prestige rose as the country came to appreciate the fact that servicemen would save the nation from enemies. In what ways were soldiers and sailors valorized, especially in movies and magazines?

9. Early in the war there appeared a genre of books depicting military life such as *See Here, Pvt. Hargrove, I Was with the Army*, and *This Is the Army* which took a comic, lighthearted view of being in the service. Read some of these works, which make army life seem like a lark. What would account for the misrepresentations of life in military service that prevailed while the draft was something of a novelty?

SUGGESTED READINGS AND WORKS CITED

Bailey, Ronald R. *The Home Front: U.S.A.* New York: Time-Life Books, 1978.

Baker, Russell. *Growing Up.* New York: Congdon & Weed, 1982.

Flynn, George Q. *The Draft, 1940–1973.* Lawrence: University Press of Kansas, 1993.

Fussell, Paul. *Doing Battle: The Making of a Skeptic.* Boston: Little, Brown, 1996.

————. *Wartime: Understanding and Behavior in the Second World War.* New York: Oxford University Press, 1989.

Hynes, Samuel. *Flights of Passage.* Annapolis: Naval Institute Press, 1988.

Keegan, John. "Going into Military Service." *Times Literary Supplement* (May 1985): 54–59.

Kennett, Lee. *G.I.: The American Soldier in World War II.* New York: Scribner, 1987.

Lay, Beirne, Jr., and Sy Bartlett. *Twelve O'Clock High!* 1975. South Yarmouth, Mass.: J. Curley, 1981.

Lowry, Robert. *The World Within War: America's Combat Experience in World War II.* Cambridge, Mass.: Harvard University Press, 1999.

Steinbeck, John. *Once There Was a War.* New York: Viking, 1958.

Wylie, Philip. *Generation of Vipers.* New York: Rinehart, 1955.

5

The Combat Zone

A Separate Peace has no actual combat scenes, yet as many critics have pointed out, it can be seen as a war novel, taking its title from Lieutenant Frederick Henry's declaration of a private truce in Ernest Hemingway's *A Farewell to Arms*. Although Knowles never takes us to the war fronts or directly describes the realities of the battlefields, he does convey the impact of the war on the minds and sensibilities of those who are not yet involved in combat. Through Gene, Finny, Leper, and Brinker, Knowles reveals the anticipation and anxiety that controlled the lives of a generation of young men who would be called to participate in the armed struggle. The selections that follow show what happened to those who answered the country's call to arms.

The U.S. Army's training programs, which were intended to convert a massive citizen army into combat soldiers in the span of a few months, often had a disorienting and depressing effect on the new recruits. The rapid buildup and hasty mobilization created almost chaotic conditions, with 14,000 men each day pouring into reception centers and training camps. But in time the army overcame the problems of inadequate housing and equipment shortages and eventually trained and equipped some ninety combat divisions of 15,000 men per division.

For those who made it through the basic training programs, the

U.S. soldiers of the 10th Mt. Division taking wounded G.I.s out of the combat zone, 1945. (U.S. Army Military History Institute)

major adjustment to military life had been made. A soldier might be assigned to infantry, engineers, or the artillery, but things would essentially be the same as far as military routines went. What would be different were the types of experiences they faced as they went overseas to various theaters of war, as the combat zones were called. Most would go to the European Theater of Operations— "E.T.O." as it was usually called—following the military practice of abbreviation. The reason most soldiers, airmen, and sailors were sent to Europe was that Franklin Roosevelt, Winston Churchill, and Joseph Stalin, the leaders of the United States, Great Britain, and the Soviet Union, respectively, had agreed that Hitler's Nazi war machine represented the greatest strategic threat, and thus Germany should be defeated first. Then full attention would be given to beating the Japanese Empire into total submission.

As the following articles, letters, and memoirs reveal, nothing could really prepare young men for the terrors and horrors they would face on land, sea, and in the air. Over 400,000 would never return, and thousands more would be physically and mentally marked by their ordeals. As Gerald F. Linderman in *The World Within War* has written, "What American soldiers in World War II failed to foresee was that battle possessed a power to impose thorough and dramatic change on those whom it did not kill" (3). Many Americans were eager to get into combat and thought that they were ready to meet the enemy following basic training. They tended to believe Hollywood war films that their enemies would be easy to defeat. The GIs had a naive disdain for the fighting abilities of the enemy. In fact, the soldiers in the German and Japanese armies had been hardened by years of combat experience in Russia and China. They were seasoned veterans, whereas U.S. troops were totally green. Americans learned several lessons almost immediately. First, the enemy forces would not be pushovers. German troops fought with fanaticism and ferocity, and Japanese soldiers, imbued with the doctrines of the warrior code, fought to the death. Furthermore, the enemy had excellent weapons. The Japanese fighter airplane was far superior to any American aircraft at the start of the war. The Japanese also employed clever weapons like the knee mortar, which gave their infantry an individual artillery piece. The Germans benefited most from superior technology, which produced the 88 mm cannon, feared for its accuracy and destructive power. The Germans also produced a machine gun that fired 1,200 rounds per minute, twice the rate of fire of the American Browning machine gun. They developed the world's first jet-powered war planes and intercontinental rockets, though too late in the war to achieve a victory through their use.

The optimistic gullibility that Americans came into the war with quickly evaporated in the fury of actual combat. In the accounts that follow, ex-soldiers provide oral and written narratives that describe battle. These writings and oral records are autobiographical and narrate a specific time in the experience of these veterans. As Samuel Hynnes points out, war stories are like travel writings in that combat usually takes a man far away from home. The soldier has to tell about the strange places he has seen and describe the experience he has in these places (18).

Furthermore, Hynnes says, those who have been through the experience of war often have undergone profound changes, the most essential being that war changes boys into men. However, soldiers who have been exposed to combat over a period of time undergo conversions of another type that change them in a more fundamental way. Robert B. Ellis describes such a moment in his book *See Naples and Die*. His platoon is ordered to advance up a mountain trail in Italy that is under heavy shelling by German artillery. It was to him "a classic demonstration of the fact that in infantry combat as practiced in modern war, your survival had nothing to do with your training, your intelligence, your battle experience and physical ability" (125). Ellis concludes that whether one lived or was killed in battle was strictly a matter of luck, since no one could predict where the next shell would land. Thus, when a man entered a combat zone, he had to face the possibility of death or injury. As James Jones, the author of *The Thin Red Line*, pointed out, each soldier must have a compact with fate, and "only then can he function as he ought to function under fire. He knows and accepts beforehand that he is dead, although may be walking around for a while" (*WW II*, 172).

Actually the odds of getting killed were directly related to what branch of the service the man was in and which theater of war he was assigned to. The infantry was the most dangerous, suffering 264 casualities for every 1,000 men. Tank men and artillery averaged 50 out of 1,000. Marines serving in the Pacific took some of the highest losses; they were the assault troops who attacked entrenched Japanese beachhead defensive positions from landing craft—the most hazardous type of military operation. Early in the war, before the United States gained air superiority, one of the riskiest missions was the daylight bombing of Europe by the U.S. Army Air Force. Bomber crews were required to fly twenty-five missions before they were reassigned, but the odds of their completing that number of flights were less than even; just 35 percent survived from 1942 to 1943. In fact, out of the 350,000 airmen who served in the Eighth Air force, some 26,000 were killed in action—a higher rate of fatalities than any other military branch, exceeding even the death rate of the marines. The reason for such devastating loss of men and airplanes was due to the Air Force's overly confident assumption that U.S. bombers could make deep penetration bombing raids against German air defenses without fighter escorts. The U.S. Army Air Force attempted pinpoint attacks on strategic targets like the ballbearing industry at Schweinfurt, Germany, and the oil refineries and fuel complexes in Ploesti, Rumania, and suffered terrible losses of crews and planes due to antiaircraft fire and enemy fighter attacks (Astor, 492). As with those who served in the infantry, the airmen soon lost their romantic notions of war as a chivalric contest where virtue and courage would prevail. Survival was a matter of pure luck in most cases. Most young men started out with a sense of their own immortality—someone else might get killed but not them. Usually their first mission would shake that assumption. Flying through the sky full of bursting shells was a totally helpless feeling because the bombers had to fly straight without taking evasive action. The shrapnel fragments from even near misses could riddle on airplane's thin aluminum skin and shatter the plexiglass that enclosed the crew.

Next to being killed or wounded, the worst thing that could happen to soldiers was to be captured and made a prisoner of war. If their captors happened to be Japanese, the worst could be expected; one out of every three POWs held by the Japanese died in captivity. On the infamous Bataan Death March, the nearly starved survivors of the four-month campaign to defend the Philippines were forced to march for eighty miles. Those who could not keep the pace were killed on the spot by the brutal guards. The Japanese did not recognize the provisions established by the Geneva Convention in 1929 for the treatment of POWs. Therefore, they did not allow the Red Cross to send food parcels or to inspect the prison camps. Even worse, they did not provide any lists of names of POWs or allow mail to be sent or received by prisoners. The Japanese were guilty of other violations of humane codes of conduct regarding POWs, such as providing starvation rations, beating and clubbing their captives, providing no medical assistance to the sick and wounded, and using prisoners as laborers to construct military roads, airfields, and fortifications, in violation of the Geneva Convention.

By contrast, Americans taken prisoner by the Germans fared much better. The German prisoner camps were under the administration of the *Luftwaffe*, or air force, and since most allied POWs were airmen, there was some fraternal feeling between the captors and captives. However, life in a German *Stalag* or POW camp was not the lark it was made to appear on the TV series of the 1970s *Hogan's Heroes*. Unlike the Japanese, the Germans allowed mail and Red Cross provisions and did not work the prisoners or subject them to beatings and humiliations. They also provided adequate housing and hospital treatment for military prisoners. However, the same could not be said for those who were sent to concentration camps because of their race or politics. These were the infamous death camps whose purpose was to provide the "final solution" to the Jewish problem. Fortunately, American soldiers of Jewish background were not treated differently from other POWs and if captured were confined to *Stalags*.

Almost all soldiers who survived combat or captivity attributed the fact that they came through their ordeal to the comradeship that existed on the battlefield or in the prison camps. This connection between soldiers was, according to Bill Mauldin, a brotherhood motivated by a sense of common purpose that lent nobility to the way that soldiers would "unselfishly risk their lives to help each other" (263). More than patriotism or hatred of the enemy, this bonding provided American troops with their strongest motivation. As William Manchester writes in *Good-bye Darkness*, a memoir of his wartime experiences in the marines, "Men do not fight for flag or country or the corps or glory or any other abstractions. They fight for one another" (391).

The bonding process began in the training camps and became stronger in combat. It is officially called "unit cohesion" and is cited as the cause for excluding women and homosexuals from the combat arms in today's armed forces. The fear is that sexual diversity in the foxhole would destroy the bond that is essential for men to function as effective combat soldiers.

As Samuel Stouffer points out in *The American Soldier*, one of the most powerful conflicts a soldier faces in battle is the struggle to stay loyal to his comrades in arms or to flee from the battlefield, a struggle that Stephen Crane so vividly depicted in Private Henry Fleming, the hero of his Civil War novel, *The Red Badge of Courage*.

The truth of this observation is clearly borne out in the personal narratives and oral histories that follow by World War II veterans. Their accounts of combat experience suggest that the violence of war had a profound effect on their imagination and memories. However, it is beyond the power of those who have not been in battle to grasp what it is like despite all the movies, books, and memoirs that have been devoted to describing the experience of combat. For the generation that fought World War II, the "war is never over," as Paul Fussell remarked on a 1999 C-Span talk show. It was the great adventure of their lives. The veterans have been labeled the "Greatest Generation" by Tom Brokaw in his best-selling book about the ordinary men who were called to take up arms to defend the country. It was the one time in their lives when they would act in a great global event, and their personal experience would intersect with the most important moment in the history of the twentieth century. Even today, over a half-century later, a man is still defined by that experience. All one need say is that "I was at Bataan" or "I landed on D-Day," or "I crossed the Rhine," or "I flew B-17s," and the deed will speak for itself. We know that what these men did mattered.

ADVICE FROM THE FRONT LINES

By the second year of the war, the army was gaining practical experience about how to fight a modern war from lessons learned on the battlefields in Europe and on Pacific islands. The following combat reports were prepared by the Army Operations Division on the direction of the chief of staff for distribution to the ground forces in September 1942. The purpose of the various sets of lessons was to give soldiers the benefit of previous battle experiences. Thus, officers and enlisted men were encouraged to read these pamphlets closely. The series was constantly being added to as new lessons were learned from combat. The army hoped that the comments transmitted from front-line soldiers would enable new troops to overcome any shortcomings in their combat training in the United States. Through these reports, replacements could see what tactics worked best against the enemy and learn how devious and deadly were some of tricks used by the Japanese and Germans.

FROM "COMBAT LESSONS"
(Washington, D.C.: U.S. Army Publication, War Department, 1942)

SECTION I INFANTRY

Battle Leadership

Again and again reports from the battlefields confirm the importance of leadership in every grade, whether it be Corporal or Colonel. Other combat lessons are important; the exercise of leadership in battle is vital. Leadership has often been defined in theory. Here are some instances of its application or its absence on the battlefield. These are but a few examples; there are many others.

Junior Officer in Battle. *Captain William T. Gordon, Infantry, Sicily*: "Since November 8, I have had seventeen officers in my company, and I am the only one who started out with it who is left in the fight. In Tunisia, from troops pinned down in the dark, I have heard enlisted men call out such things as 'Where is an officer to lead us?'—'We don't want to lie here—we want to attack—where is an officer?' . . . In each case an officer or officers have risen to the occasion, but this nevertheless shows beyond anything else the demand for battle leadership.

"A company officer must build a legend about himself. He must take calculated risks. He must, on the other hand, do what he expects his men

Going overseas: African American troops aboard a troop ship, 1942. (U.S. Army Military History Institute)

to do: he must always dig in; always take cover. His men must know that when he ducks they must duck; on the other hand, they must not believe that when the officer ducks they must run away. The officer must come through every barrage and bombing with a sheepish grin and a wry remark. Masterly understatement of hardship and danger endured plus a grin always pays dividends."

Hate Your Enemy. "Our men do not ordinarily hate. They *must* hate. They are better soldiers when they hate. They must not fraternize with prisoners—must not give them cigarettes and food the moment they are taken. Hate can be taught men by meticulous example. The Rangers are so taught."

Leaders in Front. *Staff Sergeant Richard E. Deland, Infantry, Sicily*: "We want our Captain out front; we don't care much about the position of our battalion commander."

Keep Them Moving. *Operation Report, Seventh Army, Sicily*: "During an attack officers and non-commissioned officers must never allow men to lie prone and passive under enemy fire. They must be required to move forward if this is at all possible. If movement is absolutely impossible, have the troops at least open fire. The act of firing induces self-confidence in attacking troops. The familiar expression 'Dig or Die' has been greatly overworked. Attacking troops must not be allowed to dig in until they have secured their final objective. If they dig in when momentarily stopped by enemy fire, it will take dynamite to blast them from their holes and resume the advance."

NCO Leadership. *Staff Sergeant Robert J. Kemp, Platoon Sergeant, Infantry, Sicily*: "NCO leadership is important. Leaders, NCO's, and officers should be taken to an OP [observation post] for terrain instruction and study before an attack. This had been possible in my outfit about one-fourth of the time. We have what is called an 'Orders Group,' which consists of that group of officers and NCO's that must be assembled for instruction before any tactical move."

Keep Your Mission in Mind! *Lieutenant Colonel E.B. Thayer, Field Artillery, Observer with Fifth Army, Italy*: "Difficulty was experienced in making patrol leaders realize the importance of bringing back information by a specified hour, in time to be of value. Patrols often returned, after encountering resistance, without accomplishing their mission. Sending them back to accomplish their mission, despite their fatigue, seemed to be the most effective solution to the training problem involved, although the information required often arrived too late."

Lieutenant Colonel T.F. Bogart, Infantry, Observer with Fifth Army, Italy: "Greater emphasis must be placed on inculcating in junior officers and NCO's the will to accomplish assigned missions despite opposition. A few accounts of patrol actions illustrate this point:

"(1) A reconnaissance patrol consisting of a platoon was sent out at about 1900 one evening to determine the strength of any of the Germans in two small towns, the first about two miles away and the second about three miles further on. The patrol reached the outskirts of the first town and met an Italian who told them there were no Germans in the town and then started to lead the patrol into town. A few hundred yards farther a German machine gun opened up, the Italian disappeared, three of the patrol were killed, and the others dispersed. They drifted back to our battalion during the night, and it was not until nearly daylight that the practically valueless report of the action was received. Not the slightest conception of the strength in the first town was obtained and no information of the second town. It was necessary to send out another patrol with the same mission.

"(2) A patrol was sent out with the mission of determining the condition of a road, especially bridges, over a three-mile stretch to the front. When this patrol had covered about a mile it ran into a motorized German patrol. Two of the Americans were killed, and the platoon leader claimed six Germans. The patrol leader forgot his mission, returned to the battalion CP [command post] with the remainder of his patrol, and had to be sent out again with a great loss in time in getting the information desired.

"(3) On several occasions patrols were sent out on reconnaissance missions with instructions to get certain information by a specific time. The hour would pass and sometimes several others without a word from the patrol. Sometimes it was due to difficulties encountered, sometimes to mistakes in computation of time and space factors, but in all cases there was no good reason why some information did not get back by the specified time."

COMMENT: The failure of patrols in these instances stems from a lack of appreciation on the part of NCO's and junior officers of their *missions*. In patrol actions, as in the operations of larger units, the *mission* must be kept uppermost in the minds of all ranks, and no action should be undertaken which does not contribute directly to the accomplishment of that mission. Conversely, no incidental or inadvertent contact with the enemy should deter or divert patrols.

"Notes on the Nips"

Japanese Pillboxes *Lieutenant Colonel McCormick, Field Artillery, New Georgia*: "In most cases pillboxes were built in two decks to permit the occupants to drop through a trap door during heavy shelling. They were used for heavy-weapons firing and had communication trenches which concealed light machine guns protecting the pillboxes. All were mutually supporting and very well concealed."

Superman Myth Exploded *Operations Report, 43d Division, New Georgia*: "Our troops here came to regard the Superman stories about the Japanese as ridiculous. The Jap is tricky but not so tricky as many have been led to believe. He is not nearly so ingenious or adaptable as the average American, and the truth of the matter is he's afraid of us, or our artillery, and of our sea and air power. Our troops must learn this and never forget it."

Jap Trap "We soon learned that the Japanese permitted small leading elements of the column to proceed past their effectively camouflaged fortifications and would not open fire until our main body came along."

Defensive Action *Operation Report, 43d Division, Arundel Island*: "Our first contact with the enemy was made by patrols, which encountered small groups of Japs equipped with automatic weapons. Their resistance consisted of a fluid delaying action and, during the early phases, could not be effectively fixed. After a short skirmish the Japs would withdraw several hundred yards and re-establish their temporary defense. The denseness of the jungle made such a defense quite effective in delaying our progress."

Vine Entanglements *Colonel Liversedge, U.S. Marine Corps, New Georgia*: "The Japanese used a prickly native vine for entanglements. The vines were interwoven and used to protect defensive positions in lieu of barbed wire. Results were effective and impeded attack. Vines had to be cut before progress could be made.

"*Our own troops should be instructed in the use of these vines* as a means of improvisation when wire is not available."

"Hints on the Heinie"

Reverse Slope Tactics   *Second Lieutenant S.W. Malkin, Infantry, Platoon Leader, Sicily*: "Enemy machine guns, mortars, and automatic rifles were located on the reverse side of the hills so as to catch our advancing infantry as they came over the skyline."

Don't Gawk!   *Private George Scott, Infantry, Sicily*: "Several times German planes pretended that they were involved in a dog-fight to secure the attention of the ground troops. Then they swooped down in a strafing run."

Traps and Mines   *Private First Class Edward Borycz, Infantry, Sicily*: "The enemy abandoned his tanks with motor running. When we tried to stop the motors they blew up.

"The Germans would put a mine in a road with another mine a sufficient depth under it so that it would not be seen if the top mine were removed. For a while our sappers did not run the mine detector over the area again where the first mine had been found. But after the dirt became packed down sufficiently by traffic, the second mine would go off."

Minor Tactics   *Staff Sergeants Richard E. Deland and Robert J. Kemp, Infantry, Sicily*: "Never let an apparently lone machine gun suck you into a trap. The Germans will usually not fire on the individual but will wait, watch where he goes, and get a whole flock.

"Germans always approach their positions from the end and under cover so as not to give them away.

"In the counterattack the Jerry machine gun is always well forward. German weapons are faster but are less accurate than ours; they scare you more than they hurt you. The German 81mm mortar is the worst goat-grabber; it gives you no notice when it is coming in.

"Germans use tanks to maneuver and fire from a distance in attack. When the going gets hot they pull the tanks in and, after a minute, bring them out again."

Typical Attack and Withdrawal   *Lieutenant Colonel P. H. Perkins, Tank Battalion Commander, Italy*: "The standard German attack here consists of three or four tanks in line in the lead. They are followed by infantry in trucks at four to five hundred yards. The rest of the tanks follow the infantry. When fire is drawn the infantry dismounts. The leading tanks mill about, fire, and withdraw. We have never seen the reserve tanks committed.

"In their withdrawals the Germans use tanks to good advantage. They do not have to contend with mines and blown bridges. Their tanks fire a few shots and withdraw, then move up again, fire a few more shots and withdraw, and so on."

Rearguard Action *Lieutenant Colonel Taylor, Infantry, Battalion Commander, Italy*: "My experience has been that we first meet two armored vehicles which open fire for a few minutes with everything they have on the first man of ours they see; they then withdraw rapidly down the road.

"Next we hit their outpost, which, I estimate, consists of about two squads. This outpost, protecting the road, his groups on the sides of the mountains on the flanks. It takes four to six hours to drive this outpost in due to its fine observation over us and the difficulties of maneuver."

SNAFU AT PLOESTI: SITUATION NORMAL ALL FOULED UP

In an early episode in *A Separate Peace*, Finny celebrates an Allied air raid on Eastern Europe by wearing his necktie as a belt to the headmaster's tea party. Although the exact nature and the name of this bombing raid are not mentioned, it is mostly likely that he is referring to the only such attack that was mounted by the U.S. Air Force against targets in Eastern Europe during the summer of 1943. The massive bombing mission, Operation Tidal Wave, was intended to wipe out the petroleum sources of the Nazi war machine by eliminating the huge oil refining plants at Ploesti, Rumania.

This ill-fated raid was plotted by the U.S. Army Air Force to demonstrate what long-range pinpoint bombing could accomplish. Unlike the Doolittle raid on Tokyo, which had been launched off the U.S.S. *Yorktown* largely as a morale booster, the Ploesti raid was more than a token strike. It would involve three bomber groups totaling over 175 heavy "Liberator" bombers. These planes would fly out of North African bases to reach their distant targets in Rumania. In order to evade the German radar, these huge B-24s, which were designed to bomb from 30,000 foot altitude, would be flying this mission at treetop level, a mere 50 feet over the deck.

This mission was so hazardous that the high command who planned it anticipated a 50 percent loss. The pilots who would be flying over such long distances at extremely low altitude figured that their odds of surviving would depend on the element of surprise. Everything was based on avoiding detection by the radar and hitting the target before German antiaircraft and defensive fighter squadrons could get into action.

The mission started with an omen. The lead bomber loaded to capacity with bombs and extra fuel crashed on takeoff. This was followed by further misfortune. While skimming across the Mediterranean Sea on the way to the Balkans, the B-24 carrying the chief navigator suddenly dipped a wing and crashed into the sea. This left the formation to be directed into the target by an inexperienced nineteen-year-old navigator whose ship was now the one the three bomber groups would follow. The task of accurate navigation was complicated by two factors: the lack of landmarks on the Danube Plain that the planes flew over en route to Ploesti and the extremely low altitude the formation was flying. Thus, it was not surprising that a critical error in navigation caused the bombers to swerve off course and head for Bucharest rather than the oil fields at Ploesti. When the mistake was realized, radio silence had been broken fifty miles from the target to regroup the strayed bombers. This would have fatal consequences for the success of the mission. The Germans would know the raid was coming and from which direction and have ample time to get their air defense ready to meet the threat. The Americans were heading into a death trap.

As the slow-flying B-24s lumbered in, they were shot at by small arms fire from the ground and by German fighters from above. Out of the original 178 planes, only 33 would return to their base in Bengazi undamaged. More than 300 airmen were killed, and as many more were taken prisoner after being shot down. The great loss of men and planes was not even justified by the damage done to oil refining plants at Ploesti, which were producing at 60 percent capacity shortly after the raid despite the air force's claim that the mission had been a success. No fewer than four fliers were awarded the Medal of Honor, an old military ruse for making a victory out of a defeat. Given the strict wartime censorship of news, the public never heard about all the blunders and the ill-conceived idea of using high-altitude bombers like the B-24 for a low-level attack on a strategic target.

FROM CAPTAIN WILLIAM D. BANKS, "TARGET: PLOESTI"
(*Harpers Magazine*, March 1943)

We took off at dawn. Our airfield was a small, crude affair in Libya that had been thrown together after the Italians were pushed out. At the time it was crowded with Liberator bombers, and every one that could fly was pressed into service for the Ploesti mission. My plane, the "Sad Sack," was one of them. After one last briefing, we had checked over the Sad Sack as she had never been checked before. This was to be our longest and toughest mission, and we figured we'd have enough trouble without mechanical difficulties. When we got to the plane for the take-off our ground crew were still working her over. They had been up hours ahead of us, putting the finishing touches on her with the loving care of a lot of mothers. They had been nursing the old Sad Sack along for months, and were just as anxious as we were to have her get up to Rumania and back.

Everything worked perfectly. The Sad Sack took the air easily and gracefully and we started climbing to meet the other planes that were gathering round our rendezvous spot. The sky was dark with big B24's. They were coming in from all directions, circling about and swinging into position. It took over an hour for all of them to arrive and get into their places. When our formation was finally made up we turned and headed straight out over the Mediterranean for Rumania.

My co-pilot, Carl Root, and I had a system we had been using for the five months we had been flying together in this area. I piloted for half an hour and then rested while he took over. It gave us both something to look forward to. We settled ourselves comfortably in the pilot's compartment and started counting the minutes, Carl waiting to take the controls while I looked forward to the half-hour's rest. Then we went through the old "pilot to navigator" routine over the intercom. The boys were all present and ready to go: Bombardier Joe Souza, Navigator Teddy Stewart, Engineer "Pop" Pleasant, Radioman Walt Golic, Assistant Radioman and Gunner Earl Rice, Waist Gunner Henry Richotte, Armorer-Gunner "Carburetor" Carbery, and Tail Gunner Wilson Cain. I could tell that, like me; they were doing some pretty heavy thinking about this long-distance job.

We had been practicing for this mission ever since our trip over Rome, July 19th. And this was August 1st. For an ordinary mission briefing is a matter of minutes or possibly a few hours, but for this one we were briefed for almost ten days.

Engineers had marked off areas duplicating Ploesti out on the desert, and almost every day we spent hours practicing over them. Low-level bombing was something new for these high-altitude bombers, but the Liberators were the best planes we had for the job, so we had to develop our own technique. It scared us all at first, skimming along ten feet off the ground in a big, four-engine B24, but after a few days of it we learned not to mind, and rather enjoyed the thrill. One other thing it taught us: there's nothing as safe and convenient as high-altitude bombing.

We had spent the rest of our time with intelligence specialists who reconstructed the whole Ploesti area in accurate scale on a big table and proceeded to teach us what oil refining is and how to put it out of commission. A couple of these men had helped build the Ploesti fields, so we could safely assume that they knew what they were talking about. We went into all the intricacies of refining processes and could have qualified for good jobs in the oil business by the time we got through. We learned where every cracking tower, every refining and distillation plant, and every power plant was, and practically memorized the position of every oil tank in Rumania. They taught us what the oil fields would look like from a low-flying plane, too. They made both slow and fast movies of the model oil fields, and ran them off for us so many times that we could see smokestacks rushing at us in our sleep. Part of the time was spent discussing the problems of low-level bombing, and the reasons for it. The higher-ups had decided that it would be cheaper to hit the oil fields once from a low altitude than to go after them continually from safer but less effective heights.

We had been given all sorts of escape kits, containing money in the denominations of every country we could possibly reach by plane. They also had small steel files, compasses, vitamins, and many other useful items to help us back to Libya if we were forced down. It was suggested that it would be useless to carry revolvers because we wouldn't be able to use them, but one of the pilots said later, "I don't know whether or not you guys are going to carry guns, but everybody in my plane is going to, and we're coming out shooting." We went into all the fine points of international law. They warned us to land in enemy territory, and then try to escape. If we were caught in civilian clothes after we had been captured once, we could expect to be interned again, but if we were captured in civilian clothes for the first time, we could be shot as spies. All these precautions had seemed a little gloomy at the time, but now that we were on our way it gave us some feeling of security to know all the possible avenues of escape.

In the rear of the ship the boys were kidding each other as usual, bandying such witticisms as "I'm too young to die. Honest, Judge, I'm too young to die." Joe Souza had to go through the same old stuff because of this Boston accent. Pop Pleasant, whose job it is to hand out the rather tasteless lunch rations, was taking the boys' orders. One thought he'd have a banana split. Another would settle for two dinners, while another hankered for three breakfasts and somebody's voice kept shrieking "Blue plate!" But beneath all this joking was a lot of serious thought. This was going to be no field day and we knew it.

As time went on we began to get tense. We were nearing our target and the distance was starting to tell. Several of the planes had had trouble and turned back already. Every once in a while I would look off to my left and see one or two Liberators feather a prop, wheel out of formation, and start for home. A little later one of the crew would call over the interphone, "Another plane's turned back!" Most of them went under us. We could see them about halfway down between us and the sea, headed back to the base, trying to make it to safe, Allied land before they piled into the Mediterranean. Others would turn back close enough for us to see the men in the plane. We waved good-bye, knowing how they felt and hoping they would get back safely. The Sad Sack, never in better condition, flew straight on toward Rumania.

Then, almost before we knew it, we were over the mountains and hills of Greece. We kept on altitude as low as possible, climbing over the mountains and flying down the valleys. We were so low, in some places, that we could see the people in their villages standing around and gaping up at us. We could even see that they had on their Sunday clothes. We passed some wide fields of corn and grain that looked for all the world like our own Middle West. Still keeping only a few feet off the ground, we went on up into Bulgaria. Everything was as quiet and peaceful as if there were no world war. We didn't see a single enemy plane or one puff of anti-aircraft fire. We crossed the "blue Danube," but it looked brown to us. Then we went even lower. We were approaching the oil fields.

Our group, led by Colonel "Killer" Kane, wasn't as big as it had been when we started earlier in the morning, for some of our planes were among those that had been forced to turn back. I was leading the third element, on the Colonel's left, as we roared down from the foothills towards the oil field. We kept our formation, a little tighter now, and headed in for the target. There were a lot of clouds in the sky, and the sun had been bright all the way up was gone. We went down even lower, and started clipping the tops off the trees.

Smoke was rising to meet us as we approached the refineries. The Germans had had time to set out some smudge pots, but they didn't bother us. The smoke from the oil tanks that had already been hit was a lot worse, and the sky was full of ack-ack. When we plunged in toward our refinery the smoke was so bad that we couldn't see a thing on the ground.

Our target was a power plant. If you hit that, you knock out the whole refinery. Oil tanks make a satisfying explosion and a lot of smoke, but they aren't as good strategic targets as power plants. Our pinpoint was a smokestack, and we had memorized its location so well that we didn't need to see it until the last minute. All we needed was a split second to sight it. And we had to get it with the first try; there would be no time to turn around for another run this trip.

Somebody ahead of us had bombed our target by mistake. We all felt sick when we saw the oil tanks exploding and great swirls of smoke pouring up from the ground. There was nothing to do but try to hit it again. I muttered, "Here we go, boys," and started our run. Oil tanks were still going off right under us, and on both sides German ack-ack batteries were firing in unison. We were so low that they were actually trained down on us.

We kept straining our eyes for that stack. We couldn't see it yet, and I began to worry. It looked as if we weren't going to get the damned thing after all, and we couldn't even tell if the others had hit the right spot. We just plowed on, sweating blood and not saying a word. The Sad Sack was bristling with guns for this mission, and we were firing every one of them as we roared in. The whole plane shuddered with the fire. The din was tremendous, but over it I heard Pop Pleasant yell that he'd seen his tracers knock out a whole battery.

Finally I decided to pull away. We had finished our run and hadn't even seen our pinpoint. At that moment Joe Souza yelled. He had spotted our smokestack and power plant through an opening in the smoke. I held her steady for a split second while Joe sighted and let his bombs go, and then I almost jumped out of my seat. Carl shouted, "Jesus!" and I pulled back with all the strength I had. Right in front of us, square in the middle of the windshield and looming up almost out of sight, was the tallest, hugest smokestack I have ever seen.

My heart dropped into my boots and jumped to the roof of my mouth as we drove at it. Shaking all over with the racing of her motors, the Sad Sack leapt up and climbed for the top of it. I prayed as she lost speed and the stack rushed at us. We cleared it as if we were pole-vaulting. I wiped the sweat from my eyes and almost took time off to cheer as we dropped down on the other side and sped away.

We must have missed it by inches, but it saved our lives. The Germans had just got our range perfectly, and let go with a tremendous ack-ack barrage at the moment we pulled up. The two planes behind us, which didn't have to pull up over their own targets, were knocked down by the same fire. (Apparently that's the way the Germans got most of our planes—waited for them at the end of their run.) But it was Sad Sack's lucky day. We had hit our target too, though at the moment that seemed incidental.

As we pulled away, I saw one of the planes of my element in trouble. The pilot was right over his target and had had to feather a prop [cut off the engine]. I thought, "Oh oh. There he goes." But a second later I saw Killer Kane feathering a prop too, and getting along very nicely. So I forgot about the other plane, and wasn't surprised when it joined us later. There were B24's going down all around us now. We saw two fall right in front of us that had apparently climbed up out of formation and been hit by pursuit planes. The ground was spotted with them, including some that had managed to land safely. The crews of these last were beside them, watching the planes burn and waving to us as we went by. We hated to leave them, the men were still alive. We ducked even closer to the ground and scooted for home.

There wasn't much left of our section as we started back, and two of the planes had only three engines working. German fighters were circling above, but we stayed too low for them to tangle with us. When one of them tried a pass at the Sad Sack, I couldn't resist the temptation to pull up and give him a burst with the fixed guns we had rigged up for the occasion. He whizzed by, I leveled back into formation, and Carl Root chuckled, "What the hell are you, a pursuit pilot?"

We followed the rise and fall of the land again, and it wasn't long before we had outdistanced the fighters and were over peaceful country-side. As we skimmed over the flat Danube Valley the farmers were out in their fields, waving to us as if they knew what we had been doing and thoroughly approved. We passed so close to them that it was like speed-ing by in a car. I'm sure that if I ever see them again I'll recognize them. I'm afraid we took some of their corn tops with us, though, and Pop Pleasant even claims we threshed their grain. A few of their trees are prematurely bare in the upper branches.

But the rest of the trip was no joyride. Some of the B24's were so badly shot up that Colonel Kane decided to head for Turkey instead of risking the long flight over active enemy territory. We weren't at all happy at the prospect of being interned for the duration, but we couldn't pull out and make both us and the rest of the formation easy meat for enemy fighters.

It began to rain. We were leaving the Danube Valley and nearing some mountains, so we had to start climbing. The Sad Sack was purring along smoothly on all four engines, reminding us again that we had the best damned ground crew in the Air Forces. But the two planes that had lost an engine had to start lightening their load for the climb. It startled us at first to see equipment fly out of the two planes and float back under us. The crews threw out everything that was loose or that could be yanked loose, and we left behind us a long, wobbling trail of seats, tanks, belts, shoes, boxes, and first-aid kits with gauze bandages unrolling in great circles, figure-eights, and curious, sometimes beautiful designs.

As we went over one little railroad town they surprised us by sending up light puffs of the first ack-ack we had seen since we left the target. It was too small and inaccurate to bother us much, but it made us mad. To play safe we had to duck over behind a hill and bypass the town. We reached the foothills and, flying at the lowest possible speed to keep in formation with the crippled planes, we kept easing the Sad Sack over the hills and climbing to make it over the mountains ahead.

Somehow we cleared the mountains. The Colonel's navigator, Lieuten-ant "Baron" Whalen, outdid his own record. Without even a map of the area, he led us between the mountain peaks with only a few feet to spare. I don't know how the two crippled planes got over some of those ridges, but I know the Sad Sack almost scraped her belly on a couple of crags, and the others couldn't have made it by any more. When darkness came we were out over the water again, and one of the injured planes had to feather another prop, leaving it with only two engines working. A few minutes later Wilson Cain called on the intercom to tell me that the plane had pulled out of formation. We hated to see it go after fighting its way over the mountains and getting so close to neutral land, but it was too dark now for us to help or even watch. So we headed for Cyprus. We heard later that the plane made a water landing near the coast of Turkey and that most of the crew swam to land and were interned.

I had never landed at Cyprus before, but when we came down there that night it looked even better to me than my own driveway back in Columbus, Ohio. The Sad Sack landed easily and softly, pulled to a stop without even hurting the tires, and we switched off the motors. For five long, delicious minutes Carl and I just sat there, almost crying to be back on land. We didn't speak a word—just leaned back in our seats and absorbed the sedative quiet of the pilot's compartment. For fifteen hours we had been in an earsplitting roar, weaving, climbing, diving, praying our way over mountain tops and that smokestack, every nerve strained and on the alert. Now there was calm, almost sacred peacefulness. It is one of the most beautiful things I remember.

"A PRISONER OF THE EMPIRE OF THE SUN"

The fall of the Philippines to the Japanese Army was the largest surrender of U.S. troops in history. Against overwhelming odds, an underequipped army of Filipinos and Americans had held on, but time ran out on April 9, 1942. Ironically it was Good Friday when Major General Edward King met with the Japanese commander to arrange an unconditional surrender. When asked for assurances that his men would be well treated, he was told that "Japanese soldiers are not barbarians," a remark that would be proven otherwise in the events to follow.

One eyewitness to the treatment that the Japanese dealt out to their prisoners of war was Ben Skardon, a young American infantry officer. He would survive the infamous Bataan Death March that resulted in the deaths of thousands of American G.I.s and various prison camps during his nearly four years as a prisoner of the Japanese Empire before being liberated by the Russians in Manchuria in 1945. Following his experience as a POW, Skardon remained in the army for many years. After his retirement from the service as a colonel, he began a second career. He returned to Clemson University, his alma mater, and became a professor in the English department who was distinguished for his excellence in undergraduate teaching. His story surely qualifies him as a member of the Greatest Generation. Bear in mind that the language he uses to describe the Japanese is colored by the interviewee's wartime experience and is the usage at the time of the war by the press and public.

INTERVIEW WITH COLONEL BEN SKARDON, U.S. ARMY,
RETIRED
(October 1999)

HB: We're talking about events that transpired nearly sixty years ago. Does it seem that long ago to you?

BS: Some things are as fresh in my memory as if it were yesterday.

HB: How old were you when the war started?

BS: I was twenty-one years old when I entered the army in 1939 after graduating from college with an ROTC commission. My first few years in the service were spent at army posts in Georgia and participating in the huge maneuvers held in Louisiana during 1940, the so-called war games that were the largest ever held in the United States during peacetime.

HB: How did you come to be assigned to duty in the Philippine Islands?

BS: Well, the world situation was getting pretty tense, and our relationship with Japan was going from bad to worse because President Franklin D. Roosevelt imposed an embargo on all oil to Japan in July 1941.

HB: So when did you arrive in the Philippines, and what was your assignment?

BS: I got to Manila in October 1941 and was assigned to the 91st Division of the Philippine Army.

HB: When did fighting break out in the Philippines?

BS: The Japanese hit our big air base at Clark Field in Luzon on December 8, 1941, just hours after the attack on Pearl Harbor.

HB: What were your orders now that fighting had started?

BS: We were sent up to the north in Luzon to try to fight a delaying action. This was the so-called War Plan Orange, which depended on our Pacific fleet taking control of the sea, but again the best-laid plans of mice and men went astray. We moved down into Bataan and got boxed in there. When you reached the end of the peninsula, your back was toward Manila Bay or the South China Sea. Some 2,000 would make it over to the island of Corregidor, known as "the Rock," which would resist until May 6, 1942.

HB: Where did you spend Christmas of 1941?

BS: We were still fighting up in Luzon at that point, but it was pretty a bleak situation for food. There was no regular supply of rations, and anything we got to eat we had to forage for. Some of our scouts went out and found a chicken, which we cooked for our Christmas feast. We foraged for food, and occasionally we would get a bag of rice off a truck.

HB: When did things start to get desperate?

BS: Actually, I stayed pretty optimistic through January and February 1942, although we were in a static position. Remember, we did not know anything about the destruction of the fleet at Pearl Harbor. So I thought that our relief would be coming along at any time— as soon as the Army could put a division or two on a troop ship and get it across the Pacific. But it wasn't until March, after General MacArthur left by PT boat for Australia, that hope started to fade. Malnutrition and sickness were taking away our ability to fight. I had come down with malaria, and our quinine supplies had run out.

HB: What sort of fighting was going on at this point?

BS: We did not have many combat-effective people left, mostly due to malaria and starvation, since everyone was on half-rations, which consisted of about ten ounces of rice a day with one can of fish for four men. Also ammunition was starting to run out. The Japanese were resorting to terror tactics, infiltrating small squads through the lines at night who would set up as snipers in the rear, shooting unsuspecting soldiers who assumed they were in a secure area. Furthermore, it was thought that the Japanese did not take prisoners, and any individuals who surrendered could expect to be executed. The Japanese were all veterans of years of fighting in China and were seasoned soldiers.

HB: How many men did you have left in your company by this time?

BS: Out of the original 120, we had suffered over 50 percent losses. There were maybe 60 still left in action.

HB: When the orders to surrender came on April 9, 1942, where were you?

BS: I had been taken on a stretcher to go to a hospital to be treated for malaria. We were told to take whatever we could carry and to assemble in a column to head north back up the peninsula. I picked up one can of condensed milk from the abandoned kitchen, which was what probably saved my life by giving me some nourishment to make the march.

HB: Is this the march that later came to be know as the Death March?

BS: Yes. Although I did not know it at the time, approximately 2,300 Americans were killed or died of exhaustion.

HB: How far were you forced to march?

BS: It was a long and winding road that took us up the more than eighty miles of the Bataan peninsula. We were on that road for six or seven days, I think. It seemed longer to me.

HB: Did you have to walk continuously, or did the Japanese give you rest breaks?

BS: We always stopped at night because the Nips were afraid that people would slip off into the jungle in the darkness. During the day there were pauses during the march to allow Japanese columns coming down the road to go through. Sometimes Japanese soldiers would lean out and strike at us as they went by. Therefore, I always tried to walk in the middle of the column so that I would be insulated somewhat from the guards. The most dangerous spot was to be marching at the rear. Stragglers were always in danger of being killed. Once a couple of soldiers and I stopped to relieve ourselves, and the guard started yelling at us. I ran up and tried to get lost in the column, but one of the other soldiers was not fast enough, and he was bayoneted.

HB: Why do you think the Japanese treated prisoners of war with such brutality? What was the reason for it?

BS: Well for one thing the Japanese did not expect to have so many POWs, so they were not prepared for the large number they captured on Bataan. The Death March was not a predesigned program of terror and was in some ways a case of mismanagement. Although it is not known at that time, the Japanese did not have enough food or medical supplies to take care of all the people they now had to provide for. However, this by no means excused the sadistic behavior of the guards.

HB: Did you ever see any Japanese soldiers show compassion for any of the prisoners during the march?

BS: No. All I saw were agitated and angry Japs constantly yelling "Speed-o," which was the only English word they seemed to know.

HB: Other than the constant prodding and slapping, did you witness any atrocities?

BS: One of the things that historians do not realize when they write about the Death March is that the treatment varied from one group or column to the next. Some American POWs got much worse treatment from the guards than my group did.

HB: What do you think enabled you to survive this ordeal?

BS: Well, I think the can of condensed milk that I had picked up gave me the nourishment I needed to make it. Also, I tried to avoid anyone who was acting wild or looked a little crazy, and some men were starting to behave irrationally toward the end.

HB: Where did the march end?

BS: When we reached a town called San Fernando, they put us in boxcars and took us to Camp O'Donnell, a new constructed Filipino army base that the Japanese were using as a POW collection point.

HB: Did things get any better here?

BS: Everything was very disorganized. Prisoners were just milling around. At first, there were no organized details for work parties. It was a very apprehensive time for me because I didn't know a single person, and if you were without any buddies, it could be pretty scary. Also, I was afraid that I might have a recurrence of malaria, and there wouldn't be anyone to look after me. So I tried

to conserve my strength by sleeping as much as I could and drinking a lot of water. There was one water tap from which you could
stand in line to drink from. The Japanese also provided some rice
twice a day. Nevertheless, a lot of men were dying from diseases
like dysentery and malnutrition. I had dropped in weight from 135
to about 110 pounds and was frail and very weak. Fortunately, the
Japs were not making us do very much at this point while prisoners
were coming in from all over the Philippines. It was eight to ten
days later that I was reunited with two former classmates from
Clemson College, Henry Leitner and Otis Morgan, who had been
in different outfits from me after coming to the Philippines. I was
at Camp O'Donnell from April to June 1942. It was a terrible place
because everyone there was so sick and weak. We were more like
"dumb, driven cattle," as a line in a poem goes, than like human
beings. The worst part for me was the recurrent malaria, but Henry
and Otis helped me sweat it out by lending me their blankets.

HB: What was the next phase of your captivity like?

BS: Sometime in June 1942, we were moved up to a farm camp at
Cabanatuan, where I came down with beriberi and my feet were
in agony. The only way to get relief was to rub them, and this had
to be done very gently because the pain was like ice picks sticking
in the soles of my feet. You get this disease from a lack of protein
in the diet. The only way to cure it was to eat something with
protein in it, which was not provided by the Japs, who served us
only rice. It was crucial for me to get something other than starch,
and it was here that Henry and Otis saved my life. They took my
Clemson class ring and used it to barter with a Japanese guard for
one chicken and a can of ham. We cooked it and ate it for three
days, picking even the insides of the bones clean by using a piece
of wire to dig out the marrow. It provided me the protein I needed
to get over the beriberi.

HB: After you got well enough to work, what did the Japanese require
you to do on the farm?

BS: There were different details. Some people were on water detail,
which meant carrying three-gallon buckets down to an irrigation
ditch. Some were sent out on the wood chopping detail, which
was considered a plum because you went out on trucks and the
guards would allow Americans to use their rifles to shoot a carabao
or occasionally civets, which would provide some fresh meat. The
water detail was dreaded because the weight of the buckets would
pull your arms out after carrying them all day long; you could not
lift your arms up they were so stiff. The best detail, I thought, was
weeding the okra field. We went out clad in G-strings, no shoes,

and a hat if you had one. We were not allowed to wear shoes by the Japanese in order to prevent escapes. The guards could be brutal if they thought you were loafing or not working up to speed, and they carried hoe handles and golf clubs, which they used to beat POWs for even the slightest sign of slackness. The guards did not speak any English and the Americans did not speak Japanese, so there was always a lot of confusion, and the Japs would start beating people to try to get them to do something. It was a very inefficient operation, and the Japs tried to use terror to make us do as they wanted. They were always shouting and beating POWs who could not figure out what they were expected to do.

Well, as I said, I thought working in the okra patch was a preferred detail; although you had to crawl down the rows on all fours while pulling grass and weeds with your hands, you could also sneak an okra pod into your mouth when you were sure a guard was not watching.

HB: How long were you at Cabanatuan?

BS: It was a pretty good while—over two years, from June 1942 until the fall of 1944.

HB: Why did you have to move on to other camps from there?

BS: The U.S. Army was fighting its way up from the South Pacific and getting closer to the Philippines. The Japanese were anticipating MacArthur's return as he had promised to do when he escaped from Corregidor in 1942. We were moved to Manila and incarcerated at the old Bilibid prison for a couple of months prior to boarding a transport ship to take us to Japan.

HB: Were these freighters or transports the so-called hell ships, as they have come to be called by historians?

BS: Well, that is a very accurate and descriptive term for what they were. The Japanese started to load about 1,600 American POWs on the passenger ship *Oryoku Maru* on December 13, 1944, and most of us were packed down in the deepest hold of the ship. The treatment we received was an omen of what was to come.

When we entered the ship's hold, a Jap noncommissioned officer was striking prisoners as they went by with a shovel in order to force us into this constricted space. The situation was pretty grim because the Japanese had packed men in so densely that we could not move freely. Every man was supposed to remain in a sitting position with another man wedged in front and back of him. It was extremely uncomfortable to sit this way for long; plus, it was very hot, and the air was stale and foul from lack of adequate ventilation. Pretty soon people started to get sick and pass out. Others became deranged and started to scream and become hysterical, perhaps from panic at fear of suffocation or claustrophobia, and also because we were in almost total darkness.

HB: If you were all jammed into this hold in the way you've described, how were people able to relieve themselves? Did the Japanese provide any toilet facilities?

BS: There were no toilets, not even any buckets. Since it was impossible to move, you had to relieve yourself where you sat and in your own filth. Some people used mess kits or canteens to urinate in, but it was a stinking mess in that hold that held some 900 men.

HB: Did the Japanese give you any food or water?

BS: At night they would drop a big bucket of rice and fish on a rope down into the hold, but there was such pandemonium among half-crazed prisoners that the rice was spilled and much was wasted. Very few men got anything to eat on account of the chaotic conditions. To make matters worse, the Japs did not provide any water rations, and everyone was extremely thirsty and suffering from dehydration. But as bad as things were, they got even more terrible because the next morning the U. S. Navy airplanes attacked our ship, which was in Subic Bay. The dive bombers and fighters bombed and strafed the unmarked Japanese ship, which should have been identified by signs or red crosses that indicated it was full of prisoners of war. But the Japs had not signed the Geneva Convention treaty so they were not obligated to go by any international rules. Thus, our pilots assumed these enemy ships were legitimate targets and attacked them, not knowing that many Americans would be killed. The Japanese crew and passengers started to abandon ship, but no provisions were made for the POWs, who were left to save themselves if they could. A bomb struck the ship and blew a big hole in the stern. I could see daylight through this hold, so I made my way out because the ship was on fire and filling with smoke. I dropped into the water, which was pretty close because we were down near the waterline. The ship was maybe 500 yards offshore, and I started to swim toward the beach. While I was attempting to get to land, I saw that the Japs were firing machine guns at the men in the water, apparently thinking we were trying to escape. Somehow I managed to get to land and was rounded up with other survivors and placed inside an enclosed tennis court near a place called Olongapo, where we waited for several days without any food or clothing. No one was wearing much except underclothes, and we were suffering from exposure to the hot sun.

HB: Did the Japanese give up on their plan to relocate American POWs in Japan?

BS: No, they were determined to keep us from being liberated, so they had another ship ready to sail. We were loaded aboard this freighter that had been used for transporting horses, and we were put down the ship's hold, which was filthy with horse manure. There were some slight improvements on this ship, such as some buckets for toilet purposes, but there were never enough for all the men to use, and soon this hold was overflowing with human filth, which was always underfoot. Also, there were a lot of sick and wounded people from the ordeal of the sinking of the first ship; no medical supplies were available, and many died due to starvation, disease, and wounds. The weather was also getting colder as we moved north. It was January by this time, and we had little clothing and no blankets for warmth, and, of course, the hold of the ship was unheated. The only way to keep warm was to huddle together for body heat, which wasn't much since we were all so emaciated.

When we reached Formosa, we put into harbor at Takao, where we were again attacked by U. S. Navy airplanes on January 9, 1945, during the early morning hours. Several bombs scored direct hits on the ship, one going into the forward hold containing many POWs. I was sitting in the after or near hold, which was not hit squarely but was sprayed with bomb fragments and debris, which killed and wounded many more. Several men sitting near me eating rice were killed, and I got fragment wounds and burns on my arm.

The Japanese transferred us onto the third ship for the last leg of our voyage to Japan—a troop transport this time, but again there was no provision for adequate food, water, or medical care for those who had been wounded in the previous attacks. It was a deplorable situation, with men sick and dying or freezing as it was getting extremely cold as we sailed northward in the dead of winter.

One night three of us were sleeping pressed together so as to use our body heat. During the night, I felt the man in the middle becoming very cold, which was alarming, he should have been the warmest because that was the most protected position from the cold. I tried to wake him up and looked into his eyes, but he did not stir, so I woke my other companion and after further efforts to arouse the man, we came to the conclusion that he was dead and that we had been sharing our bed with a corpse. Now this sounds kind of bad, but we very quietly stripped off all his clothes, anything you could get to wear against the cold was precious. Whenever anyone died, there were always arguments over who was to get the effects of the deceased, so that is why we were careful not to wake anyone else while we appropriated the dead man's possessions.

This ship became a sort of graveyard, with people dying every night. In the morning, the pile of bodies would be removed and dumped into the sea. One thing I admire was the fact that the senior officers tried to keep account of the names of all the deceased, so their families would know what had happened to their loved one.

HB: When did you finally get to Japan?

BS: On January 30, 1945. It was hard to know because we were down in the hold and couldn't tell whether it was day or night. We must have presented a horrible sight to the Japanese when we came off the ship. Everyone was thin as skeletons and dirty as could be. Our skin was caked in crud; only under the eyes was white. Our hair and fingernails had grown out, so we must have looked like wildmen dressed in filthy rags. Of the 1,600 who started out from the Philippines, only some 400 POWs arrived alive in Japan.

After docking at Mojii on January 30, 1945, some Japanese women standing along the side of the road started to throw small stones at us as we trudged to the tracks, but it was more humiliating than harmful. We were taken by trolley cars to Fukoka Prison Camp 3, where I remained for about three months. This place provided a kind of respite from the ordeal we experienced on the voyage. Here we were given wool shirts and army boots taken from the British and provided with some medical supplies also. This was also the first time that a Japanese camp commander (Major Rikitake) made any sort of effort to alleviate the suffering of POWs. They fed us two pretty substantial meals a day, and we were treated to curry once a week, which was heavenly. We were also allowed to take a bath—the first bathing we had done in many months. To get into these tubs was a tremendous luxury, and it also eased the pain in the joints from beriberi.

HB: So you would describe your POW experience in Japan as a big improvement over what you had known in the Philippines?

BS: Well, everything is relative, you understand. This was not any country club, and although conditions did generally improve, there was still a lot of inhumane treatment. There was one particularly vicious Japanese guard, a low-ranking corporal called Chisai, which means small in Japanese, who took sadistic delight in beating up prisoners and subjecting them to all sorts of humiliations. He never tried any of his mean tricks when Major Rikitake was around, but if he caught you alone, you were apt to get beaten up. I ran into this little tyrant once on my way to the latrine one night, and because I didn't bow deeply enough to show my respect, he took a swing at me and knocked me nearly unconscious, and as I lay there, he kicked at me. There was another bad Japanese guard at Fukoka. He was a warrant officer who conducted the head counts in the camp barracks, where we were required to count off in Japanese. If this officer did not like the way you pronounced your number or did not say it loud enough, he would slug you. He knocked me out cold one night with a punch to the jaw—again I don't know what I did wrong to displease him. The oriental mind was often inscrutable, and this was one of the dangerous things about dealing with the Japs. You never knew how they might react to something you did.

Another thing that I dreaded was what happened during air raids. We were forced to go to cave shelters that were dug in the side of a hill. These caves were low and dark and stifling when packed with POWs, and there were seventy-five to one hundred in our cantonment who were forced into these holes. After the experience on the hell ships the thought of being confined in a tight, dark space terrified me. Once I was sick during a raid and was allowed to stay in our shack. It was less terrifying there than in those caves. It was in this camp that I saw the greatest display of courage and Christian love that I have ever witnessed. This also happened during the roll call in the barracks conducted by the brutal warrant officer. One of the men was too sick to stand up for the count-off and lay coiled up in the corner suffering from pneumonia. Our Japanese guard taskmaster flew into a rage that a POW was not showing respect to a Japanese officer. He issued orders that the sick man be soaked with water and taken outside to the compound yard and remain there for the night. Well, this was no less than a death sentence to put a sick man out in the winter night. At that point, the Roman Catholic chaplain, speaking through an interpreter we called "Moon" Mullins, told the Nip warrant officer that he would take the other man's place and do his punishment for him—in other words, he would die in his place because anyone left outside who was soaking wet was going to freeze to death. To this day, the verse from John, "No man hath greater love than he who will lay down his life for another," comes to mind when I remember this episode. As it turned out, the Jap did not require the chaplain to undergo this punishment. Whether he was bluffing we never knew, but considering the inscrutable mind of the Japs, he may have been so impressed by the brave chaplain that he relented in his cruelty.

HB: This is now sometime early in 1945, and the Germans are already defeated. The Japanese are being bombed with increasing intensity

by B-29s that are making around-the-clock raids. How much war
news were the Japanese letting you all have now that things were
looking so bad for them?

BS: In April 1945 there was an announcement that FDR had died, but
we didn't know who the new president was at first; then the word
came down that someone named Truman was the U.S. president.
It was gloomy news to us because we had a lot of confidence in
FDR still. It was pretty soon after this that we were told to pack up
and prepare to get ready to move. Out of the one hundred of us
who had gone into the camp two months before, twenty-five had
died. I also got the news that my best friend, Henry Leitner, had
died of pneumonia. This was a real low point for me. From Japan
we sailed to Pusan, Korea, and were put on a train that took us
into Manchuria, although we didn't know for sure where we were.
Our treatment on the ship and in the train was much better than
during the previous move. The food rations included some meat
and vegetables served in a little *beni* box [Japanese term for a mess
kit]. Things were improving so much that I began to have hope
that I might actually survive. After we got into Manchuria, we were
put out at a big factory complex with a wall around it. This was
Hoten POW camp—my last place of imprisonment. The creature
comforts here were far better than anything I had known before.
There was a real latrine, a stove in the barracks, and, best of all,
they fed us soybeans with a bread roll, which did a lot to help
restore our health. Our skin was dry and scaly from a diet without
any protein; also, our hair had no oil in it and was wiry and dried
out. There was also a regular issue of Red Cross packages that
contained cans of salmon. The Japanese also did not require officer
POWs to work as they had previously done, and there was no harassment or humiliation by guards at this camp. My sense of op-
pression and hopelessness was lifted for the first time, as there did
not seem to be any danger from the Japs or U.S. bombers, and all
through June and July, we kept hearing that the Russians might be
coming down from the north to liberate us. Then one day a Japanese guard told us that one bomb had destroyed a whole city. This
was the A-bomb, of course. We could not imagine such a weapon.
It amazed even the ordinance officers, who assumed that the explosive had to be TNT, and such a bomb would be too big for any
known plane to carry. Then we heard the news that a second city
had been wiped out by another such bomb. One day a U.S. plane
started to circle the compound, and then seventeen parachutists
jumped out. The word came down that this was an American res-
cue team that had been sent to liberate us.

A B-29 crew had been shot down recently near Mukden. The pilot was Major Johnny Campbell, who was from South Carolina. He would give lectures to us to tell us about how the world had changed since 1941. He explained about the new jet airplanes that could fly without a propeller, which amazed us. He also mentioned a lot of new Hollywood movie stars none of us had heard of, like Ingrid Bergman and Gregory Peck.

I was evacuated from Mukden sometime in early September by a C-47 cargo plane. Those who needed medical attention were among the first to go out. My beriberi made it hard for me to walk except to hobble about. From there I went to a U.S. Army hospital in Sian, China, where they sprayed me down with DDT and I got to sleep in a bed with clean white sheets for the first time in nearly four years. I also got a shampoo, which seemed like a great luxury. The army took care of us, and we were given a special designation: "Recovered Army Military Personnel" or RAMPS.

My next stop was in Manila, in the Philippines, which I had not seen since 1941. It was in ruins from all the recent fighting in the city. The army issued us new uniforms, which had changed in style from the uniforms we had worn in 1941. I really liked the new "Ike jacket," which was very sharp looking I thought. [It was a short coat that fit snugly around the waist, making a much smarter appearance than the old-style blouse tunic that had tails.] Also I was promoted from captain to major and got all the ribbons, medals, and decorations due us. Feeling like a new man, I boarded a ship that took me back to the States. We made it home after all.

The joy of coming back to America was beyond description, and I was overcome with emotion. After debarking in San Francisco, we were sent to Letterman General Hospital. I was later transferred to Oliver General Hospital for rehabilitation. I remained there for nearly six months.

The army legal department took depositions from us about our treatment by the Japanese, and we provided names of those who were the most brutal. They were later tried as war criminals, such as Lieutenant Tashino, who played on the Japanese Davis Cup tennis team in the 1930s. He was the person responsible for our awful plight on the hell ships. There was also a Mr. Wada, a civilian interpreter, who was physically deformed by a hunched back; he was also morally deformed, I might add.

In the meanwhile, my family came out to see me, and we had a great reunion. I grew impatient with the rehabilitation and thought the army was keeping me too long, but I found out that they were holding me for observation because beriberi can damage the heart if you've had wet rather than dry beriberi.

After a thorough physical and psychological evaluation, I was accepted into the regular army.

HB: Did you feel any hatred for the Japanese people?

BS: No, I never did. I thought they had received just retribution for what they did. They were punished enough by all the destruction visited on them by our conventional bombing raids and the atomic bombs we used on them.

HB: What did you learn from this whole experience?

BS: I can't say in a few words what I've learned, but I do know that human nature is very complex, and some men are weak or evil and others are strong and noble. You can't make categorical statements about mankind.

THE STORY OF G. I. JOE

The war changed the lives of millions of people in the United States, but those whose future was most altered were the young men between the ages of twenty-one and thirty-five. As the war went on, the draft was lowered to take in eighteen-year-olds (the military having discovered that younger men without families made better soldiers than older men with domestic responsibilities). If there was one thing that a teenager in 1943 could expect, it was that as soon as he finished high school or the first year of college, he would be in uniform. There was only one prospect in the future for this generation, and that included the possibility of going to war and getting killed.

Such was the situation of Joe K. Jones, a freshman at Clemson University in South Carolina when he heard the news that the Japanese had attacked Pearl Harbor. Although he would not immediately face military service himself in 1941, his older brother, who had graduated earlier with an ROTC commission, would soon be in combat and receive a nearly fatal wound while fighting against the Japanese on Guadalcanal in 1942. Another brother would go off to the navy. He himself would be called up in 1943.

In the transcript of an interview that follows, Jones tells how he became a "G.I. Joe" and joined the "Crusade in Europe," as General Dwight Eisenhower called the campaign to defeat Hitler and liberate the captive people of Europe. Although his interview reflects an individual experience, it is really the story of a collective experience in that it recounts an episode that was typical in the lives of millions of American men who answered the call to arms. It was a call that would take many on "the most extraordinary adventure of their lives," as Kennett says in his *The American Soldier in World War II*. For each man who served, the experience was different, and yet it was also much the same: the separation from home and loved ones, the adaptation to a new life in the military, and the experience of facing the unknown, especially the unknown dangers that awaited those who went into combat. It has been said that those who have never been in combat can never truly understand it. This is no doubt true, but Stephen Crane had never been in a battle when he wrote *The Red Badge of Courage*, yet he was able to make us relive the baptism of fire that a young

Union soldier underwent. What is offered here is not fiction but an old soldier's distillation of his time on the front lines, as filtered through memory of events that took place nearly sixty years ago.

INTERVIEW WITH JOE K. JONES
(November 1999)

HB: What were you doing on December 7, 1941?

JJ: I remember I had skipped church to study that Sunday morning. It was about eleven o'clock when the news broke over the radio. Immediately there was a lot of excitement on campus, and some cadets fell out with their rifles on the drill field.

HB: In the following weeks after the war started, did many students leave school to join the service?

JJ: Students were encouraged to join the enlisted reserve so they could be deferred and stay in school a little longer.

HB: Did many join up before they were drafted?

JJ: Yes, especially those who wanted special branches. If you joined up, you got your choice of air corps, marines, or navy.

HB: Did anything else change around the campus as the country geared up for war?

JJ: Yes. There were limitations on all "war materials." Gas, metal goods, and rubber were all rationed. There were meatless meals, and you could not ride on trains or buses unless you had priority. Public transportation was used for moving troops. Also I recall we had to turn in our Springfield rifles for wooden dummy rifles to use for drilling. Another big change was the military moved onto campus and installed a unit of army air corps troops in the dorm. Then a little later, a detachment of soldiers from the Army Specialized Training Program was located on campus. These guys were on active duty, but they were going to college and taking academic subjects, mostly in math, science, and engineering, and getting instructed by Clemson faculty. They were segregated from the regular students, however, who lived in the dorms and took regular courses according to the college's curriculum, which was different from the army's.

HB: When did you get your orders to report for active duty?

JJ: It was at the end of my junior year. I finished final exams and was ordered to report with all the others in the enlisted reserve program on June 14, 1943, so I hitch-hiked down to Fort Jackson, South Carolina, where I was sworn in.

HB: What were your first impressions of the army?

JJ: At the Reception Center, I was amused at how a lot of people did not seem to know much about how to do things in a military way. For instance, our group were mostly ex-Clemson cadets who were accustomed to being in formation, and they put a corporal in charge who had been in the army just a few months. He was trying to drill us and making lots of stupid mistakes about giving commands, so we started to correct him and make fun of his errors, and he really got hot and cursed us out. This was a sort of preview of the way the army operated: incompetent people being put in charge.

HB: How long were you at Fort Jackson?

JJ: Only long enough to take all the mental and physical tests for classification, and then I shipped out to Camp Croft, Spartanburg, South Carolina, only a short distance from my home town of Deacusville. I spent seventeen weeks there undergoing basic training, prior to going on to Officer Candidate School [OCS] at Fort Benning, Georgia.

HB: What was OCS like?

JJ: Well, it was ninety days of intense preparation to be a platoon leader. It was excellent training by and large. The army was dealing with higher-quality people, and there was less humiliation and petty harassment. We were treated as potential officers. The system worked on peer review. We had to evaluate our classmates, and they rated you in turn. There was also academic work and field problems that you had to pass. I think that the army was mainly concerned with finding out who were effective leaders and had "command presence." If you were timid or not assertive, they would wash you out.

HB: When you finished OCS, what was your next assignment?

JJ: Again I was lucky because I did not have to move very far. I was sent to the 71st Infantry Division, which was in training right there at Fort Benning, so I only had to move across the post. At first I was assigned to the battalion as an S-3 officer [tactical operations officer in charge of the unit's schedule and logistics] and then to a weapons platoon.

HB: When did the division get orders to move overseas?

JJ: We were loaded on a train in January 1945, but no one knew whether we were going to Europe or the Pacific. Since the train went up through Virginia and was going up the East coast most of us thought that meant we would ship out from New York for the ETO [European Theater of Operations].

HB: Did you think you would be getting into the Battle of Bulge, which was still going on at this point?

JJ: We would arrive too late for this battle, which was winding down when we got to France in February.

HB: Where did you come ashore in Europe?

JJ: We debarked at Le Havre, France, and moved out to a tent camp called "Old Gold." The army had a number of these staging camps that were called "cigarette camps" because they were all named after various brands like Lucky Strike and Chesterfield. We spent most of February trying to get tough for combat, doing forced marches in full field packs and learning about German weapons. We knew that we were going into combat at any time, so everyone was pretty serious about what we were learning at this point. Most of the men in my platoon were eighteen to nineteen years old. Some could not read or write; only one or two had been to college. I knew how badly they were educated because I had to censor the letters they wrote back home. I had to write letters for a number of these fellows and also to read mail that they received.

HB: Did you get close to your men because you were involved with their personal lives by doing their correspondence?

JJ: Yes, I did get to know a good bit about where they came from and how they felt about being away from home and facing danger, but they were not very good at expressing their feelings in words, and some of the married men wrote very "steamy" [sexy] letters to their wives that were embarrassing to read.

HB: After your combat orientation program, when did your unit go up to the front lines?

JJ: It was sometime in early March 1945. We were ordered to replace the 100th Division in the area of the Vosges Mountains above Nancy, France. We went by train to Nancy, then in trucks up to Luneville, and then up into the mountains above the town of Bitche.

HB: What was your state of mind about this time?

JJ: I guess everyone was a little tight and also curious. If you've not had any combat experience, you don't know what to expect, so you're anxious about how you will react and worry whether you can look after your men who are depending on you. Of course, none of us, not even the NCOs, had seen any combat.

HB: What was your recollection of the first moments you spent on the front lines?

JJ: It was night and very dark when we went into the line. There was a lot of firing going on off in the distance, and you could see the flash of the big guns on the horizon. There was a smell of cordite from exploded artillery shells all over the place. I was led up to the command post by a lieutenant from the 100th Division who did not want to spend much time giving me orientation because he was eager to get away from the front since his outfit had been relieved. When dawn came, I could see that there had been some real fighting recently in their area. There were shell-holes and splintered trees and a crashed German airplane nearby with the dead pilot still in the cockpit. We stayed in that position for two or three days in a static situation. Then we started to move up in trucks toward the German frontier as they fell back behind the Siegfried Line [a fortified barrier of the Western Front]. One of the most sobering sights were the trucks coming down the road in the opposite direction loaded with the bodies of dead GIs and Germans. It dawns on you there that this is real, and these guys are out of it for keeps. However, at that point, you don't think you'll ever get killed or wounded; it's something that happens to the other person. All along the road there were dead horses, destroyed German tanks, and all types of abandoned equipment. Our planes had caught the retreating German columns in the open on the road and destroyed them. When we came up to the Siegfried Line, there were anti-tank obstacles called "Dragon's Teeth" and pillboxes, but they were not defended. I spent my first night in Germany sleeping in one of these pillboxes. It was also at this time that I was ordered to take out a daytime patrol, which was rather unusual. I was supposed to determine whether the troops on our left were Germans or Americans. We moved out in a patrol formation in that direction and discovered that they were GIs wearing olive drab uniforms. The Germans had a greenish-gray type of uniform and a very distinctive style of steel helmet that came down around the ears. It was such a good design that the modern U.S. Army helmet is almost an exact copy. The Germans were the best-equipped soldiers in the world. Their MG-42 machine-gun is still one of the fastest-firing automatic weapons ever produced, and the 88-mm field gun was legendary for its accuracy and destructive power.

HB: What sort of mood were you in—that is, were people gung-ho to get into combat with the Germans? And did anyone feel any hatred toward the enemy soldiers?

JJ: In March there was only about two months of fighting left. The Germans would surrender in May 1945, but everyone thought there would be several more big battles before it was over. The Germans were retreating all the time, and we were keeping constant pressure on their rear guard so that they couldn't dig in and set up strong defensive positions. It was still possible to get killed, though, and no one wanted to die when the war was so close to being over. Nobody was really mad at the Germans or felt they had scores to settle with them, but we had been taught that the Germans were bad people, and we were keyed up to get into combat.

HB: What sort of small unit tactics were you using during this phase of the operations?

JJ: We were always on the offensive and moving deeper and deeper in Germany. There was not a lot of organized resistance. The Germans would put a sniper or machine-gun nest in the towns to slow us down. When they fired on us, we would pull back and call in artillery fire. The shelling would usually blast them out, and if they were not killed, they would surrender or retreat. We had plenty of artillery support and didn't hesitate to use it. No soldiers can stand up very long under heavy artillery bombardment, and the German troops we were facing were Home Guards or *Volks-sturm* and Hitler Youth [units made up of men over fifty years old and boys of sixteen and younger]. The cream of the German army had pretty much been depleted after the Battle of the Bulge and the campaigns in Russia. There were still some SS units that were operational, and they were always dangerous opponents. They would fight to the last man, or until they ran out of ammunition.

HB: As you went through these German towns, what kind of attitudes did the people have toward the American troops?

JJ: If there were no German troops in the town, the burgermeister, or mayor, would come out with a white flag so that the town would not get shot up. Some German civilians were hospitable and would offer us food, but on occasion we would forage around for food by looking in the henhouse for eggs or up the chimney for hams, which was a favorite hiding place. It was much better eating than field rations. And we had some guys in the platoon who were good cooks when we found things. The troops were good at foraging after a while, and we ate well. Once we found some chickens, and we had a feast of fried chicken.

HB: Tell me what sort of routine you followed on combat duty.

JJ: We were moving out around seven o'clock and walking on the road in a columns of two, usually making about twenty miles a day.

HB: Did you pitch tents at night or just sleep out in the open?

JJ: We would try to find a barn or something with a roof, but if we were in the field, we dug foxholes and lined them with tree branches and covered up with a poncho. We were not too uncomfortable unless it rained.

HB: Were the Germans putting up much resistance at this point in the war?

JJ: No, they were on the run and shot at us just to hold up our advance. We did a lot of "sweeping" at that point, which meant all the platoons in the company would get off the road and walk in line abreast. This tactic was used to clear out wooded areas where the Germans might have set up a machine-gun to ambush us. Once we got fired on by a German machine gunner who sprayed us, but we could not see where the fire was coming from. We were pinned down for a while and could not move up until artillery fire got the range and silenced the machine-gun. When we got up and advanced, we saw that the gunner was dead. One of my men tried to take a ring off the German's body, but he couldn't get it off, so he pulled out his bayonet and was going to cut the finger off to get the ring. I saw what was going on and put a stop to it. It was considered okay to take personal possessions off the dead, but I thought mutilation of corpses was going too far. Just after this episode, we stopped to wait on the column. As we were waiting there at the edge of the woods, a couple of German soldiers in a motorcycle came up the road. I told my men to hold their fire, and we could capture these two, but when they were about 200 yards away from us, one of our machine-guns opened fire from off on the left in D Company sector. They missed, and the Germans jumped in a ditch and got away, although they were fired at by hundreds of rounds. The D Company guys got a lot of kidding for their poor shooting.

HB: Where did this take place?

JJ: I could not tell you, but it was out in a rural area south of Munich, near the Austrian border.

HB: What else happened as you neared the Rhine?

JJ: Well, once we were spending the night near a haystack and one of our men went out to get some straw. As he started to pull off the straw, a German soldier jumped out of the haystack with his hands up, and then another came out and then another, until he had five prisoners on his hands. He was without a weapon, so he started yelling for us to come out and help him accept these Germans who wanted to surrender, but no one took him seriously at first. At the last reunion of our unit, someone was telling this story, and the number of POWs who came out of the haystack had grown to twenty, so that's what people mean by "war stories"—the truth gets stretched.

HB: Do you know any more war stories?

JJ: In Speyer we came across a big wine cellar, and the company commanders told me to take a truck and get some wine to distribute to my platoon. This was a big treat for the troops, and as you might expect, some of them drank too much and were still drunk when we moved out. One guy was shooting at people on the streets as we were going through these little German villages and—this is not so funny—this drunk GI shot and killed a couple of German civilians. I was called in and told to put him under arrest, and he was held for a court-martial. He pleaded innocence saying that he had no recollection of anything he did. I'm sure that he didn't.

HB: Did our soldiers have a lot of bitterness toward the German people? Were there many criminal incidents like this one?

JJ: We had been told how badly the Germans had treated other nations, so we did not think too highly of the Krauts, but most GIs did not deal too harshly with civilians or POWs. And except for stealing, there was not much abusive behavior that I saw.

HB: Do you remember any big fights after you crossed the Rhine?

JJ: No, we had a series of scrimmages at places like Fulda, Hanau, Bayreuth, and Regensberg, but nothing major. At this point the whole 3rd Army had turned south, and we were going toward Bavaria. After crossing the Rhine, we had been moving in the direction of Berlin, but our new mission was to get down to Austria. Some of the big brass had a theory that Hitler was going to make a last stand at his "Eagle's Nest" near Berchtesgaden. This Alpine redoubt was where the Nazis would rally around him for their last stand. So the U.S. Army stopped heading toward Berlin and left it to the Russians. The decision was based on a false premise, however, the Germans never had a strategy for such a redoubt, and Hitler died in his bunker in Berlin.

HB: Where did you go cross the Danube River into Austria?

JJ: We made our crossing by boats at Regensberg, and it was here that we made our discovery of the concentration camp, in the area of Ering called Gunskirchen Lager, which was not a big *lager* [camp], but it was horrible enough. We went through it but did not stay there very long. The German guards had taken off, and all these gaunt people were standing around. We gave them some food, but we were told not to give them much because starving people should not overeat.

HB: Had you heard anything about concentration camps before?

JJ: Yes, we knew the Germans had such places, but you can't comprehend such a place until you see it and smell it.

HB: How close was this to the end of the war?

JJ: This was the end of April or early May, May 4th I think, so there were only about five or six days before the truce was signed. On May 8th the surrender was made at Rhiems.

HB: What sort of people were being held in Gunskirchen Lager?

JJ: They were mostly Hungarian Jews of all ages. There were several hundred children and teenagers among the prisoners.

HB: What size concentration camp was this *lager?*

JJ: It's estimated that there were 15,000 people in the camp, which was a sort of holding pen for the much larger death camp at Mauthausen, the biggest concentration camp in Austria. There were 110,000 prisoners there, and its inmates were sent on work assignments all over the area, but it was an extermination camp, too, with gas chambers and ovens to cremate the bodies.

HB: Where was Gunskirchen Lager exactly?

JJ: It was about 35 kilometers southwest of Linz near a market town called Lambach, which was where Adolf Hitler lived as a school boy. Gunskirchen was an isolated cluster of barracks surrounded by deep woods well off the main road. There were no gassing or cremation facilities there, but thousands of inmates had died of malnutrition and disease before we liberated them. Even after we got there, people were dying daily because they were too far gone to be revived by food or medical care.

HB: What social class were most of the prisoners from?

JJ: We learned that this group of Hungarians were made up of professional people—doctors, lawyers, academics, and intellectuals. They were people with status who had been distinguished, but they had been reduced to a primitive, animal level of existence by their treatment from the German SS guards.

HB: How long were you there?

JJ: Our regiment moved through the area, and it fell to another unit to restore order to the *lager* and to process all the displaced people and bury all the dead. Those who drew this unpleasant duty said they saw sights that would last them a lifetime.

HB: What was going on after the fighting stopped?

JJ: We were located at Steyr near the Czech-Austrian border, and one of our main functions was to accept surrenders from the thousands of Germans who were crossing the Elbe River to surrender to the Americans rather than the Russians.

HB: Was this a chaotic situation?

JJ: No, because the Germans were very orderly and organized even though they were POWs. They maintained good military discipline. All total we handled about 50,000 or 60,000 German soldiers whom we had to feed and process. They seemed very relieved to be in our hands rather than become captives of the Russians. They did not give us any trouble at all.

HB: Did you have any responsibilities toward the prisoners?

JJ: I once had to take a convoy of forty trucks loaded with about 1,500 German POWs up to Regensberg, where surrendered German soldiers were being held. Some of the trucks were captured German BMWs and had German drivers. The rest had American drivers. On the trip up to Germany, the GI guards and German POWs got along so well they swapped smokes and stories. Every day for several weeks we would run these convoys up from Austria to Germany. It was pretty easy duty, but we were all concerned that we would have to go to Japan because the war in the Pacific was still raging. It was about his time that I got to see General George Patton in person. He came down to review the unit and congratulate us on defeating the Germans. He also was attempting to psych us up to go fight the Japanese. He asked for a rifle with a bayonet, which someone handed to him. He grabbed the rifle and said that he was going with us to Japan and we were going to "stick this bayonet up the Jap's ass." Everyone laughed, but no one was as eager to go to war with Japan as Patton seemed to be.

HB: How did you feel when you heard the news about the atomic bomb ending the war?

JJ: It was a great relief because the A-bomb was dropped in August, and we were due to ship out to the Pacific in September.

HB: Was your division sent back to the United States at this point?

JJ: No. The 71st division was assigned to occupation duty in Germany, but the army had a points system that permitted men who had been overseas the longest to rotate back to the States to be discharged. Since our unit had been in Europe only four months, most of us would not go home for a while. Some American divisions had been in combat since 1942, so they went back home first.

HB: What did occupation duty entail?

JJ: It involved keeping civil order and locating and interviewing ex-Nazis. The army also allowed the troops to enroll in European universities if they wanted to, and there was the chance to travel and see the sights of Europe.

HB: When did you get home?

JJ: I came home in 1946 after three years in uniform. All the big parades were over by that time, but I had had enough of marching, so that did not bother me too much.

HB: Did the war stay with you?

JJ: Occasionally I have dreams of Germans crawling into my foxhole, and going down a road I will sometimes think how I would set up mortars or machine-guns to defend a position from attack or how I would make an advance on a hill or grove of woods.

HB: What was the major learning experience you gained from your army days?

JJ: The army taught me the value of organization. It also made me grow up fast. I was twenty-one years old and totally responsible for the welfare and safety of thirty men.

HB: Do you think yours was the "Greatest Generation"?

JJ: Well, we had a better opportunity to be great because we came to maturity during the Great Depression, and we were asked to fight the greatest war of the twentieth century. The current generation has only known good times and never been required to make any sacrifices, so I don't know what sort of stuff they're made of. America has had it soft compared to the rest of the world. World War II took the lives of 500,000 men, but no bombs fell on us, and we never had any enemy troops on our soil as invaders. [Actually some 400,000 Americans were killed in World War II.] The war was the defining moment of my life and also the most important event of the twentieth century. Everything seemed to lead up to it and from it in a historical sense. Looking back now, I am glad that I was of an age to have experienced the "big war," but I hope that there will never again be another one like it.

TOPICS FOR DISCUSSION AND RESEARCH

1. Interview someone you know who served in World War II, someone who came of age in the 1960s, and someone of your generation, and ask each if they feel there is a bond that holds their generation together. Is there any experience they have in common that only they can understand completely?

2. Many people who were in World War II say that going off to war made them feel more loyal and patriotic to the country. Read books like Ron Kovic's *Born on the Fourth of July* or Michael Herr's *Dispatches* or view some films such as *The Deer Hunter, Platoon*, or *Full Metal Jacket*, and see if these works elicit feelings of loyalty or patriotism.

3. World War I was fought to make the "world safe for democracy," as President Woodrow Wilson said, and World War II was fought to ensure the "four freedoms," as President Roosevelt said. Is there any evidence that either of these objectives was obtained? Discuss and debate.

4. People who have lived through terrible crises are often marked for life by these events. The scale of violence in World War II was much greater than any other war the United States has fought, yet Americans do not have an image of the World War II veteran as damaged from shell-shock like the Vietnam veteran is often depicted. What would account for this?

5. World War II veterans have been admired and respected because the war they fought was supported by the entire country, unlike the Korean and Vietnam wars. How was World War II different from these later wars?

6. The scale and efficiency of the regimes of the Nazis and the Japanese imperialists have been unmatched in this century, but there have been recent examples of genocide and ethnic cleansing in Asia, Africa, and Europe. In what ways are these events all alike?

7. After World War II ended, hundreds of Germans and Japanese were put on trial for committing war crimes. Many were found guilty and hanged or sent to prison. It has come to light that American soldiers committed atrocities in Korea and Vietnam. Investigate these events, and compare them with Axis war crimes.

8. In World War II, as in all other wars, both sides made blunders and mistakes. The French Maginot Line, the British raid on Dieppe, the German halt at Dunkirk, and the American bombing of Monte Cassino are all considered military blunders. Research these battles, and explain why they are considered blunders.

9. Write an essay discussing the implications of bombing cities, which results in the loss of life to civilians and the destruction of their homes. How was the bombing of Dresden justified?

10. Research the treatment of POWs by all sides during World War II. Why were the Japanese so brutal to captured enemy soldiers but less so in the case of civilians? The Germans were more correct in their dealing with captured soldiers but were they less humane in the case of civilians who were politically or ethnically incorrect?

SUGGESTED READINGS AND WORKS CITED

Ambrose, Stephen. *Citizen Soldiers*. New York: Simon & Schuster, 1997.
———. *The Victors*. New York: Simon & Schuster, 1998.
Astor, Gerald. *The Mighty Eighth: The Air War in Europe as Told by the Men Who Fought It*. New York: Donald Fine Books, 1997.
Brokaw, Tom. *The Greatest Generation*. New York: Random House, 1998.
Duggan, James, and Carroll Stewart. *Ploesti: The Great Ground-Air Battle of 1 August 1943*. New York: Random House, 1962.
Ellis, Robert B. *See Naples and Die: A World War II Memoir of a U.S. Army Ski Trooper*. New York: Mcfarland, 1996.
Hoyt, P. Edwon. *The G. I.'s War: The Story of American Soldiers in Europe in World War II*. New York: McGraw-Hill, 1988.
Hynnes, Samuel. *Soldier's Tale: Bearing Witness to Modern War*. New York: Penguin, 1998.
Jones, James. *Thin Red Line*. New York: Scribner, 1962.
———. *WW II*. New York: Grosset & Dunlap, 1975.
Keegan, John. *Soldiers*. New York: Viking Penguin, 1985.
Kennett, Lee. *G. I.: The American Soldier in World War II*. New York: Scribner, 1987.
Linderman, Gerald F. *The World Within War*. Cambridge: Harvard University Press, 1997.
Manchester, William. *Good-bye Darkness: A Memoir of the Pacific War*. Boston: Little, Brown, 1979.
Mauldin, Bill. *Up Front*. New York: Holt, 1944.
Pyle, Ernie. *Brave Men*. New York: Holt, 1943.
Slouffer, Samuel. *The American Soldier: Combat and Its Aftermath* Princeton, N.J.: Princeton University Press, 1949–50.
Tapert, Annette, ed. *Lines of Battle: Letters from American Servicemen, 1941–1945*. New York: Times Books, 1987.
Terkel, Studs. *The Good War: An Oral History of World War II*. New York: Random House, 1984.
Toland, John. *But Not in Shame*. New York: Random House, 1961.

6 ——————————————————

Contemporary Issues in *A Separate Peace*

Many of the issues *A Separate Peace* raises have application to contemporary social concerns, although the novel is set in the 1940s, over half a century ago. For example, we have seen an increase in violence on American campuses that goes far beyond anything in Knowles's book, and also we are much more concerned about the effects of post-traumatic stress on individuals. *A Separate Peace* features two acts of shocking violence: Gene's deliberate action in the tree that cripples Finny and the subsequent accidental fall that causes Finny's death. Although neither of these acts is an actual crime, each is typical of many tragedies that occur on campuses as a result of youthful indiscretion or mischief rather than outright felonious behavior, although there is more and more violence of an actual criminal nature occurring on school grounds and college campuses across the nation.

POST-TRAUMATIC STRESS DISORDER

The aspect of Knowles's story of a boyhood transgression that has the most contemporary application is the post-traumatic stress that Gene experiences for a full fifteen years after the death of his friend, Phineas. As a recent psychological study, Jonathan Shay's *Achilles in Vietnam*, shows the trauma of combat can undo a soldier's character and cause alienation that is long lasting in its effects. One of the most frequent causes of this type of post-traumatic stress is grief over the death of a comrade. Although Finny and Gene are not comrades-in-arms, they are schoolmates and best friends. While it is death in battle that cuts off a soldier's attachment to a comrade, in Gene's case it is a series of accidental circumstances that lead to the death of Finny. But Shay points out in his insightful study, "Any blow in life will have long-lasting and more serious consequences if there is no opportunity to communalize it. This means some mix of formal social ceremony and informal telling of the story with feeling to socially connect with others so that the survivor does not have to go through it alone" (39). Gene's suppression of grief and the absence of any communal mourning thwart his recovery. It is not until he tells the story that makes up the plot of the novel that he is able lay aside the anger and grief that haunted him for so long. Gene's healing and recovery come from facing the truth and creating a narrative to express it. His experience thus parallels that of Vietnam War veterans, though there was no name for it then.

Post-traumatic stress disorder (PTSD), was not classified as a psychological disorder until 1980. However, there is no doubt that Gene's problem is chronic and derived from a catastrophic experience that was similar to combat stress. These are psychological injuries that have been inflicted on men's minds rather than their bodies and have gone under different names in different wars— "soldier's heart" in the Civil War, "shell shock" in World War I, "combat fatigue" in World War II, and "post-traumatic stress disorder" after Vietnam.

In recent years there has been a major change in the thinking about who suffers from PTSD. Now experts think that it is not limited to Vietnam War veterans with whom the disorder of PTSD was first associated. It is now considered possible for victims of rape, physical abuse, disasters, torture, and the Holocaust to ex-hibit the symptoms of PTSD. Although little to date has been writ-ten about women veterans of the Vietnam and Gulf wars, there is an increased concern about women who suffer from stress-induced disorders that are not the direct result of combat experiences.

Much the same sort of situation is illustrated by the case of Leper in *A Separate Peace*, who is inducted into the army and undergoes a mental breakdown. His condition stems from the basic training, a traumatic experience for this sensitive boy who has led a shel-tered life. Like many other sufferers of PTSD, his condition is caused by a situation that overwhelms him. He reveals all the clas-sic symptoms in his encounter with Gene after he has deserted from the army, expressing moods of fear, anger, and tearful hys-teria. He also exhibits emotional numbness and a diminished in-terest in activities that once concerned him.

In addition to admitting that PTSD can be caused by something other than combat stress, psychiatrists now realize that veterans of other wars also suffer from delayed stress but that it manifests itself in different ways in World War II and Korean War veterans. How-ever, it was the unique nature of the Vietnam War that produced what are considered the classic symptoms of PTSD. Vietnam vet-erans, unlike World War II soldiers, fought in the first war America ever lost; they also suffered the stigma of being thought of as baby killers and warmongers due to the stories of atrocities committed by some units. Furthermore, they fought in a war that was widely opposed in the United States. Another factor that contributed to the unusual number of PTSD cases among Vietnam veterans, ac-cording to John Shay, was that G.I.s had no time to mourn their dead comrades, who were zipped up in body bags and whisked off the battlefield almost as soon as they fell. Thus, there was never a chance to go through grieving rituals as there had been in pre-vious wars.

Research on the subject of stress has found that violence to the human mind and body has gone under many different guises and had different names, but the consequences to those who suffer as a result of the shock of war, natural disasters, accidents, catastro-phes, rape, or "ethnic cleansing" are very similar: they suffer from haunting memories, intrusive images, and flashbacks that they can't suppress; they have feelings of rage and anger; they are al-ienated and have a sense of disassociation; and they carry guilt feelings for having survived.

The following article was posted on the Internet by the American Psychiatric Association as a public service to help those who might be suffering from PTSD by defining the symptoms of this syndrome.

FROM AMERICAN PSYCHIATRIC ASSOCIATION, "POST-
TRAUMATIC STRESS DISORDER"
(http://www.amerrescue.org, 1998)

It's been called shell shock, battle fatigue, accident neurosis and post rape syndrome. It has often been misunderstood or misdiagnosed, even though the disorder has very specific symptoms that form a definite psychological syndrome.

The disorder is post-traumatic stress disorder (PTSD) and it affects hundreds of people who have been exposed to violent events such as rape, domestic violence, child abuse, war, accidents, natural disasters and political torture. Psychiatrists estimate that up to one to three percent of the population have clinically diagnosable PTSD. Still more show some symptoms of the disorder.

While it was once thought to be a disorder of war veterans who had been involved in heavy combat, researchers now know that PTSD can result from many types of trauma, particularly those that include a threat to life. It afflicts both females and males. In some cases the symptoms of PTSD disappear with time, while in others they persist for many years. PTSD often occurs with other psychiatric illnesses, such as depression. Not all people who experience trauma require treatment; some recover with the help of family, friends, a pastor or rabbi. But many do need professional help to successfully recover from the psychological damage that can result from experiencing, witnessing or participating in an overwhelmingly traumatic event.

Although the understanding of post-traumatic stress disorder is based primarily on studies of trauma in adults, PTSD also occurs in children as well. It is known that traumatic occurrences—sexual or physical abuse, loss of parents, the disaster of war—often have a profound impact on the lives of children. In addition to PTSD symptoms, children may develop learning disabilities and problems with attention and memory. They may become anxious or clinging, and may also abuse themselves or others.

The symptoms of PTSD may initially seem to be part of a normal response to an overwhelming experience. Only if those symptoms beyond three months do we speak of them being part of a disorder. Sometimes the disorder surfaces months or even years later. Psychiatrists categorize

PTSD's symptoms in these categories: Intrusive symptoms, avoidant symptoms, and symptoms of hyper arousal.

Often people suffering from PTSD have an episode where the traumatic event "intrudes" into their current life. This can happen in sudden, vivid memories that are accompanied by painful emotions. Sometimes the trauma is "re-experienced." This is called a flashback, a recollection that is so strong that the individual thinks he or she is actually experiencing the trauma again or seeing it unfold before his or her eyes. In traumatized children, the reliving of the trauma often occurs in the form of repetitive play.

At times, the re-experiencing occurs in nightmares. In young children, distressing dreams of the traumatic event may evolve into generalized nightmares of monsters, of rescuing others or of threats to self or others.

At times, the re-experiencing comes as a sudden, painful onslaught of emotions that seem to have no cause. These emotions are often of grief that brings tears, fear of anger. Individuals say these emotional experiences occur repeatedly, much like memories or dreams about the traumatic event.

FOR SOME THE WAR NEVER ENDS

The National Center for PTSD conducts research and provides information to victims and families of those who suffer from the disorder. The fact sheet quoted below was published over the Internet specifically to help veterans of World War II whose cases had gone unreported, unlike those of Vietnam veterans.

FROM NATIONAL CENTER FOR PTSD, "POST-TRAUMATIC STRESS
AND OLDER VETERANS"
(http://www.neptsd.org, 1997)

From as long ago as Homer's ancient story of the battle between the Trojans and the Greeks, and the times of the Bible and Shakespeare, military personnel have been confronted by the trauma of war. Recent books and movies have highlighted the impact of war trauma for veterans of the Vietnam war and the Persian Gulf war, but the traumas faced by veterans of World War II and the Korean conflict have been publicly acknowledged in the media less often and less clearly. With the release of the movie, "Saving Private Ryan," the reality of war trauma in World War II has come front and center for veterans, their families and our society at large. The phrase, "war is hell," only begins to describe how terrifying and shocking that war was for hundreds of thousands of Americans military personnel. For most World War II veterans, those memories still can be upsetting, although only occasionally and for brief periods, more than 50 years later. For a smaller number of World War II veterans, the war trauma memories cause severe problems still, in the form of "post-traumatic stress disorder" or PTSD.

War is a life threatening experience that involves witnessing and engaging in terrifying and gruesome acts of violence. It also is, for most military personnel, a patriotic duty to protect and defend their country, their loved ones, and their values and way of life. The trauma of war is the shocking confrontation with death, devastation, and violence. It is normal for human beings to react to war's psychic trauma with feelings of fear, anger, grief, and horror, as well as emotional numbness and disbelief.

We know from numerous research studies that the more prolonged, extensive, and horrifying a soldier's or sailor's exposure to war trauma, the more likely that she or he will become emotionally worn down and exhausted—this happens to even the strongest and healthiest of individuals, and often it is precisely these exemplary soldiers who are the most psychologically disturbed by the war because they are able to endure so much of it with such courage. Most war heroes don't feel brave or heroic at the time, but simply carry on and do their duty with a heavy but strong heart so that others will be safer—despite often feeling overwhelmed and horrified.

So it is no surprise that when military personnel have severe difficulty getting over the trauma of war, their psychological difficulties have been described as "soldier's heart" (in the Civil War), or "shell shock" (in World War I), or "combat fatigue" (in World War II). After World War II, psychiatrists realized that these problems usually were not an inborn "mental illness" like schizophrenia or manic depressive illness, but were a different form of psychological disease that resulted from too much war trauma: "traumatic war neurosis" or "post-traumatic stress disorder" (PTSD). Most war veterans are troubled by war memories, but were fortunate enough either not to have "too much" trauma to recover from our to have immediate and lasting help from family, friends, and spiritual and psychological counselors so that the memories became "livable." A smaller number, probably about one in twenty among World War II veterans now, had so much war trauma and so many readjustment difficulties that they now suffer from PTSD.

Because most World War II veterans came home to a hero's welcome and a booming peacetime economy, many were able to make a successful adjustment to civilian life. They coped, more or less successfully, with their memories of traumatic events. Many had disturbing memories or nightmares, difficulty with work pressure or close relationships, and problems with anger or nervousness, but few sought treatment for their symptoms or discussed the emotional effects of their wartime experiences. They were expected by society to "put it all behind them," forget the war, and get on with their lives. Delayed PTSD occurs in subtle ways: for example, a World War II veteran who had a long successful career as an attorney and judge, and a loving relationship with his wife and family, might find upon retiring and having a heart attack that he suddenly felt panicky and trapped when going out in public. Upon closer examination, with a sensitive helpful counselor, he might find that the fear is worst when riding in his car, due to some unfinished trauma memories of deaths among his unit when he was a tank commander in the Pacific theater in World War II.

ACADEMICS VERSUS ATHLETICS

Another issue that the novel raises that has great relevance to our own times is the role of sports in education and whether academics and athletes can be mutually beneficial to an institution or an individual. Does the old Greek ideal of *mens sana in corpore sano* (a sound mind in a healthy body) have any contemporary relevance? Finny, the prime example of the campus hero-athlete, claims that "you always win at sports" (26). He means that the joy of playing a game is the only reward that counts and that "it matters not who won or lost, but how you played the game." This was the belief of Grantland Rice, an early sports writer who made the phrase famous, but his view is a far cry from a remark attributed to Green Bay coach Vince Lombardi: "Winning isn't everything; it's the only thing." Today we seem to be more in accord with the famous coach's philosophy than with the older concept that the joy of competition is a sufficient reason to play sports. American schools with athletic programs are driven by a win-at-all-costs mentality that prevails down to the grade-school level and even on the sandlot. Everyone wants to be number one, and many people, from school administrators to athletic staffs to the athletes themselves, are willing to do whatever it takes to have a championship season. This kind of ambition often means making many compromises in academic integrity and the basic morality of an institution.

As Murray Sperber shows in *Onward to Victory: The Crises That Shaped College Sports*, there is a long history of conflict between the athletic departments of schools and the faculty; moreover, no other branch in the educational establishment has experienced so many scandals and disgraces as the athletic departments of various institutions over the years at all types of institutions, large and small, public and private, military and civilian.

There is a great deal of emphasis on sports in *A Separate Peace*. Finny is an outstanding athlete who breaks swimming records and invents new games at which he excels. Despite Finny's optimistic outlook that "sports are always good," much that happens in athletics these days refutes this naive premise. In fact, if one looks at the history of sports in the United States, it is disheartening to see that sports and sportsmanship have seemingly always been at loggerheads. As Hank Nuwer, an investigative journalist, shows in his wide-ranging examination of scandals in American sports, many of the problems surfaced with the emergence of organized sports around the turn of the twentieth century. By 1895 it was common practice for "boosters" to pay the tuition and pocket money for prize college athletes (35). Some schools used nonstudents in varsity football games or professional players, playing under assumed names.

Of course, unethical practices can be found in any type of human endeavor, but it is always shocking when it is exposed in athletics because sportsmanship and sports stars are held up to society as being supremely virtuous, and yet both amateur and professional sports are constantly being tarnished by scandals that result from gambling, drug use, sexual abuse, and recruiting and academic cheating. Recently athletes have been involved in more than just misdemeanors that would bring a reprimand for rules violations. There seem to be increasing numbers of violent crimes committed by both amateur and college athletes, ranging from the brutal hazing of rookies, to sexual assault, armed robbery, and even murder. In fact, two pro football players are currently facing trial for first-degree murder. Ironically, rather than being held to higher standards expected of those that society holds up as heroes, the reverse is true today: sports stars often get special treatment and seem to be above the law. One only has to look at the former Indiana University basketball coach, Bobby Knight who until recently had gotten away with verbally and physically abusing his players, or recall that Florida State allowed Peter Warfield, a blue chip football player, to stay on the squad even though he was guilty of grand theft. In each situation the institutions decided to retain these individuals despite their disgraceful conduct because their services were deemed essential by boosters and alumni, whose influence often dictates how universities decide their priorities.

Murray Sperber, an English professor at Indiana University and a frequent critic of athletic corruption, gives a brief overview in the following excerpt of the strained relationship between athletes and academics and shows some of the negative effects that the sports industry has had on higher education.

FROM MURRAY SPERBER, *ONWARD TO VICTORY: THE CRISES THAT SHAPED COLLEGE SPORTS*
(New York: Henry Holt, 1998)

Intercollegiate athletics have existed on American campuses for well over one hundred years. However, the explosion of television entertainment during the last two decades of the century has amplified the size and importance of college sports to an unprecedented degree. In the 1980s, with the breakup of the NCAA's monopoly on TV rights and the emergence of ESPN and other cable networks, the electronic media began to hype college sports in high-tech and innovative ways. The wall-to-wall televising of college basketball and football games and the frenetic merchandising of college sports paraphernalia provided a synergy between the media and university athletic departments, expanding both and engrossing sports fans and undergraduate students as never before.

Many university officials permitted or encouraged the increasing commercialization of their schools' athletic programs in the futile hope that the added revenue would offset their athletic departments' chronic annual deficits. In fact, because the TV networks insist that athletic programs provide them with the best possible sports product to televise, most schools entered an athletics arms race, spending more money than ever before on the recruiting and retention of intercollegiate athletes. Such expenditures, including immensely expensive training facilities, produced even greater deficits. This economic absurdity exists within the context of massive public and private cutbacks to higher education, and a shortage of funds to hire faculty and staff as well as to maintain many basic university services and even the physical plant. Some schools with large enough endowments have managed to avoid these problems, but most have not.

The expansion of big-time college sports affects many areas of university life, one of the most obvious being scholarships. Since 1980, at most schools in NCAA Division I-A, athletic scholarships have increased by almost 900 percent, while, at many of these institutions, academic merit scholarships have decreased. The debate of the 1940s and 1950s on whether athletic scholarships should exist now seems as antiquated as the controversy over right-to-work laws. The only current argument on athletic scholarships concerns their size and perks: is the stratosphere the limit, or the ionosphere? In fact, many big-time sports schools spend much more on grants for jocks than on academic merit scholarships. According to the most recent *Chronicle of Higher Education* study on this topic, Duke University awarded $4 million annually to its 550 intercollegiate athletes, but only $400,000 in academic merit grants to its 5,900 other undergraduates; the nearby University of North Carolina at Chapel Hill gave almost $3.2 million a year to 690 athletes, and $636,000 in academic merit scholarships for its almost 15,000 other students.

Colleges and universities claim to be in the education business; however, when they fund athlete scholarships so much more lavishly than academic ones, they send a contradictory signal. They indicate that they place a higher priority on sports than education, and they also tell prospective students, particularly those from minority groups, that because the main chance of obtaining a free college education is through sports, they should first develop their athletic skills and then their academic ones.

Although the proponents of big-time college sports see its effects on higher education and on student life as positive or benign—they never support their position with any research. The few studies done in this area on the impact of big-time college sports on undergraduate education, indicate many negative effects from college sports. A decade ago, Ernest Boyer, the head of the Carnegie Foundation, concluded from his organization's research that, on college campuses, "the cynicism that stems from the abuses in [intercollegiate] athletics infests the rest of student life, from promoting academic dishonesty to the loss of individual ideals. We find it disturbing that students who admit to cheating often excuse their conduct as being set by the college example . . . [of] athletic dishonesty." Recent research, as well as much anecdotal evidence, indicates that this situation has become worse at the end of the twentieth century. In their attitudes toward big-time college sports, a majority of undergraduates, particularly at large state universities, exhibit a doublethink mentality, an unstable combination of cynicism and sentimentality that began in the 1950s and has increased every decade since. Many students understand the unresolvable problems in college sports, illustrating their perception with stories on how athletes at their schools cheated academically or received outrageous perks. Yet these students also claim to "love college sports" and boast of attending every game to which they can obtain tickets (a majority of these are sold to boosters and alumni), watching all other games on TV, usually with classmates at a sports bar, and organizing their extremely active social lives around their schools' sports activities.

Students also exhibit doublethink on many other college sports issues, including "special admits" for jocks: many schools use baseline SAT/ACT numbers when considering regular applicants for admission, e.g., an SAT total of 1300 at UCLA; but these universities enroll athletes with SAT and ACT scores far below those of normally admitted students, e.g., in the 850 and lower range at UCLA. To the statement "Athletic scholarship winners should meet the same college entrance requirements as regular students," a large majority of undergraduate respondents (83 percent) agreed or strongly agreed. Yet, many of these same students approved of the "Prop 48 Casualties" [nonqualifying athletes] at their schools—athletes with SAT scores below 850—and happily cheered for them when they suited up for the varsity.

To the statement "Regular students should have the same access to academic assistance as athletic scholarship winners—i.e., free unlimited tutoring, enhanced test files, etc. . . . ," 87 percent assented, some out of egalitarianism, others wanting the same advantages for themselves. "Enhanced test files" is a euphemism for copies of exams supplied to the athletes for the actual tests. That some faculty members cooperate in this deception is one of the disgraces of Big-time Sports U.

A favorite argument of the proponents of big-time college sports is that at huge, impersonal institutions, it provides a central rallying point, bringing all elements of the university together in true community. On occasion, particularly when a school's team wins a national championship, this appears true; however, in a deeper sense, because of the idiosyncratic and artificial nature of the event—the necessity of sweeping through an entire season and/or tournament, and the immense amount of media attention—if Big-time Sports U can only develop these random, occasional communities, then it offers a sad commentary on its achievements.

The following selection examines the problems facing student-athletes in the light of the way the university treats their "education" and the way athletics reflects the ills of society in general, particularly the belief that winning is all that matters.

FROM GARY D. FUNK, *MAJOR VIOLATION: THE UNBALANCED PRIORITIES IN ATHLETICS*
(Champaign, Ill.: Human Kinetics, 1991)

One School of Architecture academic offering . . . is open to all students enrolled in the university. Introduction to Architecture, which fulfills a university humanities requirement, is a lecture class taught in a large auditorium with audiovisual aids. In contrast to the stringent academic requirements and work standards of the architecture program itself, the approach to Introduction to Architecture is, to say the least, more lax. Students who quickly perceive this laxity flock to the course in hopes of fulfilling general education requirements and garnering easy credit. The resulting large classes hold enrollment figures up, keep departmental budgets healthy, and present an unfortunate professor with the prospect of spending an entire semester with several hundred students who can't distinguish between an arch and a fresco—and couldn't care less. This university's athletic department is a perceptive lot, and many athletes take the class in search of hours of eligibility. Football players are the most predominant and obvious athletic group in the class. Large and often black, the gridders provide sharp contrast to the rest of the mostly white class as they lounge in the back of the auditorium, taking up two or three seats each.

During one past semester, class attendance was terrible, especially among the football players, and those players who were present carried on conversations, fell asleep, even snored loudly. As the semester dragged on, the professor became furious with the situation. He instructed his assistant, a fourth-year female architecture student who helped prepare the class slide shows, to quiet the football players who were conversing and awaken those who were napping. The next lecture found the athletes behaving as usual. With trepidation, the student assistant approached the inattentive, snoring, hulking horde and quietly and politely asked for cooperation. Mildly speaking, she was treated with disdain, and she hurried back to the safety of the slide projector, where she devised a new strategy that the irate professor eventually agreed to implement. Toward the end of each class period, a one-question quiz would be administered to determine attendance and consciousness. The quizzes, worth 10 points apiece, would go a long way toward determining semester grades. The obvious strategy behind the quizzes was to reward those attending and awake and punish those absent or napping.

After each lecture, the student assistant graded the quizzes, and the professor recorded the zeros with a gleeful vengeance. The strategy was mildly effective, as attendance improved. But it soon became apparent that, although their attendance had improved somewhat, the football players were still missing the answers on the quizzes. The professor had not considered the ramifications of failing 20 football players en masse; therefore, he decided to make the questions so simple that they would be impossible to miss. The student assistant, responsible for developing and administering the quizzes, pondered her new instructions and decided to ask the following question: What is the name of this class?

It was a piece of cake, right? It meant 10 easy points for everyone, even the football players. Wrong! The responses included "Engineering," "Art," "History," "Middle Ages," "?," and "I don't know." As the astounded assistant graded the quizzes, it soon became apparent not only that some of the student-athletes failed to pay attention, but also that many hadn't a clue as to what class they were attending.

That the win-at-all-costs philosophy has undermined collegiate sports and that many institutions have been tainted by scandals in their athletic departments is all too obvious. As the news account below shows, we see the same attitudes filtering down to the nation's sandlots as overzealous parents take their children's activities for too seriously.

FROM "WHEN CHEERS TURN INTO JEERS"
(*U.S. News and World Report*, May 15, 2000)

In nine years as president of the Subdivision Sports youth baseball league, the low-pressure alternative to Little League he founded, Mike Finneran of Naperville, Ill., has had many memorable moments. Like the time one coach in a second-grade game began choking the other. Or the

numerous encounters with parents who hurled the "F" word faster than
Randy Johnson's fastball, berated their kids from the sidelines, and dis-
puted every umpire's call. "We were the laid-back league," says Finneran,
50, who canceled this spring's baseball season for third- through eighth-
grade boys. "I've had three heart attacks, triple-bypass surgery, and a
stroke. I don't need the stress of these guys fighting."

Subdivision Sports isn't the only league stressed out by parent spoil-
sports these days. Across America, along with the idyllic scenes of kids
scrambling after line drives or booting soccer balls around the park, there
are the heckling hubbub and ferocious temper tantrums from adults taking child's play far too seriously.

Hardly a game goes by without an ugly example—or two or three. Last
fall, a "midget league" football game in Pennsylvania ended in a melee
involving nearly 100 players, coaches, parents, and fans. A Maryland father, disappointed that his son had been left off the all-star team, knocked
down and kicked a coach, while an Oklahoma coach had to be restrained
after choking the teenage umpire during a T-ball game for 5- and 6-year-
olds. In fact, attacks on umpires have grown so common that the National
Association of Sports Officials recently began offering a new benefit to its
19,000 members: assault insurance.

But they're not the hardest hit, says Fred Engh, president of the National Alliance for Youth Sports and author of *Why Johnny Hates Sports*:
The players are. He cites a recent survey by the Minnesota Amateur Sports
Commission in which almost half the young athletes said they had been
yelled at or insulted, 17.5 percent reported being hit, kicked, or slapped,
and 8.2 percent were pressured into harming others. No wonder 7 in 10
kids quit organized sports before their 13th birthday. "You'd never hear
this at a child's piano recital: 'Erin, you bum, you can never do anything
right!' " notes Engh, who likens the unrealistic expectations adults place
on young athletes to child abuse.

Alternatives. Alarmed by the escalating epidemic of aggression,
thousands of communities are embracing measures to quash the "win at
all costs" mind-set and restore a sense of recreation to childhood's fields
of dreams. West Des Moines's youth baseball league recently adopted a
zero-tolerance policy toward obnoxious adults; cuss or brawl, and the
kid leaves the team. "We're going to stand tall on this," vows league
president Mike Linn, who hopes to stave off violence before it occurs
with other measures, such as giving every young player a turn at bat and
running coaching clinics. Albuquerque fines abusive spectators $5, while
soccer leagues nationwide now observe "Silent Saturdays"—sometimes
with duct tape or lollipops to muzzle sideline shouters. In Florida, the
Jupiter-Tequesta Athletic Association is really playing hardball: It just became the first in the nation to require that parents attend an ethics class
and sign a code of conduct if they want their kids to play.

So far, such measures have scored big with the unobstreperous parents who make up the vast majority of coaches and spectators. Jupiter-Tequesta didn't lose one of its 2,000 players because a parent shunned the sportsmanship class, for example. And while incidents still arise, they quickly get resolved—often by the parents themselves. "It's eerie how quiet it's been because the parents are trying to figure out where to draw the line," says JTAA President Jeff Leslie, who calls the overall effect "a blessing for our league."

But sports historian Gerald Gems, chairman of the health and physical education department at North Central College in Illinois, considers these temporary palliatives at best. He says that efforts to bring civility to youth sports ultimately will strike out unless they also attack America's win-at-all-costs mentality. What's also needed, he suggests, are programs to teach coaches child psychology and strategies for dealing with parents. Jim Thompson, founder and director of the Positive Coaching Alliance in Stanford, Calif., which has launched a 10-year campaign to boost sportsmanship, agrees. "We don't want parents just to learn not to be jerks," he says. "We want them to learn to be positive motivators."

CRIME COMES TO THE CAMPUS

The days are long past when the schoolyard and the college campuses were considered secure oases of quiet and contemplation
far removed from the distractions and dangers of the outside
world. A wave of violence has swept over America's schools, with
shootings in classrooms in all parts of the country leaving many
students dead and wounded, shot down by their own classmates
in most cases. There has also been an increase in certain types of
crimes on college campuses such as rape, assault, theft, and even
murder. It has been reported that for every 1,000 students on campus, there will be twenty-six crimes committed against them an-
nually. Furthermore, violent crimes are committed twelve times a
day on college campuses across the United States ("campus crime,"
www.bpinews.com/edu). The *Chronicle of Higher Education* conducted a study in 1999 that revealed that drug and alcohol violations increased for the sixth consecutive year, with 7,897 arrests in
1997. The same study showed a 4.4 percent rise in weapons law
violations for the years 1996–97. There is no agreement among
experts on the cause of these increases, but most observers see it
as an indication that American schools are no longer ivory towers
and suffer from the same ills as the larger society. It is frightening
to learn that in 1998, there were 21 killings on college campuses,
1,240 rapes, 1,068 robberies, 2,267 aggravated assaults, 13,745
burglaries, 539 arsons, and 179 hate crimes. These incidents were
reported by 481 four-year colleges in compliance with new federal
laws. The dimensions of the campus crime problem were largely
unknown until 1990, when Congress passed a law requiring
schools to report their annual crime figures and the Department
of Education was required to publish a nationwide report on
crimes that occur on campus.

Yet despite the growing concern about safety, most students are
safe, and, paradoxically, those who attend larger institutions are
safer than those at smaller schools. The Department of Education
report cited above in the *Chronicle of Higher Education* shows
that students are more likely to be victims of crime at small
schools, which is attributed to the fact that most small colleges are
private and lack the resources for security. According to the most
recent statistics, it is safest to attend a public two-year nonresiden-

tial school, which indicates that students who reside on campus are potential victims of crime twenty-four hours a day. However, students who live off campus are not considered victims of college crime because the Campus Security Act requires that only crimes that occur on the school grounds be reported. Thus, if students are mugged, assaulted, or murdered in the vicinity of the campus, these crimes are not counted. Since many crimes against students occur near but not on the actual campus, Congress has expanded the Security Act to require colleges to include these crimes in their annual reports.

Finally there is another type of violence that prevails in many American schools: physical and psychological abuse known as hazing. This type of activity is not limited to schools, however; it is practiced by the military, athletic, and even civic organizations, but it is most identified with Greek letter societies. Hazing in different forms has been around a long time, as Hank Nuwer points out in *Broken Pledges*, which examines hazing of all types, from sororities, athletic teams, secret clubs, and societies to even school bands. For a long time, hazing was regarded as a form of youthful high spirits and ritual that shaped group loyalty and built character. When Clemson University, for example, decided to abandon the "Rat System" [hazing of first-year students] after it ceased to be a military academy and became a coed civilian college, many alumni thought that dropping hazing would spell the end of school spirit, or "Tiger Pride" as it was called.

With attitudes like these, a lot of reeducation was needed to show that pride in belonging to any group is not dependent on humiliation and physical abuse. Nevertheless, recently there has been an epidemic of hazing across America's schools, colleges, and athletic fields. The National Collegiate Athletic Association (NCAA) found in 1999 that 80 percent of college athletes had been hazed in some form that usually involved drinking contests or humiliation and brutality. Many coaches turn a blind eye to such rites in the belief that they build team spirit and toughen players (see Huffer). Many people do not realize what a serious problem hazing is and do not see it as a crime since the victims of hazing willingly submit to these situations because they want to belong to the group. Yet if some of the practices followed by those who perform initiation rituals were conducted outside the academic or athletic context, they would be considered criminal.

In fact, numerous deaths have occurred as the result of hazings that got out of control. For example, a Morehouse College fraternity roughed up a pledge with a heart condition, causing his death. A pledge at the University of Texas was forced to drink huge quantities of alcohol, then handcuffed and taken for a ride, where he was dropped off in a remote spot. He was found dead the next morning. As Nuwer shows in his book *Broken Pledges*, these kinds of fatal incidents have a long history, and they are still happening, which is ironic since schools have been so quick to suppress hate speech and any language that might hurt students, and yet behavior that does actual bodily harm is allowed to continue.

Having been hazed as a fraternity pledge and having hazed others, Hank Nuwer has developed a deep commitment as a journalist to illuminating this societal problem as a means of eliminating it. Nuwer offers insights into these problems that very few people can address with authority. He is considered the national expert on hazing and is frequently asked to be a guest commentator on national news programs.

FROM HANK NUWER, *BROKEN PLEDGES: THE DEADLY RITE OF HAZING*
(Atlanta: Longstreet Press, 1990)

European harassment of students wasn't called hazing. Early in the fifteenth century a system known as pennalism flourished on the continent. By the seventeenth century, master's degree students needed to obtain a document that affirmed they had gone through the equivalent of a Middle Ages hell night. Under the system of pennalism, older students regarded newcomers as savages who needed to undergo hardships to prove themselves worthy of admission into the company of educated men. Veteran students extorted money from the younger men, abused them physically, and forced them to dress in odd garb. One such French custom that emigrated to our universities was the cap or the beanie that American freshmen and many Greek pledges routinely wore for a term or a year. (The custom still exists on a voluntary basis at a few American colleges, including Phillips University in Enid, Oklahoma.) The system of pennalism, fortunately, disappeared from the continent, but not before many young men were humiliated, injured, and killed.

The English aristocracy's practice of fagging [the humiliation and persecution of new boys] flourished in [British public] schools and was occasionally practiced at Cambridge and Oxford. Fagging was defined in *The Spectator* in 1891 as "the right exercised by the older boy to make the younger do what he likes, and what the younger one generally dislikes." *The Spectator*, in an article defending fagging, said that human nature—not corruptness—makes boys in groups behave abominably. "Boys, even when honest and honourable, are very queer cattle," it said. "A boy may still be as honest, as good, as simple-hearted, and as loveable as the day that he left his mother's side, and yet the little wretch will bow his little knee in the temple of custom, and be found aiding and abetting his small school-fellows in malpractices that at home he would have considered criminal."

Each new student was to learn humility and etiquette by becoming a fag, or man-servant, to an upperclassman. The newcomer did chores, ran errands, cleaned digs, or quarters, and anything else that came into the upperclassman's mind. The senior men physically abused and mentally harassed their fags. Suicides, serious injuries, and deaths sometimes resulted. The practice, condemned by the poet Percy Bysshe Shelly as "brutal and degrading," wasn't stopped at Britain's celebrated Eton until 1980. American colleges had a form of fagging although anti-British sentiment during the eighteenth century prevented the word's being used. Vocabulary distinctions notwithstanding, Kershner found that freshmen at Harvard, for example, were expected to run errands, refrain from sauciness, and never use the upperclassmen's privy.

The practice is occasionally found today in high-school athletics in the United States. Some coaches have rationalized that fagging is good if it is supervised. In 1985, for example, the Manheim [Pennsylvania] High School head football coach and the assistant athletic director sent parents initiation policies in writing for a football camp they planned to hold at Juniata College. According to the document, the arrangement teamed sophomores to seniors in a so-called little brother–big brother relationship, but in practice there was nothing to distinguish this system from fagging. Among other duties, sophomore boys were expected to carry team equipment and seniors' luggage, cart food on trays for the big brother, and bring a food package [no more than five dollars] to camp for the big brother.

Another practice at Oxford University in England during the 1600s was called salting and tucking. An upperclassman would scrape the skin off a younger lad's chin with the knife just before a traditional drinking ceremony, according to a *Smithsonian* article by Michael Olmert. The young man then chugged a schooner of salt water. The water spilled from the vessel and stung the youth's exposed flesh.

Olmert also quotes Martin Luther as he initiated new students to Wittenberg in 1539. Luther made neophytes wear silly "yellow bills" (horns) on their heads and basted them in wine to wash away, symbolically, their pasts and "former unbridled natures." Said Luther, "You'll be subjected to hazing all your life. When you hold important offices in the future, burgher, peasants, nobles and your wives will harass you with various vexations. When this happens don't go to pieces. Bear your cross with equanimity and your troubles without murmuring. . . . Say that you first began to be hazed in Wittenberg when you were a young man, that now that you have become a weightier person you have heavier vexations to bear. So this test is only a symbol of human life in its misfortunes and castigations."

By about 1850 hazing was common on Eastern campuses, perhaps spread by young men who had quit West Point and Annapolis to attend public and private colleges. The jargon of hazers varied from campus to campus. At one time the practice was called dibbling at West Point. During the late 1860s, the most serious form of hazing was a practice known as yanking, which occurred when upperclassmen picked up the blankets upon which a cadet was sleeping in order to do mischief to him. Fraternity hazing was not a major problem during the nineteenth century at public and private universities although it was hardly nonexistent, as some Greeks have claimed. The most serious hazing arose from class rivalries, particularly those between freshmen and sophomores. These took the form of battles royal, known as scraps. Often there was a form of warfare called the cane rush, in which the two classes vied with each other to get the most hands on a cane. Many college presidents and faculty members deplored the practice, but others condoned it or looked the other way, believing it built school spirit and class unity.

The beginning of American fraternity existence goes back to Phi Beta Kappa in 1776 (although it has even earlier social antecedents). The original purpose of this literary society was to give students a forum of their peers to express their views at a time when American was breaking away from British rule. Thus, the original concept of fraternities had both an intellectual and social appeal; later, its leaders would add a system of noble and worthy values. One Phi Beta Kappa rule that was subsequently lost forever was a ten-shilling fine for drunkenness. The so-called "Union Triad" (so named because they were popular at Union College) of Kappa Alpha, Sigma Phi, and Delta Phi flourished next. Writer Stephen Birmingham has noted that fraternities then spread across America and part of Canada like wildflowers. In time fraternities broke with other fraternities, and young men visited other colleges with the zeal of Mormon missionaries to form new chapters. Kershner says that these forebears of the fraternity movement thought nothing of taking a six hundred-mile train ride to visit another chapter or school. When there were sufficient chapters, national associations were the result, and fraternities in time became a successful business.

Fraternal hazing became more common by the 1800s. The University of Georgia Zeta Chi, for example, tossed pledges high in the air on a quilt held by members; one heavyset pledge was shaken up when a quilt split in two, dropping him on his buttocks. On another occasion Georgia Zeta Chi brother Donald Fraser played a practical joke on his fellow members.

The candidate he had been instructed to bring to an initiation backed out at the last second. Fraser donned the mask and quilt of the candidate and entered the initiation ceremonies. The members were clad in sheets; a single candle barely illuminated Phi Kappa Hall. The supposed initiate was introduced to the mysteries of the brotherhood, docilely submitting to some absurd hazing practice until a voice ordered him to stick out his tongue so that it might be branded. The members tried to force him to comply, and the jokester whipped out a pistol. Unknown to the membership, the gun contained blanks. Fraser took aim at the panicked Zeta Chis. Two men jumped out a window, dislocating their ankles in a fourteen-foot fall. Others were bruised or suffered wrenched arms. What happened to the prankster when his game was discovered is unrecorded.

Significantly, hazing was slow to take hold on the Pacific side of the Mississippi, possibly because Westerners despised a custom they saw as typical of effete schools back east. The University of Colorado student paper boasted in 1893 that the institution "has never has a case of genuine hazing." But in 1895 the attitude at Colorado flip-flopped when the school hired Eastern professors who decried the lack of school spirit in their new students. By 1899, the student paper at Colorado said hazing was "a natural part" of student life, so much so that the faculty unsuccessfully tried to abolish it in 1900.

The word *hazing* has a colorful history. The term was used by English sailors to honor a man's first trip across the equator. Another popular use of the term was on the American Frontier. Old-timers frequently subjected greenhorns to hazing in the form of cruel pranks and verbal abuse. The term *hazers* also came to be used by western ranchers to refer to men on horseback who used whips as they cornered a horse they were trying to break.

Hazing deaths occurred during the nineteenth century. Eileen Stevens's C.H.U.C.K. files contain a letter from a woman who claims that her ancestor, John Butler Groves, died in an 1838 hazing at Franklin Seminary in Kentucky. Since all school records were lost in a fire, the claim cannot be easily refuted or affirmed. Without doubt the first hazing death to receive extensive newspaper coverage occurred in 1873 at Cornell University. A pledge, Mortimer N. Leggett, son of the U.S. commissioner of internal revenue, was blindfolded and taken for a long walk in the country by members of Kappa Alpha. Two members eventually took off his blindfold, and they all tried to return to campus in the darkness. Unfamiliar with the terrain, the three plunged down a slope to the edge of a cliff. Leggett died of injuries sustained in the fall.

As if to prove that few people are aware of what constitutes hazing, the death was ruled an accident. The Kappa Alpha members testified that there had been no drinking or hazing. They argued—successfully, since no charges were placed—that the death was the result of an initiation rite. The father of the dead youth, General M. D. Leggett, accepted initiation into the fraternity in place of his dead son.

In 1899 the Kappa Alpha fraternity at Cornell again required a pledge to walk through unfamiliar terrain near Geneva, New York. Edward Fairchild Berkeley of St. Louis perished when he accidentally fell into a canal. In 1912, a London *Morning Post* correspondent wrote that "Death at a fraternity initiation" or "Seriously injured while being initiated" were almost standing headlines in American newspaper offices.

Hazing dropped drastically during World War II (as it did during World War I) when fraternity membership plummeted as college men went off to war. Following the war, many veterans would not tolerate being hazed by students younger than they were, recalls Mark Steadman, now writer in residence at Clemson University. But ironically, these same veterans introduced strenuous physical hazing that gave some fraternity pledge programs a boot camp atmosphere. When fraternity membership boomed during the late 1940s, hazing also increased dramatically on many campuses. Instances of freshman hazing and cadet hazing in service academies also rose during this era. Hazing "had become worse than it had been for the last ten years," a Texas A&M dean complained to the press in 1947 (Nuwer 1990). The school blamed hazing for a whopping 48 percent dropout rate of dormitory students after a single semester.

Different forms of hazing have been going on for a long time, but have recently become an issue that more people hear about. Although there are laws in place that govern hazing, it seems that more needs to be done.

Currently individual campuses are seeking to reduce hazing incidents. Most have policy statements on hazing and related incidents and have tried to lay out exactly what they consider hazing to be and what action they will take. For example, the University of Texas system lays out very clearly state law and Board of Regents policy. The Texas State Legislature has also set forth a policy for hazing connected with any educational institution in the state. Many of these policies, though, have been in place for some time and have not greatly reduced reported hazing incidents. Many individual Greek and other campus organizations have also adopted anti-hazing stances. In some cases, initiation rites even include date rape sensitivity training and alcohol awareness seminars. But in fact, most policies are not always followed. Students are too wrapped up in tradition to want to change their ways. In a book entitled *Rush: A Girl's Guide to Sorority Success*, Margaret Ann Rose gives the advice that "hazing activities are always mandatory unless a girl is physically unable to take part, gets sick during the activity, or is terribly upset about the hazing. Girls who are unable or have the courage to refuse to participate in hazing are less a part of the pledge class." Attitudes such as these make hazing a continuing problem.

One organization that is not affiliated with any campus group, C.H.U.C.K. (Committee to Halt Useless College Killings), founded by a woman whose son died in 1985 as a result of hazing, strives to bring about awareness, sharing information on laws and proposed legislation, and researching and documenting deaths and injuries related to hazing. Since its campaign began in 1991 many states have finally recognized hazing fatalities as felonies.

All of the efforts of campus leaders, campus organizations, state and local governments, and other organizations like C.H.U.C.K. are apparently not enough to make the groups change. Hazing will be stopped only when students' attitudes change. They are the ones that have to stop these horrible practices in the name of tradition and loyalty.

FROM EILEEN STEVENS, "HAZING: A GREEK TRAGEDY"
(http://www.alphaphi.org, 1993)

The work that I do began because of a personal experience. I speak from the heart, as a mother, who learned about the ugly tradition of "hazing" in the worst possible way. I lost my son Chuck, fifteen years ago in an alcohol/hazing incident in New York State. He was kidnapped from his dorm, locked in a car trunk in freezing weather with the other pledges, and forced to consume a lethal mix of bourbon, wine and beer. Chuck was dead within hours of acute alcohol poisoning and exposure to the cold. Other pledges were hospitalized but fortunately they lived. Since that time I've spoken at over 500 campuses **not** against fraternities—but against hazing! The organization I founded, C.H.U.C.K., Committee to Halt Useless College Killings, has a definite purpose: to increase awareness, to work to find alternatives to hazing, to encourage educational programs and to lobby for anti-hazing laws.

If Greek life is to remain in existence it must rid every chapter, on every campus, of hazing in all its ugly forms. They very survival of fraternities and sororities depends on that simple fact. This is not an easy task because students entering fraternal organizations, as well as existing members, are receiving a mixed message. Until there is a clear signal from college administrators, national headquarters and lawmakers that even the most subtle, seemingly innocuous forms of hazing will not be tolerated the problem will remain and it will worsen. Hazing in any form has no place in any fraternity. It defeats the very spirit of brotherhood and friendship that Greeks represent and violates the very premise on which they were founded.

Fraternal life was founded on strong values and ideals for good and pure reasons and the founders would hang their heads in shame were they to realize that the ugly practice of hazing entered the pre-initiation programs. This fraternity signifies honor, leadership and brotherhood. Hazing is an aberration of all you stand for and must be stopped.

The past decade has seen dramatic, precedent-setting change. Thirty-nine states have outlawed hazing. Federal attention is taking place right now and the judiciary committee is reviewing two drafts that would criminalize hazing and put mandates on universities. Legally the landscape is seeing laws being tested in the courts and litigation that is jolting the financial foundation of national fraternities resulting in an insurance crisis. Some university boards are seeking the abolishment of Greek-letter organizations on their campuses and some have succeeded in doing just that! Some courageous fraternities have eliminated the pledge process and may be setting the tone for the future. The ever-present media continues to report the hard truth, abuses, indignities, injuries and fatalities (60 in the past decade). These are frightening facts that cannot be justified, blemishing the innocent along with the guilty. Adverse publicity, lawsuits and public pressure have put Greeks under fire and Greek life in jeopardy.

Being a Greek is an honor. One that commands responsible behavior. No member of a fraternity should allow hazing to go on in their chapter. Even seemingly harmless activities have led to problem situations. Most reported hazing incidents involve alcohol.

Subservience, ridicule, verbal abuse, intimidation, sleep deprivation, forced calisthenics, unfair tests are all hazing and should be reported. No one should compromise their dignity to belong to any group. If you are allowing yourself to be hazed, or looking the other way when someone else is being hazed, you are enabling this ugly practice to continue and jeopardizing the emotional and physical well being of others. You are the future of fraternity. You have rights and an important voice. This is a time of growth and personal development. You are in a unique position to strengthen your chapter, implement change and set a tone for the future. Only you can eradicate the cancer of hazing. You will face many challenges and choices. I implore you to do so with leadership and courage.

I speak to you as a mother who lost a fine son needlessly to hazing and alcohol. I believe in you or I would not do the work that I do. I ask you to do your part, respect and value life and each other so a tragedy like Chuck's is never repeated.

GENDER ISSUES IN EDUCATION: SINGLE SEX VERSUS COEDUCATION

Since the 1970s all-boys schools have almost disappeared in the United States and the same is nearly as true for all-girls schools. The arguments for coeducation seem sound. Mixed-sex schools are cheaper and more efficient to operate, thus saving money; single-sex schools are not in keeping with modern culture, where men and women have to work together and need to learn to understand the opposite sex. Thus boys and girls should be educated together. Coeducation also promotes sexual equity, argues Anne Conner, the president of the National Organization for Women, who said at at recent conference that single-sex education does not promote tolerance, multiculturalism, or gender sensitivity. The American Association of University Women claims that the formation of single-sex schools would take this country "two giant steps backwards . . . to a time when sex stereotypes upheld by public institutions prevailed in society at large" (*AAUW Newsletter* 1995).

While many people might consider single-sex schools an anachronism, others would disagree, and they are likely to be regarded as hopelessly reactionary. However, recent research shows that there are some clear advantages to single-sex schooling. It has been shown, for example that single-sex schools are better in terms of academic achievement and social adjustment, especially during the high school years. The reason is that teenagers are often controlled by anti-intellectual adolescent culture in mixed-sex schools and conform to the social expectations of the peer group rather than to the academic expectations of the institution.

Ironically single-sex schools started to be relieved of the sexist onus that had been placed on them as it was shown that girls often performed better in an all-female classroom. The same fact was demonstrated in the case of minority students and in 1992 attracted the attention of the U.S. Department of Education, then under Diane Ravitch, secretary for educational research, who launched a project to evaluate the value of single-sex education that was later scrapped.

The issue was revived again in 1994 in the U.S. Senate, where the lawmakers debated an amendment introduced by Senator John Danforth who proposed that grants be given to create ten single-sex programs for low-income minority students and that Title IX, which had prohibited public single-sex schools, be suspended. The measure passed by a vote of sixty-six to thirty-three. Nevertheless, the Danforth amendment was killed in the House. It appears that the demand for diversity applies in all areas except education, where the insistence is that single-sex schools should give way to more progressive and politically correct mixed-sex schools. As former Secretary Ravitch put it, the current system acts on the premise that we must stamp out diversity in the name of diversity (see Ruhlman, 352). The following promotion of an all-male academy in Philadelphia, Pennsylvania, reveals the special appeals that such institutions must make today to justify their existence.

FROM "THE CHA ADVANTAGE," *CHESTNUT HILL ACADEMY TODAY*
(http://www.chestnuthillacademy.org/chaadvanage.htm, 2000)

At Chestnut Hill Academy we understand boys, appreciate their range of characteristics, and enjoy steering their energy into productive channels. Throughout all grade levels we plan curricula and activities that will help them grow into young men who will be prepared to face the challenges of the 21st century in their colleges, their workplaces, and their families. We agree with the words of Michael Gurian, the author of *The Wonder of Boys*, "The fact is, that masculinity, if appropriately parented, mentioned, and educated, is one of life's most nurturing and creative forces."

We know through both science and experience that body chemicals, brain differences, and hormones cause boys and girls to develop at different rates and employ different learning styles. To ignore this in education makes little sense. In the early years we see differences in motor skills, the performance of language arts, the ability to read social cues, and organizational skills, among others. At CHA we create educational programs which challenge boys intellectually and excite their curiosity without causing unnecessary frustration in performance areas which are still maturing. Across the country, in tests administered in public schools, many boys lag significantly behind girls in all phases of language arts. At CHA, where boys' timetables and styles are respected, they read and write across the curriculum with clarity and enthusiasm.

In Middle School, the needs of early adolescent boys continue to be well-served in academic programs which give students the opportunity to gain confidence and skills more oriented toward self-improvement than social acceptance. Active, rigorous learning in specific subject areas is supported by a focus on organizational, study, and collaborative skills.

In extracurricular activities such as drama, orchestra, community service, assemblies, and dances, the boys begin interacting with their grade level counterparts at nearby Springside School for girls.

As they approach adolescence, one of boys' primary drives is to clarify the concept of masculinity. In coed situations it is safer for most boys to identify primarily with more stereotypical male interests such as science, math, and sports. In a boys' school, boys enjoy these pursuits but are also intensely involved with a wider variety of interests including writing, music, art, and drama.

As young men enter the Upper School years, some developmental differences become less pronounced. Boys are more intellectually ready to understand and respect the differences between men and women. At this point Chestnut Hill Academy and Springsdale School begin to weave classes together as The Coordinate Program. . . . Boys now have the experience of coeducational classes as they prepare for coeducational colleges and a coeducational world. They remain, however, part of a boys' school with exceptional programs, role models and opportunities for nurturing the boys who will follow in their footsteps.

The following argument for single-sex education was written by Robert L. Maginnis, a policy analyst for the Family Research Council. He refutes the view that same-sex schooling is a form of bigotry and holds that both men and women would benefit from single-gender education.

FROM ROBERT L. MAGINNIS, "WHY SINGLE-SEX EDUCATIONAL
EXPERIENCES OFTEN WORK BETTER"
(http://www.frc.org, February 1994)

Just as males and females differ anatomically in obvious areas like genitalia, they also differ in less apparent areas like brain development and functioning. These differences can and do affect the way males and females learn.

According to Harvard sociologist David Riesman, males learn most when they perceive their teacher as a disciplinarian and competitor. They respond better to teaching based on the adversary model of education, which incorporates contest and competition in a disciplined atmosphere. "Girls learn in different ways than boys, and, up until now, educators have failed to recognize that," says Chris Mikles, the female founder and teacher of a successful all-girls math class in the public school system of California. Generally, females are more likely to thrive in a learning environment that offers high levels of positive reinforcement, support, and cooperation.

Thus, single-sex environment can be the most effective educational setting for at least some students. Among the academic benefits of single-sex schools are these:

- Students of both genders enrolled in single-gender schools enjoy higher academic performance, increased interaction with faculty, increased verbal aggressiveness and higher intellectual self-esteem.

- Women at single-sex schools are more likely than their peers at co-ed institutions to pursue majors such as science, math, management and economics. They have more opportunities for leadership and aspire to higher academic degrees.

- Men at single-gender schools are more likely than their peers at co-ed institutions to get good grades, participate in honors programs, graduate with honors and pursue a career in business, law or college teaching.

- Both men and women at single-sex schools are more likely than students at co-ed institutions to be satisfied with curricular variety, student and faculty relations, quality of instruction and friendships with other students.

Apart from these advantages, the experience of the United States Military Academy at West Point should give pause to those advocating that VMI [Virginia Military Institute] and The Citadel be made co-ed.

According to Col. Patrick A. Toffler, director of the office of Institutional Research at West Point, the U. S. Military Academy has been altered significantly by the eradication of its single sex program. Unit morale has been adversely affected by jealousies arising out of emotional attachments. Physical standards have been lowered to accommodate female cadets. Drop out rates have increased. Women have received special consideration when competing for leadership positions. Consequently, almost half the men and more than half the women believe the experiment has not been successful.

CONCLUSION

Many argue that same-sex classes are a form of bigotry and a civil rights "retreat." But the truth is that single-gender schools diversity America's educational and provide the option of a single-sex education to individuals—both women and men—that might benefit greatly from it.

In the fall of 1993, Michael Ruhlman returned to his old prep school to see how much the school had changed since he had been a student. In his view, single-gender schools are more effective academically than coeducational schools.

FROM MICHAEL RUHLMAN, *BOYS THEMSELVES: A RETURN TO
SINGLE-SEX EDUCATION*
(New York: Holt, 1996)

American education has been primarily coeducational since the mid-nineteenth century, and it had become so not because coeducation was deemed better for children but rather because coeducation was more economical than teaching boys and girls in separate buildings. What single-sex high schools had formed and lasted were independent—either small, rich, private schools or religious, and largely poor, schools. These lasted for decades unquestioned, largely ignored—anomalies in an otherwise democratic, religiously free country.

Then the country's mood changed. The great wave of conversions from single-sex to coeducation which began in the 1960s and continued well into the 1980s occurred not because researchers and sociologists had scrutinized the single-sex form and found it harmful to children, but rather because it seemed like a bad idea to separate boys and girls, to keep them away from each other in separate schools. Because the mood changed, single-sex schools found it difficult to attract enough students to fill their schools; most could stay alive only if they became coeducational. American independent schools, more than half of which were single-sex, did what public schools had done a century earlier—again, not out of concern for the students but rather economic necessity, a move further enforced by the belief that coeducation was more egalitarian.

Yet the few all boy schools that survived did so because they were strong, and when the winds, slowly, began to turn again, these schools sailed—girls' schools, in a political climate dominated by feminist thinking, leading the way. Backed by research, organized into a strong coalition, and bolstered by reports of intractable sex bias within coed schools, girls' schools no longer needed to justify their existence, and enrollment boomed.

Boys' schools followed the girls' schools, first in a sort of dim-witted, hey-wait-a-minute recognition that they didn't have to sit in the corner anymore, and then in a stumbling, pro-active way, in which they began to promote themselves as actually being good for boys. Finally in the spring of 1994, boys' schools found their voice. Following the Belmont boys'-school conference, a new group would solidify—Boys' Schools: An International Coalition. It's goal: to understand and promote "The development of school-age boys." In a matter of months, the newborn coalition, would comprise 140 schools from the United States, Canada, England, Australia, and Japan. Its mission statement would be lofty enough to support is physical size: ". . . Boys' Schools aim to insure a future in which humane and capable boys will being their gifts to bear on the creation of a just and livable world."

Mary Baldwin College in Virginia is one of the few remaining all-women's schools in the United States. The following selection reveals why this institution advocates single-sex education for women at the college level.

FROM "SINGLE-SEX EDUCATION FOR WOMEN"
(Mary Baldwin College Bulletin, 2000)

Since the 1960s and 1970s, the number of women's colleges in the United States has dwindled. In 1960, there were 268 women's colleges in the United States. Today, there are only 83.

This movement away from single sex education evolved from a variety of economic and societal concerns, and those women's colleges that remain have moved forward with the times, incorporating innovative learning opportunities for their students.

An impressive body of recent studies on single sex and mixed sex education at both pre-college and college level confirms the continued importance of these institutions in American education today. These studies demonstrate that single sex schools lead to higher achievement and self-esteem in women, encourage women to pursue traditionally male-dominated careers, and alleviate some of the disadvantages women may suffer in a coeducational setting.

On the whole, research reveals that compared with women at coed schools, women's college students:

- Participate more fully in and out of class (AAUW study: females receive significantly less attention from instructors than males; teachers call on males twice as often and are three times more likely to praise males)
- Develop greater self-esteem
- Score higher on standardized achievement tests
- Are more likely to major in traditionally male-dominated disciplines, such as math or science
- Are more likely to graduate from college
- Are more likely to enter medical school
- Are twice as likely to receive doctoral degrees
- After graduation tend to have more successful careers, hold higher positions, be happier and earn more

TOPICS FOR DISCUSSION AND RESEARCH

1. Despite the growing evidence that post-traumatic stress is a disorder, some psychiatrists still think that it is a fabricated disease for the purpose of getting compensation from the government or sympathy from the community, especially among Vietnam veterans. Debate this issue, considering how society tends to look at veterans of this war as either war criminals or psychological cripples.

2. A number of films have featured ex-soldiers who suffer from PTSD, among them *The Deer Hunter* (1978), *Born on the Fourth of July* (1989), *Taxi Driver* (1976), and *Heaven and Earth* (1993). Check out any of these movies from a video store to see how post-traumatic stress is depicted and decide if Hollywood distorts the disorder or creates a greater awareness of it.

3. Just as film treatment of PTSD indicates a growing awareness of the victims of this disorder, so do the following works of fiction: *Rumor of War* by Philip Caputo (1977), *Paco's Story* by Larry Heinemum (1986), and *In the Lake of the Woods* by Tim O'Brien (1994). Read one of these novels and write an analysis of a character suffering from PTSD.

4. Those who study youth sports say that parents and coaches bear the most blame for the lack of good sportsmanship in junior leagues and high schools. Do you think this view is correct? Debate what factors contribute to poor sportsmanship. Is there too much emphasis on winning?

5. Some critics of big-revenue, high-profile sports programs in football and basketball say that schools should give up the charade that athletes are really students and create a nonacademic environment that would make colleges and universities into a minor league where football and basketball players could pursue their dreams of becoming professionals. Debate the pros and cons of such a plan for (a) the athletes, (b) the schools, and (c) sports fans.

6. Two traditional reasons for including sports among the extracurricular activities that schools sponsor was the belief that students should have a sound mind and a healthy body and the assumption that athletic competition builds moral character. Debate whether these values are upheld by the events in *A Separate Peace*.

7. According to a recent FBI Crime Report, more crimes are being committed on America's school grounds and campuses than at any previous time. Also, much crime occurs off campus as students return to their apartments. Why are students such frequent and easy victims of crime, and what do you think could be done to prevent it? How safe is your school?

8. Many people trivialize hazing and don't recognize the danger of it. Do you think that hazing is good or bad for building team or club or school spirit? Why do people submit to hazing, and would you engage in it if given the opportunity? Write an essay from the perspective of a (a) victim and (b) perpetrator of hazing.

9. Much evidence based on recent research shows some advantages to all-girl and all-boy schools. Make an argument urging that coeducation be discontinued for educational reasons; make a counterargument that coeducation should be continued for social reasons.

SUGGESTED READINGS AND WORKS CITED

POST-TRAUMATIC STRESS DISORDER

Fullerton, Carol S. *The Structure of Human Chaos*. New York: Cambridge University Press, 1994.

Hansel, Sarah. *Soldiers' Heart: Survivors' Views of Combat Trauma*. New York: Sidran, 1995.

Lifton, Robert J. *Home from the War*. New York: Simon & Schuster, 1973.

Shay, Jonathan. *Achilles in Vietnam: Combat Trauma and the Ongoing of Character*. New York: Simon and Shuster, 1995.

Trim, Steve. *Walking Wounded: Men's Lives during and since Vietnam*. Norwood, N.J.: Ablex, 1993.

Zaczek, Ron. *Farewell Darkness: A Veteran's Triumph over Combat Trauma*. Annapolis: Naval Institute, 1994.

ACADEMICS VERSUS ATHLETICS

Funk, Gary D. *Major Violation: The Unbalanced Priorities in Athletics and Academics*. Champaign, Ill.: Human Kinetics, 1991.

Miracle, Andrew, and C. Roger Dees. *Lessons from the Locker Room: The Myth of School Sports*. New York: Prometheus Books, 1994.

Nuwer, Hank. *Sports Scandals*. New York: Franklin Watts, 1994.

Putnam, Douglas T. *Controversies of the World of Sports*. Westport, Conn.: Greenwood Press, 1999.

Sperber, Murray. *College Sports, Inc.: The Athletic Department vs. the University*. New York: Henry Holt, 1990.

———. *Onward to Victory: The Crises That Shaped College Sports*. New York: Henry Holt, 1998.

Telander, Rick. *The Hundred Yard Lie: The Corruption in College Football and What We Can Do to Stop It*. New York: Simon & Schuster, 1989.

Wiggins, David K. *Glory Bound: Black Athletes in White America*. Syracuse: Syracuse University Press, 1997.

CAMPUS CRIME

Beadle, Muriel. *Where Has All the Ivy Gone*. Garden City, N.Y.: Doubleday, 1972.
"Education Department Releases Data on Campus Crime." *Chronicle of Higher Education* (May 28, 1999) pp. 35–37.
Huffer, Richard. "Praising Hazing." *Sports Illustrated*, September 13, 1999.
Nuwer, Hank. *Broken Pledges: The Deadly Rite of Hazing*. Atlanta: Longstreet Press, 1990.
Rose, Margaret Ann. *Rush: A Girls' Guide to Sorority Success*. New York: Villard, 1985.
Wolfe, Linda. *Wasted: The Preppie Murder Case*. New York: Simon & Schuster, 1989.

GENDER ISSUES IN EDUCATION

Hall, Roberta, and Bernice Sandler. *The Classroom Climate: A Chilly One for Women?* Washington, D.C.: Association of American Colleges, 1982.
Howe, Florence. *Myths of Coeducation*. Bloomington: University of Indiana Press, 1984.
Riordan, Corneluis. *Girls and Boys in School: Together or Separate*. New York: Columbia University Teachers College, 1986.
Ruhlman, Michael. *Boys Themselves: A Return to Single-Sex Education*. New York: Holt, 1996.
"Separated by Sex: A Critical Look at Single-Sex Education For Girls." *AAUW Newsletter* (1998).
Tyack, David and Elizabeth Hansot. *Learning Together: A History of Coeducation in America*. New York: Russell Sage Foundation, 1990.

Index

About the Author

HALLMAN BELL BRYANT is a Professor of English at Clemson University where he teaches American and British literature of the Victorian period. He is the author of *A Separate Peace: The War Within* (1990).